HOW TO HELP YOUR CHILD PLAN A CAREER

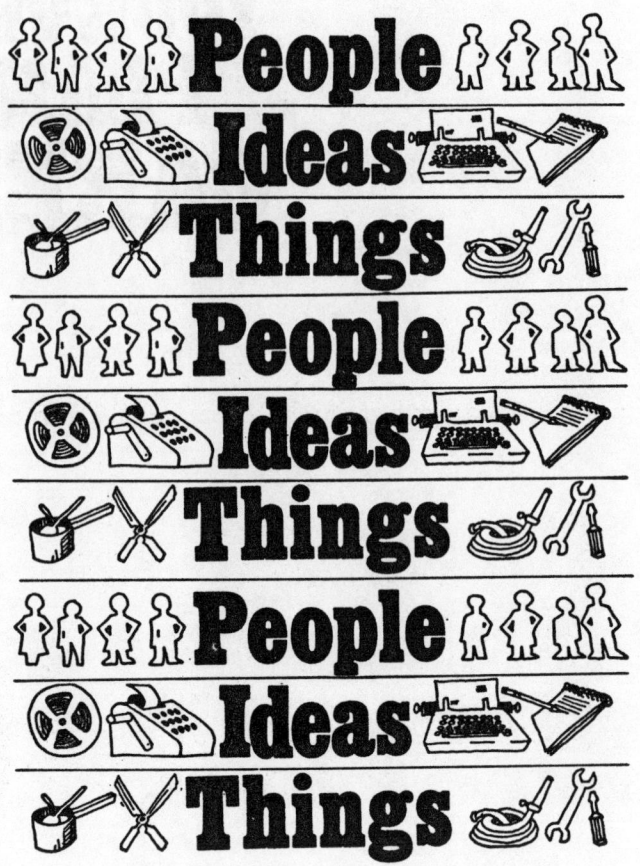

HOW TO HELP YOUR CHILD PLAN A CAREER

foreword by
GEORGE GALLUP, Jr.
The Gallup Poll

Dean L. Hummel and Carl McDaniels

Published by **ACROPOLIS BOOKS Ltd.** • Washington D.C. 20009

© Copyright 1979 by Dean L. Hummel and Carl McDaniels

All rights reserved. Except for the inclusion of brief quotations in a review, no part of this book may be reproduced or utilized in any form or by any means, electronic or mechanical, including photocopying, recording or by an information storage and retrieval system, without permission in writing from the publisher.

ACROPOLIS BOOKS LTD.
Colortone Building, 2400 17th St., N.W.
Washington, D.C. 20009

Printed in the United States of America by
COLORTONE PRESS, Creative Graphics Inc.
Washington, D.C. 20009

ACROPOLIS BOOKS
are distributed in

CANADA
by Carlton House, 91 Station Street,
Ajax, Ontario L1S 3H2

EUROPE AND THE BRITISH COMMONWEALTH
by Paul Maitland, 2/16 Mount Sion,
Tunbridge Wells, Kent TN1 1UF, England

JAPAN
by Atlantic Book Service, 23-17 Akabane Kita,
3-Chome Kita-Ku, Tokyo 15

PAKISTAN
by SASI Ltd., State Life Bldg #5
Zaibunnisa Street, GPO 779, Karachi 3

ELSEWHERE IN ASIA
by ICTO PTE Ltd., Wing On Life Bldg.,
150 Cecil Street, Singapore 1

second printing July 1979

```
Library of Congress Cataloging in Publication Data
Hummel, Dean L
   How to help your child plan a career.

   Bibliography: p.
   Includes index.
   1. Vocational guidance.  2. Parenting.
I. McDaniels, Carl, joint author.  II. Title.
HF5381.H846          331.7'02           79-1303
ISBN 0-87491-227-X
ISBN 0-87491-228-8 pbk.
```

Acknowledgments

A special appreciation is expressed for the availability of Bureau of Labor Statistics, United States Department of Labor materials which have been utilized in this book. The Bureau continues to develop and publish excellent and current reports which are mainly used by professionals in the career guidance field. We have incorporated, and in some instances, adapted the Bureau's materials so that parents and their children can benefit by their use.

Also, we acknowledge the many parents and students for their participation in field testing out materials and for their enthusiastic encouragement of our efforts.

Dedication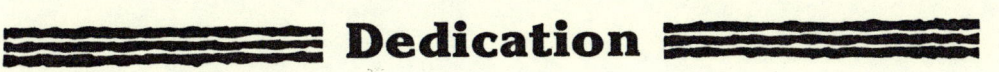

Dedicated to Gretchen, Eric, and Krista Hummel and to Lynn, Lisa, and Diane McDaniels whose uniquenesses have been great joys in our lives. Your continuing search for identity in diverse careers suggests that we and your mothers provided homes in which freedom of choice was possible, if sometimes difficult.

From you we learned that sustained faith, feelings of worthiness, and successful experiences create a foundation for healthy career development. From you we also learned that career decisions are not always easy to make, but ultimately each person must decide for himself.

We trust that what we learned from you, and from the numerous children and youths with whom we have worked, is translated in this book for other parents to use with their children.

Foreword

Gallup Poll findings support the conviction of authors Hummel and McDaniels that career choice and development should not be left to chance. For example, in our surveys we find more than one-third of Americans saying they would go into another line of work if they had it to do over again. And certainly many others, while not actively unhappy with what they are presently doing, would be happier and more productive in other pursuits.

Hummel and McDaniels give us a careful look at the process of career choice and development in the home, stressing the point that meaningful decisions can best be made in the context of a loving relationship between parents and children.

Importantly, their book is a readable and practical book in which they outline specific steps that should be considered in bringing young people to career awareness and decision. It is a much needed book because it is essential for a society not only to maximize the talents and interests of its citizenry, but to avoid the serious problems which can arise when people are unhappy in their life's work.

I can pay the book no higher compliment than to say that I have put it to use in trying to help my own three children think constructively about their future roles in life.

George Gallup, Jr.
President
The Gallup Poll
American Institute of Public Opinion
Princeton, New Jersey

Are You an Occupational Ignoramus?

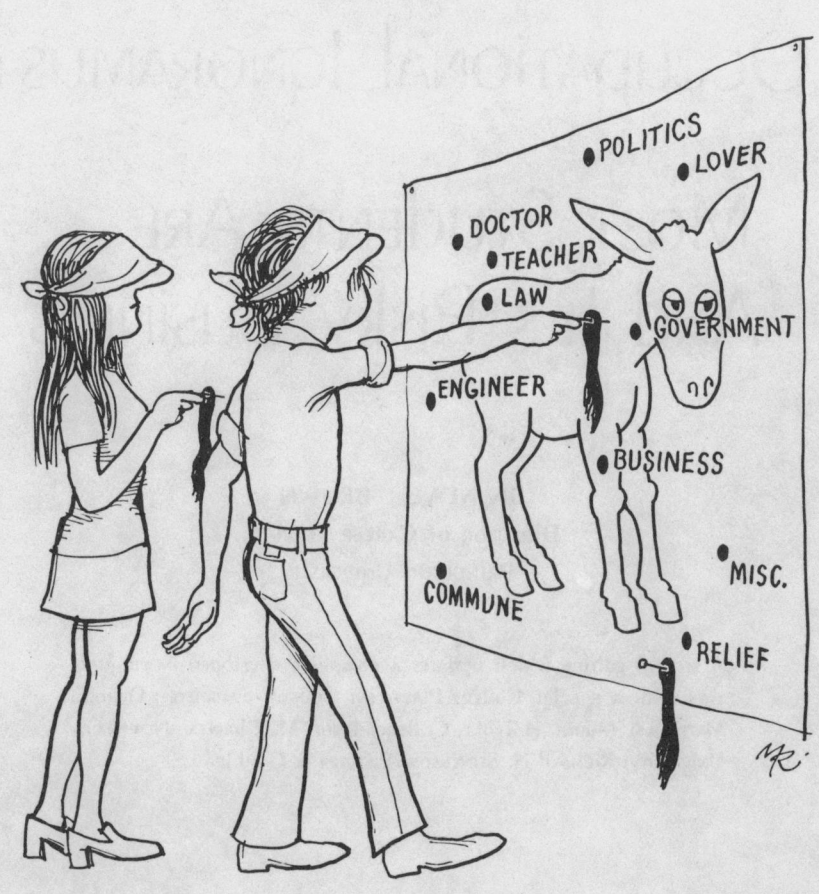

Most Students Are...
And It's Risky Business

Are You an Occupational Ignoramus?

Most Students Are... And It's Risky Business

By NEWELL BROWN
Director of Career Services,
Princeton University

A second edition which updates a pamphlet developed in conjunction with a special College Placement Council committee: Drue E. Matthews, Mount Holyoke College; Irene M. Charles, New York University; Richard N. Stevenson, Procter & Gamble.

Copyright 1971, 1977 by
The College Placement Council, Inc.

Chart on the centerspread reprinted from After College...Junior College...Military Service...What? by Newell Brown. Copyright 1968, 1971 by Newell Brown. Published by Grosset & Dunlap, Inc.

"I guess the best advice I can get is from my parents."

Inevitably, parental advice is colored by emotion; concern for your welfare; a desire to feel pride in your accomplishments and aspirations; anxiety when you seem to be on the wrong track. Further, some parents may have a limited and inaccurate understanding of today's world of work. But they're not to be tuned out entirely. Much of what you are and know you inherited or learned from them. And they know a lot you don't. The trick is to be able to glean the wheat of solid, useful information from the chaff.

"The objective of career planning, as I understand it, is to reach, by graduation, a fixed idea on where I want to go and of the steps I need to take to get there."

Not necessarily. Many of you are not ready to "fix" on a plan. For some the best objective is only to decide on a sensible first step after graduation. That's a step which heads in approximately the right direction, considering what sort of person you are and what your alternatives are. This reduces the chance of having to double back later and leaves open a variety of appropriate next steps. Chance and the constantly changing nature of work opportunities are going to have a lot to do with where you are 40 years hence. Most of the movers and shapers of tomorrow will be those who get going but stay loose, not those with one-track goals and minds.

"My parents say I should be able to make up my mind. 'After all,' they keep saying, 'you're old enough to vote, so get with it.' I guess they're right but so far I haven't gotten anywhere."

They're not right. All this kind of talk does is breed anxiety. There's nothing about reaching 18, or even 21, which automatically produces a hitherto missing capacity to make a comfortable decision about the future. This capacity comes to some individuals before college, to many during college, to many more later, and to some, never. And it can't be forced overnight through logic and will, or a quickie investigation of job alternatives. Early and leisurely exploration of alternatives and of oneself, however, can speed the decision. For those still uncertain at the end of their senior year, the best decision to make is to make no firm decision but rather to simply try to choose a next step in the right or, at least not wrong, general direction, leaving as many doors open as possible.

"I don't know what I want to do so I'm going to take some aptitude tests."

Except for tests which measure your capacity to do several kinds of academic work at the graduate level, aptitude tests probably won't tell you much about yourself that you don't already know. Besides, no single aptitude test, or even a battery of tests, can give a clear answer, much less make a decision for you. You'll have to find your own answers, starting out by jotting down what you do well and easily and what you do poorly and painfully. Your aptitudes, of course, must enter into the choice of next steps, but there are other aspects to consider — your achievements to date, for example. Keep in mind also your interests, personality, temperament, and values. Some of this you can do yourself with some honest self-appraisal, but you may want to talk it over with others and do some reading about the kinds of work that fit in with your whole being. Where they are available, you may want to take some special tests of your interests. But don't expect a neat printout to follow. To be promising, the eventual decision must be your own.

"As a woman I'm getting a lot of conflicting signals: prepare for and plan on a professional career; marriage and careers don't mix; careers I might like won't be open to me. I guess I'll relax until I see which way the ball is going to bounce."

Waiting to see what happens doesn't make much sense because nothing much could happen! Besides there's a 50/50 chance that what turns up will start you down a path that leads nowhere, and in 10 or 15 years you'll find yourself saying, "Why didn't I . . .?"

Today women have more options from which to choose. A substantial number are going from college into professional training and careers. Many of these women also have successful marriages, some of the dual career sort, including children. Others either interrupt their careers for a short period or manage to pursue them on a part-time basis while their children are very young.

It is important for you to decide for yourself which of the options makes the best sense for you. Even if you decide on marriage and a family, keep in mind that in your mid-thirties you will probably have your last child out of the house for all or part of the day. How are you going to occupy yourself for the next 30 years or so?

All career fields now are legally open to women but it is also true that to make significant achievements women will have to work with dedication and push back the barriers that still exist.

"Why worry now? I'll fall into something or take somebody's offer, and after that it will depend on how hard I work, how bright I am, and the breaks I get."

You may well be able to fall into something but, with shrinking opportunities for the college-trained — how rewarding it will be at the start — how far you go from there — and how satisfied you'll be with what you're doing — will depend on more than brains, brawn, and breaks. It will also depend on how the job fits you, your aptitudes, interests, physical capacities, your need for security, freedom, prestige, your feelings about making money, being of service, where you want to live, your preferred ways of dealing with people. "Falling in" without thought to such considerations usually leads either to getting "locked in" to an unrewarding work life or to having to back off and start again with loss of time, momentum, and maybe opportunity.

"Short of your junior year, you can't get a summer job that's career-related. For underclass students, summer jobs are for making money — and having a ball, if you can work it in."

Upperclass students obviously have two big advantages. They have more to sell by way of know-how, and they may be available for permanent employment next year. But the lowly jobs need not be a total loss. For instance you either supervise or are supervised or both. How do these roles fit you? Camp counseling is basically teaching. How do you react to having to sell yourself (waitress), or a service (bank teller), or a product (pots and pans)? Does the ghetto turn you on as strongly when you're in the ghetto as it did from the ivory tower of college? Make some bread and have a ball during the summer, but some simultaneous self-enlightment is available too — if you're looking for it.

"I have to decide on my major soon so I've got to make up my mind about what I want to do after college. What you major in is the important thing to employers and graduate schools you apply to."

To graduate schools, so far as their offerings in arts and sciences, and engineering are concerned, yes. As to admission to such graduate schools as business, law, social work, and journalism, no particular undergraduate courses are required. Even in medicine you can major in a non-science field, if you get in the pre-med courses as electives. Do what comes naturally, especially if you can't make up your mind as to what you want to do after college. No particular major is required for the large majority of occupations of interest to college graduates. Whatever your major, if the business world is an option, consider taking some courses in business, economics, or computer science, for two reasons: the exposure will test your interest in and aptitude for business-related disciplines; and, if business becomes your goal, this exposure will strengthen your attractiveness as a candidate.

62 Kinds of Work for College Graduates

FIELDS OF WORK

as students who think in terms of career "Fields" commonly describe their interests.

CAPITALS show the six general Fields of Work which comprehend all the others

	Accountant	Actuary	Advertising Worker	Architect	Artist: Creative and Performing	Bank Worker	Buyer	Chiropractor	City Planner and related	Computer Scientist (Programmer)	Conservation Worker	Counselor	Criminologist and related	Curator	Dentist	Dietitian	Education Worker (Non-teaching)	Engineer	Environmentalist	Foreign Language Worker	Fund Raiser	General Manager (Executive, Administrator)	Home Economist	Humanist	Industrial Designer
	†	†	†	†		†	†		†	†	†	†	†				†				†	†		†	†
Advertising	*	*							*												*		*	*	*
Airlines	*	*	*						*							*		*	*	*					
Banking	*	*				*			*							*			*	*					
Business	*	*	*	*	*	*	*	*	*	*	*	*	*	*		*	*	*	*	*	*	*		*
Communications	*	*							*							*	*	*	*		*			
EDUCATION (96)	*		*	*	*		*	*	*	*	*	*	*	*	*	*	*	*	*	*	*	*	*	*	*
Farming	*	*							*		*					*			*	*	
Finance	*	*	*			*			*									*	*	*	
Foundations	*			*					*				*			*	*		*	*	*	*
GOVERNMENT (100)	*	*	*	*		*	*	*	*	*	*	*	*	*	*	*	*	*	*	*	*	*
Industry	*	*	*	*			*		*	*	*				*		*	*	*	*
Insurance	*	*	*	*					*	*			*		*			*		
International Work	*		*	*	*	*		*	*	*			*			*		*	*	*	*	*
Journalism	*		*		*													*		*		*	*
Manufacturing	*	*						*	*		*		*			*		*
MILITARY SERVICE (122)	*	*	*	*		*		*	*		*		*	*	*	*	*	*	*	*	
Motion Pictures	*		*	*	*												*		*	*	
PRIVATE NONPROFIT (121)	*	*		*	*	*		*	*	*	*		*		*	*	*	*	*	*	*	*	*
PROFIT-MAKING (104)	*	*	*	*		*	*	*	*	*	*	*	*	*		*	*	*	*	*	*
Politics	*		*						*										*	*	
Publishing	*		*	*					*							*		*		*	*
Radio-TV	*		*	*	*											*	*	*	*	*
Recreation	*		*	*		*	*		*		*					*	*			*	*
Retailing	*		*	*			*		*							*	*			*	*
SELF-EMPLOYMENT (116)	*	*	*	*	*		*	*	*	*	*	*	*	*		*		*	*	*	*	*
Urban Redevelopment	*			*					*	*	*	*	*			*	*	*	*	*	*
Utilities	*		*	*					*	*						*			*	*
Writing, Editing			*		*				*								*	*		*	*	*	*

†Careers which liberal arts graduates can pursue with little or no more postgraduate training than is required of those from other undergraduate disciplines.

6

The accompanying chart covers jobs in which virtually all college graduates are employed. One or another of these jobs which you haven't heretofore considered might be your cup of tea. Do you know what they all do: actuary, curator, production manager, personnel manager, systems analyst, for instance?

"Senior year's time enough to get busy deciding what next. Right now I've got too many other irons in the fire."

The best commentary you can get on this one is from your senior friends who entered their senior year undecided as to the next step. Quite a few use the word "panic." Not a surprising emotion when, after 15 years of playing the familiar role of student, one focuses for the first time on the fact that a few months hence (unless grad school is a clear and certain path) it's going to be a whole new ball game. The possibility of senior panic is generally inversely related to the amount of thought given to the hereafter before the senior year.

"I'm on a big scholarship and a bigger loan which I'll have to start repaying soon after I get out. That kind of rules out grad school, which is too bad, because everyone seems to think you have to go to grad school to get anywhere."

Lots of angles to this. It's true that in the future most people who get to the top, whatever they're doing, will have had additional formal education beyond college — on-the-job experience won't usually give them all they need to know. Continuing education of some sort will be a must for many in our technological world. Without it, there's risk of being underqualified or of becoming occupationally obsolete. But the schooling doesn't necessarily have to be taken in year-sized bites or in academic settings. Programs at night, on weekends, or in the summer — often company training programs, too — can do the trick. A quarter of the nation's lawyers got their degree while working full-time. Many of the country's MBA aspirants are studying part-time. Often employers help pay the costs. Further, a variety of financial aids may be available to graduate students and, more, and more will be granted on the basis of need. Finally, many graduate schools prefer applicants who've been "out" for two or three years.

"I'm going to drop my education major. The word is that all up and down the line teachers, especially at the elementary and secondary levels, can't find jobs."

It is true that many aspiring teachers can't find jobs these days. But that doesn't mean that there are no jobs. In fact, at the elementary and secondary levels there are some 150,000 openings each year. These result from the departure of teachers who die, retire, or leave teaching. The problem is that there are a lot more than 150,000 trained teachers looking for jobs. The point is that a well-trained, able, flexible, and persistent teacher can probably find a job teaching. Weaker candidates will have to do something else. The same is true in other tough-to-enter fields, that is, not a lack of openings but too many aspirants. Don't give up if you're really interested.

"When I came to college, I planned to major in business. I like the business courses I've taken so far, but now I've decided I don't want to work in business or industry. I think I'll switch to social sciences or something so I can get into some other kind of work."

Most business majors go into business (in the sense of profit-making enterprise) as do most other non-education majors. That's where most of the jobs are and will be for a long time to come. But graduate schools in most professions welcome an able business major — and straight out of college. So do educational, governmental, and non-profit institutions like hospitals and the Red Cross.

"The way to get involved in urban or environmental problems after college is to take as many courses as you can at college in all the relevant subjects."

Such an over-all but necessarily superficial comprehension of the problems will probably get you nowhere. Governmental and other organizations in these fields are looking for people who know their stuff in one or another of the relevant disciplines, usually at the graduate-degree level. To become, one day, an environmental or urban generalist you will have to start as a trained architect or economist or ecologist or social worker or biologist or geologist or political scientist or master of city planning or demographer or publicist or engineer or professional in some other pertinent area.

"I'd like to get into education or maybe government. But let's face it, I want to make enough to live well, and I couldn't do it on a teacher's or government worker's salary."

Your information is dated. Today starting salaries in private enterprise and government, at the federal level and in the larger states and cities, are very comparable. And beginning teachers can bring home annually nearly as much if they work during their summer vacations. Further, government and teaching raises remain competitive with business through the first three or four years. At that point, of course, business and industry salaries, especially at middle management levels, begin to pull away. But even so, people at the top of the government and education ladder today make as much as many private enterprise vice presidents. Ask your placement officer for the figures.

"I just love people and talking with them so I guess I'll go into personnel work or maybe social work."

Personnel work — and social work, too — require a lot besides love and conversation. (Incidentally, these aren't the only two people-oriented occupations! In fact, working with people is part of nearly every job.) But as to these two fields, tough-minded, knowledgeable analysis of individuals, situations, and institutions as well as compassion are required. A personnel officer fires as well as hires; prepares statistical analyses, budgets, and reports; administers wage and training plans; often bargains with unions — all these plus lending a sympathetic ear. Social workers have comparable varieties of responsibilities and may find themselves in difficult if not hostile environments. Furthermore, graduate work is virtually a must in both occupations if one wants to move up.

"The law isn't for me. Digging through dusty books; legalese; splitting hairs; working for some big corporation on contracts; making out wills; getting divorces for people; getting some criminal off. Not for me."

Those are certainly some of the things some lawyers do. But they aren't all the things all of them do. There are at least a dozen different varieties of lawyers: environmental, patent, urban, psychological, poverty, international, labor, corporation, tax, general practice, criminal, maritime, and governmental (prosecutors, solicitors, legislative assistants). And law isn't alone in having facets not apparent to the casual observer. The same is true for the professions of writing, teaching, educational administration, library work, advertising, accounting, and counseling, to name a few. Don't turn down a possible career that might fit you on the basis of off-hand knowledge about it. Take a careful look at all the possibilities first.

"I can't stand bureaucracy. Otherwise I'd be tempted to look for a job in the federal government."

Bureaucracy — if by that you mean buck-passing, intricate hierarchies, clock-watching, pressures for conformity, committee decision making, red tape — certainly exists in big government. But it can exist wherever more than a handful of people work together. It's a matter of human nature. Its incidence seems to relate more to an organization's size than to its nature. It is certainly not unknown in big business, big foundations, big church organizations, big educational organizations, or the army. If you really can't stand bureaucracy, avoid big organizations of any kind or, better still, hang out your own shingle. But a lot of big and satisfying jobs can only be done from positions in big organizations.

"I want to move fast when I get out so I've been trying to find out what the growth industries are. In particular, I've been looking into trucking and manufacturing. Manufacturing is creeping but trucking is booming. Trucking is for me."

Your conclusions about relative growth rates are accurate, but in the forseeable future there will be a greater number of positions in a large field such as manufacturing. For example, there are some 20,000,000 people presently employed in manufacturing and only 1,000,000 in trucking. The larger the current employment in any field of work, the greater the number of deaths, retirements, and transfers out each year and thus, other things being equal, the more numerous the openings from top to bottom. There'll be 10 to 20 times more openings each year in manufacturing than in trucking in spite of the latter's faster overall growth rate.

"Somewhere there's just the right job for me. I'm going to work at it until I find it."

The woods are full of the wrong jobs for you, to be sure. On the other hand, your chances of finding a one-and-only right job are remote. A variety of jobs undoubtedly contain the ingredients essential to your basic happiness. It's a matter of, first, determining what those ingredients are, then finding out what jobs contain them, and finally picking that one which best combines feasibility and fit. Square pegs won't be happy in round holes but they can be in reasonably square ones, give or take an inch.

"My hang-up is that there are three or four things I'd like to do for a living when I get out of college. I suppose I've got to decide on one and pursue it and let the others go if I'm going to get anywhere."

There isn't much place in the world of work, at least at the start, for one who would be a Jack-of-all-trades. But sometimes multiple talents can be put to good use — for example, the engineer who also is a good writer and becomes a technical writer. And, looking ahead, a variety of interests and abilities can be valuable as one moves into administrative responsibilities. What's more, the manpower experts say the day is here when many people can expect to have two or three distinctly different careers in their lifetimes. Finally, if one thing seems certain, it's that people are going to work fewer and fewer hours on their regular jobs and have more and more time for whatever else they want to do. Mathematicians, for instance, are frequently musical. The day could well come when our fiddlers are moonlighting mathematicians or vice versa.

If you have the impression that this is all a come-on, you're right — and with no apologies. If many of the boldface assumptions quoted in this pamphlet seemed to you sensible at first blush, you run a real risk of getting off on the wrong foot after college. The aim of the pamphlet is to persuade you to start doing some thinking now about where you go from here and to begin using the career planning and placement office on your campus. There you'll find reading material on career fields and employment opportunities, and, perhaps, on graduate schools and summer jobs; also personal counsel if you want it, and possibly tests and other aids to help you to decide on a major — or on how to get off on the right foot when you graduate. Drop by in the next few days and see what the career planning and placement office has to offer.

COLLEGE PLACEMENT COUNCIL, INC.
P.O. Box 2263   Bethlehem, PA 18001

CONTENTS

Introduction: You Can Make a Difference..........................11

PCQ: Parent Career Quotient....................................13

1 Understanding the Basic Question "What Are You Going
To Do When You Grow Up?"......................................15
    The Influence of Parental Attitudes   18
    The Developmental Phases of Choosing a Career   19
    Career Development "Helping Skills" Questionnaire   21

2 Developing Your Child's Feeling of Worthiness................23
    Qualities that Promote Feelings of Worthiness   24
    Parent Worthiness Qualities Profile   28

3 Reinforcing Your Child's Success — In Work and Play..........29
    Building Successful Experiences   30
    Hill-to-Climb Checklist   33

4 Teaching Your Child How To Make Career Decisions............35
    SWING: A Step-by-Step Process   37
    The SWING Test for Parents   39

5 Exploring the World of Work: Data Cues......................41
    Data Work Defined   44
    Occupations Relating Primarily to Data   45
    Noticing the Cues in Your Child   46
    Occupations Relating Primarily to Data and Things   46
    Noticing the Cues in Your Child   47
    Conversation Corner   48
    Data Exploration Checklist   49

6 Exploring the World of Work: People Cues...................51
    People Work Defined   51
    Occupations Relating Primarily to People   53
    Noticing the Cues in Your Child   54
    Occupations Relating Primarily to Data and People   54
    Noticing the Cues in Your Child   55

	Conversation Corner	57
	People Exploration Checklist	58

7 Exploring the World of Work: Things Cues 59

Things Work Defined	59
Occupations Relating Primarily to Things	62
Occupations Relating Primarily to Data-People-Things	63
Noticing the Cues in Your Child	63
An Occupational Example	64
Conversation Corner	66
Things Exploration Checklist	67

8 Taking Part In Your Child's Career Planning Process............69

Helping in Stages	70
Exploring Through Leisure	71
Exploring at School	75
Options Other Than a Four-Year College	76
Points to Ponder	78
The Data-People-Things Game	81

9 Forecasting the Labor Market: Trends and Predictions 85

Recent Job Changes	85
Women at Work	86
Where the Jobs Are	87
Where the Information Is	88
Industrial Profile	88
Occupational Profile	92
The Job Outlook	97

10 The Other Data: Standardized Tests, Extracurricular Activities..127

Tests	128
Other Data: Grades and Extracurricular Activities	130
Other Data Test	132

11 The Other People: Counselors, Teachers, Role Models.........135

Parents and Their Frustrations	136
Counselors and What They Do	136
Other Important People	137
"Other People" Resources List	140

12 The Other Things: Resources For Further Information 141

General Career Planning	141
Military Service Opportunities	147
Special Help for Women and Girls	148
Special Help for Minority Youth	150
Special Help for the College Bound	151
Vocational School Guides	153
College and Universities Guides	154
Job Search, Interviewing, and Resume Writing	155

13 The Career Sort: A Game To Help Your Child Screen Career Interests 159

Career Sort Instructions	159
Career Sort Example	161
Other Career Sort Games	170

PCQ: Parent Career Quotient — A Recap 173

Index. 175

Career Sort Cards 177

Introduction

You Can Make A Difference

Our own careers in business, management, guidance, career development, teaching, occupational information, and counseling psychology have convinced us that parents need assistance—sometimes desperately—in helping their children plan careers. This conviction has been reconfirmed by the tenth annual Gallup Poll on Education conducted in 1978, which reported that parents list the need for help with their children's career development as a high priority.

We know that a major struggle in most individuals' lives is a search for identity. We also know that in the United States identity is a product of what a person does, the nature of a person's work, and the lifestyle supported by the rewards of work. The foundation of the great American dream is a belief in opportunity and freedom of choice. For most persons, the dream is possible, the opportunities exist, and the knowledge is available to exercise freedom of choice in one's career—if help is at hand when needed. We believe parents are the greatest potential helpers for their children's career planning—if they know how to help. This book is designed to help parents provide that needed help.

Most of all, we hope the material in this book will persuade parents that they *can* help their children gain control over the career development process and not drift aimlessly about in a sea of occupations and opportunities. A major way to do this is to create a positive atmosphere in which children can make free choices—choices not bound by lack of information or sex and race stereotyping. This accepting home climate also encourages career exploration and realistic experience in planning. We hope to show you how to do all of this.

Many sources have been tapped in the development of this book. We have analyzed hundreds of research studies, interviewed persons in successful careers during the past 25 years, and studied more than a thousand self-career sketches written by adolescents and adults. From these sources we conclude that most persons wish in retrospect that they had had greater understanding and more useful career planning help from their parents. We also found that most parents want for their children the opportunities they believe they missed.

This book is more than a do-it-yourself guide for parents and their children. It is intended to help parents better understand career development as a vital aspect of human growth and development. The book includes pertinent up-to-date information about occupations, usable resources, career games, predictions about career opportunities in the future, and a Career Sort exercise useful in refining career interests.

We must caution parents that simply reading this book is not enough. If you wish to be your child's number-one career planning helper, you must complete the exercises and apply the techniques you have learned in working with your child.

At this point, we depart from the traditional book introduction. Before you begin your study of the contents of this book, complete the following Parent Career Quotient exercise. You will have an opportunity to retake this little quiz again at the end of the book, after you have completed your study. We have faith in you, as your child will, if you apply what this book attempts to teach about career development and career planning. We wish the best for you and your child.

Dean L. Hummel
Carl McDaniels

PCQ: Parent Career Quotient

Place a check mark beside each question you feel deserves a "yes" answer.

_____ 1. Do you provide a good sounding board for your child's dreams, fantasies, and plans for his/her career? (See Chapter 1.)

_____ 2. Do you build on your child's faith in himself/herself and his/her feeling of worth? (See Chapter 2.)

_____ 3. Do you try to provide reinforcement for successful work and leisure experiences and help relate them to career planning? (See Chapter 3.)

_____ 4. Do you help your child learn about the process of career decision-making? (See Chapter 4.)

_____ 5. Do you help your child understand the world of work and himself/herself through *data*? (See Chapter 5.)

_____ 6. Do you help your child understand the world of work and himself/herself through *people*? (See Chapter 6.)

_____ 7. Do you help your child understand the world of work and himself/herself through *things*? (See Chapter 7.)

_____ 8. Do you assist your child in exploring various work and leisure options through school courses, hobbies, reading, part-time and summer jobs, and volunteering? (See Chapter 8.)

_____ 9. Do you know where to look for timely information on projections for future employment? (See Chapter 9.)

_____ 10. Do you understand how to relate your child's interests, aptitudes, and achievements to his/her career planning? (See Chapter 10.)

_____ 11. Do you know the career planning resource persons in your child's school and how best to work with them? (See Chapter 11.)

_____ 12. Do you know ten good resources for further reading about career planning? (See Chapter 12.)

_____ 13. Do you know a fascinating game to sort out your child's career interests? (See Chapter 13.)

_____ 14. Do you know which occupations are expected to have the best employment opportunities over the next ten years? (See Chapter 9.)

_____ 15. Do you know a neat game that can help get across the Data-People-Things concepts to your child? (See Chapter 8.)

_____ Total checks: Score 10 points for each check. (Example: 4 checks = 40 points total.)

_____ TOTAL SCORE

What is your score? The following outline may give you a general idea of where you stand. Top score is 150. Low score is 0. The important thing is how you score after you have finished reading the book, when you will have a chance to take the quiz again.

P.C.Q.	Where You Stand
130-150	You must have had outside help.
100-120	You can still use a little help.
70-90	You should get some good ideas from this book.
40-60	You ought to enjoy getting some helpful ideas.
0-30	You have the right book.

No matter what your score, each chapter should give you some new clues and ideas to explore with your child in helping plan his/her career.

Chapter 1

Understanding The Basic Question:

"What are you going to do When you grow up?"

"Faith becomes the first source of power for youth in developing self confidence and career planning."

"Most persons attain identity from the work they do—from the kinds of careers they have."

"Parents want for their children the chance they believe they didn't have themselves."

From the time a child learns to talk, parents and others ask, "What are you going to do when you grow up?" In fact, many parents develop dreams and plans for their children, even before they are conceived. Most parents know that persons attain identity from the work they do—from the kinds of careers they have. But beyond dreams and plans, many parents experience frustration in their attempts to help their children plan a career. They lose faith in their ability to understand their children and to utilize fully the information and resources that can be so helpful in a youngster's step-by-step development of a career. Still, studies reveal that youth faced with a problem of planning and decision turn first to their parents for advice and counsel.

Faith—in their parents and in themselves—becomes the first source of power for youth in developing self-confidence and in practical and realistic career planning. It is the ever-present underpinning that provides the acceptance, hope, and motivation to pursue a realistic and satisfactory course. "No step in life," said Frank Parsons, the "father" of vocational guidance, "unless it be the choice of a husband or wife, is more important than the choice of a career."

It should be obvious that growing boys and girls need to develop and maintain faith in themselves if they are to experience healthy progress toward seeking identity through career development. Career development is something that happens to people—by choice or by chance. What a person does is an expression of what that person is. How well a person is doing is the measure of what that person will become. How well a person likes what he/she is doing becomes an expression of individual happiness. Career development is a process that begins at birth and extends to death. However, according to psychologists, the formative years in a person's life set the pattern for individual living. Parents' love and understanding, acceptance, and assistance in these years are potent factors in who and what the child becomes. Dr. Anna Roe, eminent psychologist and career development authority, has found that early childhood experiences and parental relationships are the greatest influences affecting healthy career development. And, according to Dr. Robert Hoppock, noted job satisfaction expert and former New York University professor, persons make choices based on their *needs*.

Parents must become effective counselors and proficient consultants in using career information resources to help keep the light of faith burning in their children's struggle to achieve identity through career development. They must have knowledge themselves and join others (counselors and teachers) in furthering their children's quest to become what they are capable of becoming. A biblical quotation expresses well the importance of multiple sources, noting that

"without counsel purposes are disappointed; but in the multitude of counselors they are established" (Proverbs 15:22).

Career development, involving a pattern of work experiences over a period of time, is a major factor in the age-old adherence to a work ethic. But the work ethic means different things to different people, and questions persist. Why do people work? Why do you as a parent work? How do youth attitudes seem to be different or in conflict with parent attitudes about work?

Generalities are usually suspect, but it may be helpful to think about this: Paul Nash describes youth attitudes as changing from

(1) puritanism to enjoyment,
(2) self-righteousness to openness,
(3) violence to creativity,
(4) politeness to honesty,
(5) bureaucratic efficiency to human relations,
(6) objective truth to personal knowledge,
(7) ideology to existential decision-making and actions,
(8) authority to participation, and
(9) tradition to change.

Does all this mean that youth attitudes are eroding the work ethic? Does it mean that youths attack our "old-fashioned" attitude in an attempt to destroy the work ethic? On the contrary, a recent study reported in *Time* magazine supports most other findings that a majority of youth prefer work to unemployment, that personal identity can be found in meaningful work. They are all aware, as Liebow's *Tally's Corner* shows, that to be denied work is to be denied far more than the things that paid work buys; it means being denied the ability to define and respect oneself. This fact could explain why an estimated 100 million person will be at work in America in 1980—most of them from among today's youth and young adults.

Clearly, the answers to the question "Why do people work?" are complex, reflecting multifaceted human values. The reason for working is inevitably related to the meaning of work for the individual. In schools and colleges the meanings will be as varied as the diversity of the student body; even for the individual, the meaning of work may be made up of a combination of elements. In any case, the developing student must, in the process of understanding self in relation to the world of work, come to grips with the reasons or reason why he/she plans to work.

The Influence of Parental Attitudes

Parents are people—designated as either "Mother" or "Father." They come in all sizes, shapes, colors, and may be found in varying age brackets—although most are thirty-nine or under at least until their children grow into adolescence. Parents are the conceivers of red, wrinkly little things called babies for whom they generally provide home, food, care, and a great deal of love. Sometimes they are understanding, accepting, and almost human. At other times they are irritable, rejecting, practically impossible. As their offspring approach school age, they release them to the charge of teachers, principals, bus drivers, and counselors. They send them off to school each day with a sigh of relief for a few hours of freedom, only to experience a longing for their return at the end of the school day or before. It is probably safe to categorize most parents of the last half century in this way.

To generalize any further about parents of yesteryear and today would be pure folly, for we see change all about us. A reminiscent glimpse at the influences that shaped our thirty-nine-year-old parent, however, may help us identify the bold changes in parental attitudes in general and attitudes about work in particular.

The thirty-nine-year-old (give or take a few years) was probably born in a family that had been shaken to its roots by the Great Depression of the 1930's. His parents may have lost their jobs or their businesses, experiencing for the first time in their lives the fear of not having work or not being able to put food on the table.

Our thirty-nine-year-old thus grew up in a home where the work ethic was strong; he learned that it was important to have a job—almost any job—to be respected as a worker and a person. Furthermore, in his youth almost everyone was patriotic; flags and uniforms were respected and honored. Almost all believed that God was alive, that He cared deeply for mankind. Toil and hard work were man's reasons for being. Few questioned the Judeo-Christian work ethic. And for most, God was white, pro-American, and male, and He rewarded hard work.

And almost everyone was for motherhood—abortion and the burden of children in a family did not enter most people's minds. In adolescence, the thirty-nine-year-old never viewed sexual intercourse or nudity at the local movie house. He had never heard of marijuana; polio was a dread disease; the moon was a romantic but unreachable dream; and the sky was really blue. The women's place was in the home, and work was something every able-bodied man did.

Parental attitudes were formed under these influences, but changes were in the making. Although most adults still support the work ethic, and the majority express job satisfaction according to studies and polls, a recent study showed only 43 percent of a cross-section of white-collar workers and 24 percent of blue-collar workers would choose the same kind of work if given another chance. Most parents want for their children the chance they believe they didn't have themselves.

The first and most essential ingredient in helping a child in his/her career development process is *faith*. If the parent has faith in his/her child and shows it, the child will develop faith and confidence in his or her own capabilities.

The Developmental Phases of Choosing a Career

According to career development experts, children and youth progress through three general phases of development. In each of these phases and their substages, a parent can help instill and maintain the faith a child needs to succeed.

Fantasy Phase, Before Age 11

During the fantasy phase, children believe they can do whatever they like. Needs and desires are transformed into occupational choices. At this time it is very important for parents to listen to their child's expression of dreams about who they want to become and to take part in child fantasy games acting out jobs.

Tentative Phase, Ages 11-17

In the tentative phase, interests, abilities, and values are used in making choices. Reality is not adequately considered, and choices are tentative. During this period, parents should be able to accept their child as a growing person, regardless of strengths and weaknesses. Parents should relate to jobs and things children like to do, regardless of the parent's earlier experiences in various fields. Substages of the tentative period are:

Interests. During this time, interests are the first bases for choice, but children begin to understand that abilities are necessary. Parents should be able, during this period, to supply books, magazines, and games related to the child's interests, values, and capacity. Parents should serve as career models and introduce the child to other vocations outside their own work.

Capabilities (about ages 13-14). After the interest substage, adolescents also take their understanding of capacities into account in their plans. Knowledge of capacities is not total, and choices are tentative.

Values (about ages 15-16). Next, values begin to influence the choice process, and interests and capacities become less powerful factors.

Transition (about ages 17-18). In this substage, the factors above are brought together and used in choosing. Reality factors have not yet influenced the choice process to a great degree, and there is a certain amount of hesitancy in plans. The person, however, usually realizes that current decisions have an effect on the future. At this time, parents as well as others should help children find and use job information.

Realistic phase, 17 to Young Adulthood

Choices are usually made during the realistic phase. Compromises are made between reality factors—educational opportunities or job requirements—and personal capabilities. Reality factors are changing, and parents should understand that biases against nontraditional occupations for boys and girls are disappearing. Substates of the realistic period are:

Exploration. The realistic phase starts with exploration; opportunities are investigated for almost the last time and options are considered. To reinforce parental faith, the child should be permitted to try out a variety of work, even if the parent may not like it. Parents can help by supporting the school's efforts in career education.

Crystallization. During this substage the person actually takes a giant conscious step. Compromise is an important consideration.

Specification. Choice is narrowed, and the person becomes quite specific. Steps are taken to put the decision into action.

At any time during these developmental phases and substages, you can help your child develop and maintain faith in his or her personal ability to plan a career in specific ways. The following questionnaire is provided to help you as a parent evaluate your career development helping skills.

The remainder of this book will help you become an expert in exerting the power of faith to sustain a feeling of worthiness in your child and to provide the expert help that will reinforce his or her successful experiences in developing a career plan.

Career Development Helping Skills Questionnaire

		Yes	No
1.	Do I listen to my child's expression of dreams about who he/she wants to become?	___	___
2.	Can I accept my child as a growing person, regardless of his/her strengths and weaknesses?	___	___
3.	Do I take the time to participate in my child's fantasy games acting out jobs?	___	___
4.	Can I relate to jobs and things my child likes to do, even if I have had no experience in those fields?	___	___
5.	Do I supply my child with books, magazines, and games from which interests, capacities, values, and job skills can be experienced and learned about?	___	___
6.	Do I serve as a career model and introduce my child to other vocations outside my field of work?	___	___
7.	Can I permit my child to try out work experiences, even though I may not like the work myself?	___	___
8.	Can I find and use job information resources in helping my child learn more about specific occupations?	___	___
9.	Do I support the school's efforts in career education?	___	___
10.	Can I permit my child to explore interests in nontraditional occupations regardless of sex or social or economic background?	___	___

Each *yes* is worth 10 points. Add up your Career Development Helping Skills score.

If you scored 100, you are superb.
If you scored 90, you are excellent.
If you scored 80, you are OK.
If you scored less than 80, you can get help by consulting your child's school counselor.

Chapter 2

Developing Your Child's Feeling Of Worthiness

"Essential to healthy and successful career planning is a feeling of worthiness.

"For all things we learn only from those we love."

"Parent qualities promote a feeling of worthiness in offspring."

Most psychologists and teachers would probably agree that persons experience several basic psychological needs throughout life. One such need, essential to healthy and successful career planning, is a feeling of worthiness. This feeling is a kind of "I'm OK" identity that most persons strive for in their work places and throughout their careers. Like most other good kinds of feelings, it is fostered by love. Goethe wrote, "For all things we learn only from those we love."

Parents should be the greatest lovers, especially of their offspring. But what are the essential factors in communicating love in ways that will nurture a feeling of worthiness and facilitate healthy and productive growth in career development? Are there prescribed and specific ways to show love and maintain the faith a child has developed? What qualities are required in the transmission of parent messages that will develop and maintain a child's feeling of worthiness? We believe that at least thirteen qualities of positive parental behavior are required in the career planning process to foster a worthwhile identity in growing boys and girls. These qualities were gleaned from analyses of hundreds of self-sketches written by youngsters and adults about their personal career development.

The importance of feelings of worthiness are illustrated in the following anecdote, which should provide a clue to parents who serve as teachers in the career development process. At our family dinner table, where we frequently exchange expressions about the day s experiences, our ten-year-old daughter blurted out, "Miss Hoy is really a great teacher!"

Her mother responded, "You must have some pretty good reasons to say such a nice thing about Miss Hoy."

"Well, yes. Besides knowing her stuff, Miss Hoy makes each one of us fifth graders feel important, that we are somebody special, that she cares for each of us."

Perhaps Kahlil Gibran, in *The Prophet*, knew children when he declared, "The teacher. . .gives not [only] of his wisdom but rather of his faith and his lovingness." A feeling of worthiness builds a foundation of confidence and motivation in career development.

Qualities That Promote Feelings of Worthiness

For many years we have collected and analyzed student writers' sketches about their personal career development. The following thirteen qualities stood out as prominent parent behaviors that promoted a feeling of worthiness in offspring. The lack of these behaviors was also identified as contributing to children's negative feelings about themselves. We will illustrate both positive and negative aspects of these qualities.

Respectfulness

Can I, as a parent, respond to my child's career ambitions in such a way as to convey my feeling of respect for them? Said Joan in her self-sketch, "When I was little, my parents never seemed to take my career dreams seriously. When I showed an interest in art, I was told that that stuff is for someone else who can afford such frills. Become a teacher, a nurse, or a secretary in which there is security. I wanted their respect, so I dropped my activities in art. After ten years, I still wonder how much respect my parents had for me and my career ideas. On the sly, I am now taking some art classes at a local community college."

Responsiveness

Can I, as a parent, respond directly to the content and feelings expressed by my child's career ideas? Or do I base my responses on my past experiences and possible biases I may have developed? Peggy, in her self-story about careers, wrote, "Whenever I asked my parents about a profession and schooling it would take, I was told that my ambitions would require more money than the family budget could afford, and besides I would probably get married soon after high school anyway. When I finished school, I might better plan to get a job in the local textile factory like my older sisters have. Well, I did what they said to do years ago, and I hated every day of it. So, after three years in that factory, I got a scholarship to college. About my parents, well. . ."

Empathy

Can I, as a parent, attempt to perceive my child as he or she really perceives himself or herself, and can I understand, feel, and be a part of this child's world? Jim, in his autobiographical sketch, told how his father always seemed to feel and understand as he did.

"When I expressed an interest in leaving the farm and joining the Peace Corps, dad seemed to know what I was thinking, feeling, and hoping. So, we sat down and talked about what I might do if I joined the Corps. One thing, for sure, my dad pointed out, I need some technical skills, either through schooling or experience. Now I am in Agriculture in college and I may really be able to make a contribution if I decide to join the Peace Corps."

Acceptance

Can I, as a parent, demonstrate acceptance of my child in a way that will foster dignity and self-respect? Will my child feel that he or she is special and worthy? Don wrote in his self-sketch that his dad seemed to be able to accept the almost unacceptable in him. "I told my dad, who was a former all star athlete, that I wasn't really interested in following our family male tradition in sports because it interfered with my studies and science projects. I know it must have been a disappointment to him, but he saw my interests and career ambitions as more important than his own desires. It was good to feel accepted, even though I appeared to be different. As it turned out, I went to college as a student athlete and succeeded in my studies and in sports. What was really important, at the time I expressed a lack of interest in sports, is that my dad accepted me. Because of this, I felt more free to discuss other problems with him."

Trust

Can I, as a parent, demonstrate trust in my child's career interests, self-assessment, and career life goals? Or do I object to youths' fantasies, their need for exploration, their sense of values? Teresa revealed in her career development sketch that she was constantly aware of her father's lack of trust in her career exploration ventures. "I had decided that I was a 'people-oriented' person and to gain some experience, I volunteered to participate in a community chest fund raising drive. My father's objections to taking a night shift were misinterpreted as a lack of trust, and the participation in the drive became a less meaningful experience. How could I get people-oriented experiences if my parents didn't trust me?"

Expressiveness

Can I, as a parent, be expressive enough so that what I believe will be communicated clearly and understandably? Or do differences of opinion with my child on career topics overshadow true meaning and rational thinking? Hank wrote in his sketch about his aptitude and interest in electronics: "When I told my parents of my intentions to drop a second language in my junior year in high school and enroll in electronics shop instead, they blew their respective stacks. They dwelled upon their shop biases rather than a set of reasons why, or why not, my plans were sound in pursuing my interest and in testing out my degree of aptitude. Now, as a second year student in engineering, I sure could have used the electronics shop experience."

Dependability

Can I, as a parent, create a feeling on the part of my child that I am dependable, that I am there when needed? Mary Ann explained that "the most anxious time in my career planning happened when I was about to enter my tenth year in school. The peer pressure was so strong. When I decided to take typing and shorthand, many of my girl friends made fun of me for taking a 'vocational' course of study. They said it would wipe out my chances of going to a good college. Good old dependable mom and dad; they were right there when I needed them. They agreed that the skills I would learn could be a real advantage when I went to college. We confirmed our thinking with my school counselor, and of course I really used my typing and shorthand skills in college, and I still do when I am taking notes or preparing reports."

Consistency

Can I, as a parent, relate to my child in a way that is consistent and that will build confidence in his or her knowing what to expect of me? Krista wrote in her autobiography that "the confidence I developed in exploring career ideas came from the even-mannered and even-tempered behavior of my parents. No matter how 'far out' my fantasies about what I wanted to be were, they would handle it. When I once told them I would like to become a rock singer, they encouraged me to explore my potential. Of course I learned soon enough that I didn't have either the aptitude or the temperament for that kind of a career. Now, I still enjoy singing and playing guitar with our office group."

Perceptiveness

Can I, as a parent, gain my child's confidence through acts and judgments that confirm my ability to understand his or her interests, ambitions, and goals? Jerry complained in his sketch that his father "never seemed to understand, especially the connections between my interests and long range goals. Like one time, when I told dad that I wanted to visit the U.S. Congress while we went on vacation. He said the idea was lofty but foolish. All important decisions in Washington, D.C., are made behind closed doors. Anyway, can't you just study government in school? He didn't understand the seriousness of my interests and judgment, and this occasion sure did shut me up about my long range ambition to go into politics. Now, I'm stuck in engineering, dad is paying some of the bills, and I'll have to delay my career plans until I get out on my own."

Genuineness

Can I, as a parent, respond to my child in such a way that what I know and what I believe will be conveyed? Bill, in his career development essay, told how he and his parents had disagreements about his career plans. "The thing about it was that we could always sit down and talk through our differences. They always leveled with me; they didn't beat around the bush. I convinced them that I was serious in my interest in automotive technology and they agreed to my enrollment in our local community college. Here, I can give it a try and if I learn this isn't for me, I can choose another alternative.

My parents' honesty is the thing that makes us get along together."

Positiveness

Can I, as a parent, display positive attitudes toward my child's career desires? George recalled that his dad had a positive attitude about his ideas—most of the time. "When I was little, I was a nut about science fiction, always recording, building, or playing games about science fiction stuff. About the only time dad wasn't positive in his reactions to my games was when I planned to fire my little brother into orbit on a rocket from the back yard. Almost no matter what I dreamed aloud or showed my dad in science fiction, he took me seriously and showed an interest. Actually, it was his positive attitude and interest in my school science project in microbiology that helped me decide on my studies later."

Objectivity

Can I, as a parent, allow my child to see himself/herself objectively—to face reality and weigh the pros and cons? John, in his essay, remembered the painful evaluating sessions he and his parents went through at almost every career decision step from choosing high school subjects and activities to selecting part-time jobs. "These were painful, but helpful because they forced me to go through reality testing with parents who could be objective enough to see more than one side of an issue. When I thought I would set a goal to make the ice hockey team, they helped me to realize my sense of balance and strength hardly would let me develop into an expert skater. Through their objectivity, I learned to be more objective, and it helped me to keep from being disappointed in trying without success."

Sensitivity

Can I, as a parent, act with sufficient sensitivity that my behavior will not be perceived as a threat to my child's ideas and sense of worthiness? Henry recalled in his sketch that his parents always seemed to make him feel worthwhile when he raised questions about schooling and planning for the future. "They were sensitive to my feelings and ideas. When they disagreed, they always helped me look at alternatives. The time I was going to drop out of our school photography club because I had a conflict with the club president, they didn't say, you shouldn't do that. They did help me look at alternatives to working out the conflict. I learned that differences with people shouldn't influence long range career decisions."

The previous thirteen qualities are not by any means the only parent qualities necessary to foster the feeling of worthiness in children and youth. As you can see from the sample self-sketches, however, these qualities can have significant effects on the individual and his or her future career plans and development.

The following rating scale is designed to help you assess the qualities in yourself that can help promote feelings of worthiness in your child.

Parent Worthiness Qualities Profile

Rate yourself on each quality and circle the appropriate number on the line opposite.

Quality	Bad	Poor	So-So	OK	Great
Respectfulness	1	2	3	4	5
Responsiveness	1	2	3	4	5
Empathy	1	2	3	4	5
Acceptance	1	2	3	4	5
Trust	1	2	3	4	5
Expressiveness	1	2	3	4	5
Dependability	1	2	3	4	5
Consistency	1	2	3	4	5
Perceptiveness	1	2	3	4	5
Genuineness	1	2	3	4	5
Positiveness	1	2	3	4	5
Objectivity	1	2	3	4	5
Sensitivity	1	2	3	4	5

Now draw a line joining all the numbers you have circled. This represents your worthiness qualities profile. If it is mostly on the *OK-Great* side, you are doing well in helping your child maintain faith and develop a feeling of worthiness. These parent qualities indicate very high expectations, and we know that we can't all be perfect. However, a parent can develop or improve these important qualities in many ways. Examples are participating in parent study groups sponsored by schools and PTAs; studying parent-child relationship books; group and family counseling; and working with your wife, husband, or a friend to improve in one or more of the qualities.

Now that we have presented steps in helping your child maintain faith and develop a feeling of worthiness in career planning, the next step is to concentrate on feelings of success.

Chapter 3

Reinforcing Your Child's Success In Work And Play

"Childhood and youth experiences in success build personal confidence."

"Poor motivation is due to lack of success."

"Success is a hill to climb."

In the step-by-step process of successful career planning and development, we have acknowledged that step 1, building and maintaining *faith*, is of vital importance throughout the life span. Step 2, developing the *feeling of worthiness*, is the ingredient that maintains that faith. Parents' awareness of these steps and their own behaviors become the most important influences in the process during the periods of early childhood and youth.

The struggle of growing up in an adult world is not easy for most children. Favorable experiences result in *success*, which supports faith and feelings of worthiness. Childhood and youth experiences in success can build or destroy personal confidence in decision-making (discussed in Chapter 4).

But what is success to a growing child? For most boys and girls, success, or the lack of it, is what they are and what they become. Another anecdote illustrates. A three-child family was preparing to have dinner at a local restaurant. Seated at the table were a girl age 13, a second girl age 11, a small boy age 4, and, of course, mother and dad. We couldn't help but overhear mother's instruction to the small boy, whose name was Greg. "This is a nice restaurant, and you are a good boy, and today you can order your own dinner, just like your dad does."

Mother then reviewed the menu with Greg, and the waitress took the orders. When she came to Greg, he said, "I'll have a coke and a hot dog."

The mother scolded Greg, making something of a scene, and authoritatively ordered a "nice meal" for Greg. When the waitress served Greg, she set a coke and a hot dog on the table before him. After a considerable silence and a show of mother's embarrassment, Greg in a shrill voice said, "Wow, she [the waitress] thinks I'm real!"

Success is feeling real. It is knowing that it is OK to make harmless mistakes. It is climbing a hill, getting to the top, and knowing how you got there. It is feeling accepted as a person. It is learning and getting a signal of joy from others that you have learned. It is confidence to try again after not doing so well.

The bottom line, step 3, is *success*. The following poem shows how success was expressed by one sixth-grade (11-year-old) girl.

Success Is a Hill to Climb
Krista, 6th grade
May 1967

A hill is to climb.
   The farther you climb,
   The higher you find yourself.
Sometimes you trip and fall.
   But pick yourself up
   Keep trying.
   Don't abandon the task.

There are many kinds of hills
   One, a hard rocky hill,
   The hill of success and belief.
Another, a not so easy, yet not too hard
   hill to climb,
   The hill of families and friends.
And yet another,
   A smooth and easy hill to climb,
   The hill of fun and games.
But, maybe YOU are the most rugged hill
   of all.

Building Successful Experiences

Successful experiences provide a basis for expanding interests and for the courage to try out new things. Fear of exploration and of trying is reduced when parents can walk hand-in-hand with their child through his/her exploratory attempts with work- or leisure-related tasks. It is with successful climbing that children become reinforced in their acceptance of themselves and in the confidence that success is possible.

Chapter 2 provided a glimpse of thirteen youths' life experiences in career-planning incidents; some were experiences of success and others related to failure. During the fantasy period of career development, the child develops a vital self-concept related to career awareness—the *self-concept of success*. Ironically, the concept of failure is often first learned in school. Hardly any parents say to a young child, "You are a failure!" But other, more subtle behaviors influence the formation of a child's self-concept of success or failure.

Parents must keep in mind that all hills to climb can be learning experiences, and that successes and lack of successes can be the bases of important decisions about the next hill to attempt. Although reinforcement of successful play activities and assigned and volunteer jobs done by children at home prior to school age are foundation factors in building self-concepts, school work and related social experiences become the self-structure of career development.

This self-structure becomes crucial during the tentative phase and the exploratory activities of career development. These periods begin during the junior and early senior high levels and can carry through adulthood. At those times, the acknowledgment of and feelings of success become confidence builders. The effects are important in the child's receptiveness to alternative choices and are supportive of freedom of choice. In effect, the influence is one of self-motivation.

William Glasser, noted psychiatrist and school consultant, declares that poor motivation is due more to lack of success than to any other one thing. How, then, can parents nurture childhood and youth motivations built on success? What parent signals and activities are basic?

First, parents must help their children learn that basic work attitudes of promptness, respect, responsibility, and interest in school work are expected both at home and at school. The development of work habits may be influenced by family, religious, or ethnic training and may influence the extent to which one develops such work habits on the job.

Second, the work a child does in school is good, important, and related to the larger world of work. All work requires use of basic skills, and both work and school contain elements related to data, people, and things.

Third, not all persons can be completely competent in all things, nor is it expected by parents that they should be. Skills required in one kind of occupation often are transferable to others.

Fourth, doing one's best is being successful as a person, and parents will not punish their children by comparing their work with others'—even brothers', sisters', or parents'—accomplishments. People in jobs derive a variety of satisfactions from their work—wages, personal relationships, prestige, challenge, competition, service to others, control, responsibility, dependence, and outlet for energy.

Fifth, children will be respected for doing what they are capable of doing, not for excuses they may make for not doing. One way to learn about work is to try different kinds of activities in different work situations to see what they are like, how one likes the activities, and how skillful one is in such activities.

Sixth, children can expect parents to get involved in their school work in almost every way except doing it for them. A person's career choice may be affected by learning about careers and getting accurately interpreted information; on the other hand, decisions may also be affected by how one feels about the choice or what others feel about that choice.

Seventh, the basics—reading, writing, and arithmetic—are related to all the kinds of work people do. All work relates, in varying degrees, to the production of materials or rendering of services. Generally, those who have the appropriate education and training are the ones who get the jobs.

Eighth, a climate conducive to study will be maintained in the home as well as in school; that means some routine budgeting of time and limitations on such interferences as too much television viewing. Generally, the more schooling one has, the greater one's earning power. Most entry jobs require at least a high school education or its equivalent.

Ninth, parents are home teachers, and to the degree possible, they will help with resources and materials. Some jobs require a certain kind and amount of experience (apprenticeship, on-the-job training, internship, and so on) before a person is accepted as a qualified worker. The work force structure tends to be changing so that more jobs require people to provide services rather to produce materials and equipment. Even with greater automation and cybernation, projections of manpower needs suggest that most people will work. As science and technology advance, a greater variety of occupations tends to be developed.

Tenth, parents will be the connecting link between home and teachers and schools, and they will take part in parent-school involvement programs. The necessity of formal education (learning in school) tends to increase in importance as technology expands.

Eleventh, children should try their hand in school activities outside the classroom, and parents will help all they can. Hobbies and leisure time activities may lead to occupational opportunities if children are given the appropriate exposure and demonstrate ability in such activities.

Twelfth, work is something everybody can do and enjoy, and school is work and can be enjoyable. The kind of work one does can be a personal decision, based on the individual's knowledge of his own capacity to develop skills and to develop them so that they may be salable.

Thirteenth, school is a place to learn, and if a child learns what he/she can, be it a little or a lot, he/she has not failed. The child will be a success with parents and with himself. Almost all jobs require people to have certain skills in symbol learning—that is, reading, writing, computation, and communication. Basic symbol skills and communication skills may be acquired through the study of subjects offered in schools, kindergarten through postgraduate work. Most jobs have educational or training requirements.

These are thirteen "signal items" parents can use to *build success*, which supports the *faith* and *feelings of worthiness* so important to healthy career planning.

Hill-to-Climb Checklist

Here is a hill to climb—for parents and their children. Check the blanks before each step that applies to you to evaluate your effect on building success experiences.

              _____ 13. Recognize school as place to learn
            _____ 12. Recognize school as work
          _____ 11. Encourage extracurricular activities
        _____ 10. Maintain school link
      _____ 9. Serve as home teacher
    _____ 8. Provide study climate
   _____ 7. Encourage mastery of basic skills
  _____ 6. Become involved in child's school work
 _____ 5. Express respect for doing
_____ 4. Recognize doing one's best as success
_____ 3. Recognize degrees of competency
_____ 2. Emphasize importance of school
_____ 1. Encourage basic work attitudes   *Bottom Line—Success*

For each blank without a check, analyze the importance of the item to your child's success self-concept. A talk with the child about your checklist, or even a comparison of how the child would mark it for the parent, will give you ideas on how you rate and on how you can help.

Chapter 4

Teaching Your Child How To Make Career Decisions

"Many people change their goals and career directions while growing up and even during adulthood."

"Career decision-making requires a step-by-step plan of action."

"Decisions should be realistic, based on sound information."

Healthy career development and realistic career decision-making seldom occur by chance. Most successful persons decide what they want in a career and how to get there based on firmly established faith in themselves, on a personal feeling of worthiness, and on the reinforcement gained through successful experiences. To be sure, some children seem to know what they want to do in life even before they enter school. This is rare, however, and many people change their goals and career directions many times while growing up and even during adulthood.

Just as "man does not live by bread alone," neither do child and youth decision-makers act on information and plan on their own. They are influenced by parents, who can help in planning and using information for decision-making. Parents should be warned, therefore, of two dangers in decision-making that, if not recognized and overcome, can result in unrealistic and unhappy choices. First, early specific occupational decisions may not be wise, because they can close the doors on future opportunities. Second, parents have told us that they have difficulty obtaining accurate, understandable information about possible careers, and without it, realistic planning is almost impossible.

Making a premature job decision may require a person to pay a painful and long-term price if change is desired later on. As just one example, many small boys are unduly pressured to participate in early organized childhood sports with the hope of winning a "student athlete" college scholarship or becoming a professional athlete. In the majority of such cases, physical growth, coordination, and competition keep the growing child from excelling in sports, and result in a waste of time and effort that might have been applied otherwise—for example in sports that might provide leisure time satisfaction in later life. With greater sports opportunities for girls today, they can be caught in the same kind of trap. As another example, you may remember Peggy in Chapter 2, whose parents discouraged her from seeking post-high-school education because she "would probably get married soon after high school anyway." A decision based on such reasons may be a great drawback to Peggy's career development and is certainly based on limited, if not false, information about the role of women in careers and at home.

Career decision-making requires a step-by-step plan of action based on accurate information. Charles ("Boss") Kettering, the famous inventor and automobile giant, once advised: "The future is what we are all interested in, because all of us are going to spend the rest of our lives there, and the future begins two seconds from now." He meant that all important decisions are based on a series of smaller decisions, which become the foundation for choice. Kettering's attitude is important in successful career decision-making, for most people spend over 100,000 hours of their lives working. Obviously, anything your child will devote so much time to should be carefully planned, and decisions should be realistic, based on sound information.

Dr. H.B. Gelatt, director of guidance for the Palo Alto Unified School District in California and, consultant since 1971, with the College Entrance Examination Board, proposed a decision-making plan widely used in school guidance programs. In his research, he found that a "conceptual frame of reference" is basic to the decision-making process. His plan has become known under the label "Decide" and is widely used in schools offering courses and learning activities for career planning and exploration of decisions and outcomes. Basic to the deciding process are: (1) personal aspects of the "deciding self" (examining and recognizing personal values); (2) "prior to deciding" (gaining knowledge and using appropriate and adequate information); and (3) "applying skills" (knowing and using a workable strategy for putting information into action). In his research, Dr. Gelatt has found that a "conceptual frame of reference" is basic to the decision-making process.

A most important concept in decision-making is that it is a process, a series of action steps resulting in a realistic and appropriate choice. Frank Parsons, as long ago as 1909 in his book *Choosing a Vocation*, prescribed a three-step process. First, a person should engage in self-analysis—that is, examine personal interests, aptitudes, achievement levels, and personal characteristics. Second, a person should analyze the world of occupations—that is, the nature of work tasks in jobs and the personal, physical, and educational requirements. Third, a person should, from what he has learned in the first two steps, match person to occupation. This three-step process seems simplistic and suggests a danger in matching persons with jobs at the expense of learning and development. It also suggests a one-time action rather than a developmental career planning process. Other career decision-making plans abound in books and magazines, many of which are valuable to the career planning helper.

SWING: A Step-by-Step Process

What follows is our frame of reference for a step-by-step approach to career decision-making for children and youth. We use the acronym SWING for the decision-making process leading to a career goal:

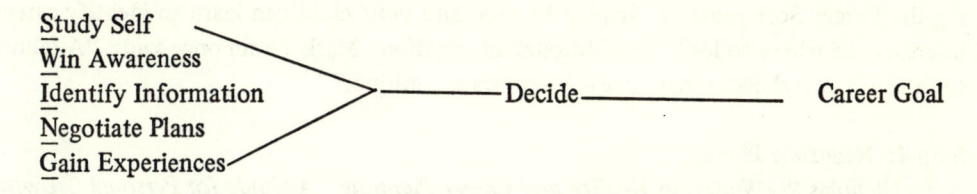

<u>S</u>tudy Self
<u>W</u>in Awareness
<u>I</u>dentify Information ⟩————— Decide ————— Career Goal
<u>N</u>egotiate Plans
<u>G</u>ain Experiences

SWING is a process that incorporates a series of steps, sometimes interchangeable, sometimes backward or forward, but always career-goal-oriented. It is partly attitudinal and partly a matter of planning. From an attitudinal point of view, it emphasizes that learning can come from trying and even temporary failure. Nancy Lopez, sensational 1978 golf rookie who went into a tailspin after setting records for eight major tournament victories in early summer, said: "I'm always learning how to improve my game, and I'll be back on top because I learn from my defeats." Later in the summer, she won the European Women's Open Golf Tournament by three strokes. Pete Rose, the "hustling" Cincinnati Red, after his 1978 National League record hitting streak ended at 44 consecutive games, said: "Tomorrow, I'll *swing* and hit again." And in his next game, he had four hits, including two singles, a double, and a home run. And again, Charles E. Kettering, whose more than one hundred major inventions influence all our lives, said: "For each of my successes, I had a hundred failures, but I always learned enough from them to try again. For, like Edison, Ford, and many others, that's the story of my success and of my life." As we pointed out in Chapter 3, success is the "bottom line" but it is also a "tough hill to climb."

SWING suggests ways you can help in your child's career decision-making and goal-setting.

Step 1: Study Self

According to Dr. William W. Purkey, well-known educational psychologist, "the ways in which a person views him/herself and his/her world are products of how others see him/her and are the major forces in his/her achievement." Parents will be helpful to their children if they develop and practice the worthiness qualities described in Chapter 2.

Step 2: Win Awareness

Richard Bolles, in his best-selling career decision book, *What Color Is Your Parachute?*, declares that only you can decide, but you must win an awareness of who you are and what you can do. You can help your child by understanding and using interest, aptitude, achievement, and personality factors in your career advice (see Chapter 10). It is the shades of these data, as we suggest in Chapter 10, and their relation to your child's self-concept that aid in healthy career decision-making.

Step 3: Identify Information

We have found in our research and that of our students that good decisions can be made without sound information, but that *accurate information is necessary* in order to assure good decisions. You should help your child understand Data, People, and Things cues (Chapters 5, 6, 7) and help them get accurate information on these factors. By playing the Career Sort game in Chapter 13, you and your child can learn to identify career interests and where to look for additional information. Mark Twain once said: "A fellow can't think or feel accurately unless he knows something."

Step 4: Negotiate Plans

Nicholas W. Weiler, in *Reality and Career Planning: A Guide for Personal Growth*, points out that one needs a carefully devised plan if one expects to "take charge" of one's career development and life growth. You can help your child negotiate plans by weighing all the factors related to his/her self-concept and his/her potential with Data-People-Things aspects of work activities (see Chapters 5, 6, 7). Like Robert J. Ringer, in his best-selling book, *Winning Through Intimidation*, you can help your child by sizing up the situation, developing a plan of action, and then negotiating a winning decision.

Step 5: Gain Experiences

Ben Franklin advised that "Experience is the best teacher!" You can help your child in career development and decision-making if you really put this book to use. A career is more than just a job. It is what persons do in their total life experience. As we will see in Chapter 8, exploration is a healthy, almost "fail-safe" way to learn about job functions related to Data-People-Things and to oneself. In most applied work—teaching, bricklaying, selling, and so on—early tryout experiences are required before special training is scheduled. Try to help your child gain experience through exploration.

We have found that SWING, these five steps, can be repeated without paying a dear price. SWING provides an awareness that can help your child learn without experiencing the pain of great failure. SWING develops a parent-child partnership like the ones described in self-sketches by Jim, Don, Mary Ann, Krista, Bill, George, John, and Henry in Chapter 2.

A footnote in bold print should be added to the SWING process in decision-making steps. Each of the steps will be affected by change—change in economic, social, educational, and your child's personal condition at any given time. It is important, therefore, to stay current and to use the most up-to-date information in support of each SWING step.

Now, parents, test yourselves and see if you have learned the SWING steps for the decision-maker.

The SWING Test for Parents

In the blanks below, complete the five-step decision-making process:

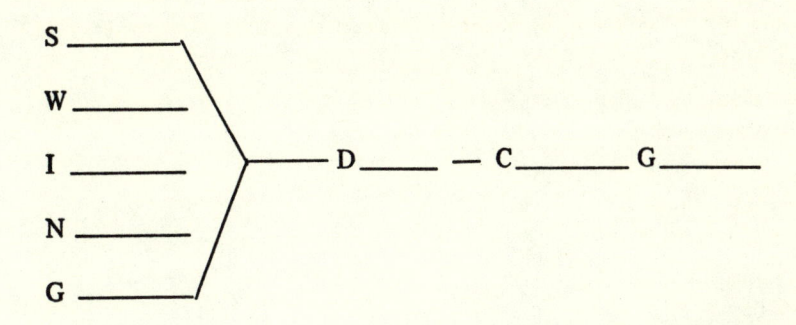

```
S _____
W _____
I _____  >----- D _____ -- C _____ G _____
N _____
G _____
```

Scoring:

    All blanks correct: home run
    All but 3 blanks correct: on base with a hit
    More than 3 blanks incorrect: strikeout*

*But remember, the game isn't over and you can get to bat again if you review this chapter for the correct answers.

Chapter 5

Exploring The World of Work: Data Cues

"All people are involved in one way or another with job activities that relate to Data-People-Things."

"Various relationships with Data-People-Things can be described as worker functions."

You can approach the matter of helping your child examine the world of work in many ways. One of the most direct and universal ways is to look at the work a person does on the job. All people are involved in one way or another with job activities that relate to *Data-People-Things*.

The *Dictionary of Occupational Titles* (DOT), fourth edition, 1977, is published by the U.S. Department of Labor. This book classifies every major occupation in the country—some 20,000—by the degree to which it relates to *data, people,* or *things* on a scale of 0 (high) to 8 (low). This reference is one of the two or three most widely used career information resources in the United States and is usually found in public or school libraries, career resource centers, and guidance offices. We recommend the DOT for in-depth exploration of occupational information. We have chosen to use the DOT and the Data-People-Things approach because:

1. It relates to all occupations
2. It relates to all individuals
3. It relates to most government publications
4. It relates to school subjects
5. It relates to leisure activities.

Figure 1

Activities in the Data-People-Things Hierarchies

		Data	People	Things
Complex	High	0 Synthesizing 1 Coordinating 2 Analyzing	0 Mentoring 1 Negotiating 2 Instructing 3 Supervising 4 Diverting	0 Setting Up 1 Precision Working 2 Operating-Controlling 3 Driving-Operating
	Average	3 Compiling 4 Computing 5 Copying 6 Comparing	5 Persuading 6 Speaking-Signaling 7 Serving 8 Taking Instructions-Helping	4 Manipulating 5 Tending 6 Feeding-Offbearing 7 Handling
Simple	Low	7 No Significant Relationship	9 No Significant Relationship	8 No Significant Relationship

In Chapter 13, the "Career Sort" provides you with a series of card cutouts based on the 83 major occupational groups and their relation to Data-People-Things. These cards should be used by your child as a sorting game to identify likes and dislikes and to help narrow interests for the purpose of further career search.

The next two chapters will provide some background on this approach to the world of work and will tell you how to help your child understand and relate to it in his/her own career development and decision-making. The various relationships with Data-People-Things can be described as worker functions—what the workers do with data, people, or things. Each chapter lists worker functions ranging from relatively simple to more complex tasks. Individuals relate to Data-People-Things in the same way occupations do. Each of us relates to data in some degree from simple to complex in work or at leisure. We may, for example, like to do crossword puzzles—a fairly complex activity—but not like to be around people or put things together with tools. Or we may like all three activities; either way, the experience provides insight and cues to self-understanding and understanding of the world of work at the same time. The overall organization of the Data-People-Things hierarchies is shown in Figure 1.

Data Work Defined

Data work can be defined as working with or dealing with *information, knowledge, ideas*, or *concepts*. These may be obtained by *observation, investigation, interpretation, visualization* (mental pictures or images). Data cannot be touched or handled but may be expressed in numbers, words, or symbols. Data also may be expressed by the spoken word, or may be in the form of ideas and thoughts.

In other words, data work involves mainly working with *words, numbers*, or *ideas in a variety of activities* that range from simple to complex. Each of us relates in some degree to data in our work or leisure. Every occupation also relates in some degree to data. Here is the way the *Dictionary of Occupational Titles* organizes the functions from complex to simple.

High (Complex)

0 Synthesizing: Discovering facts and/or developing logical conclusions or interpretations of ideas by bringing together the analyses of data (results of examining and determining the value of data).

1 Coordinating: Determining the time, place, and order of operations or actions to be performed as a result of analyzing data (see item 3, Analyzing). Carrying out and/or reporting on actions decided upon.

2 Analyzing: Examining and determining the value of data, which sometimes results in a need to choose the best course of action to be taken.

Average

3 Compiling: Gathering information about data, people, or things and putting it together in proper order. Frequently involves reporting and/or carrying out activities indicated by the information.

4 Computing: Performing arithmetic operations, reporting results, or carrying out activities as indicated by the results. Does not include counting.

5 Copying: Transcribing data (rewriting from another copy or from shorthand notes), or posting data (entering it in ledgers or account books).

6 Comparing: Judging data, people, or things according to what can readily be observed, such as what they do, how they look, or how they are made, and whether they are usual or differ from the usual.

Low (Simple)

7 No Significant Relationship

Remember, these are some of the worker functions carried out directly on the job. Each level indicates the degree of occupationally significant relationship with data for an occupation. You may notice some of these levels of functioning in your child's school work, club involvement, and chores around the home, as well as in a host of leisure activities. They are important clues to look for in your child's career development and to encourage as it seems appropriate.

A great many occupations are involved in a significant way with data. Sometimes a worker deals mainly with data alone—a typist, for example. Some estimates place the number of such occupations at nearly 10 percent of all available employment, and such occupations have increased in recent years. Some workers are involved with both data and things in a significant way—a floral designer, pharmacist, or machinist, for example. Some estimate the number of such jobs as high as 30 percent. So the emphasis on words and numbers found in the schools is reflected in the requirements for many occupations.

Occupations Relating Primarily to Data

In occupations relating primarily to data, the worker is mainly involved with information or conceptual knowledge. There is no significant relationship between these jobs and people or things. Some such occupations are:

Production Planner	Clerk-Typist
Accountant	Bookkeeper
Abstractor	Insurance Clerk
Contract Clerk	Mail Carrier
Stenographer	Billing Machine Operator
File Clerk	Typist
	Meter Reader

Noticing the Cues in Your Child

As you can see, these jobs mainly involve working with words and numbers. If your children at an early age begin to enjoy playing number or word games, it is a cue to their interests in the area of data. If they like mathematics and English in school at a later date, you have another cue to their data pursuits. As your child gets older, he/she may express special interest in clubs involving numbers, such as math clubs or neighborhood or religious organizations requiring record (books) keeping. Should you sense these interests, you as a parent may want to encourage the exploration of these leisure activities as a tryout for more serious interaction with data. Interest in a pocket calculator also may serve as a cue to an interest in data for your child.

Occupations Relating Primarily to Data and Things

In the following occupations, the worker has a double involvement, relating primarily to information or conceptual knowledge and relating in a significant way to objects or things. One's relationship with people is not *occupationally* significant—a person may work around people but not relate to them in a significant way. Some such occupations are:

Chemical Engineer	Pathologist
Mining Engineer	Food Chemist
Dairy Herder	Parts Clerk
Tool and Die Maker	Keypunch Operator
Automobile Mechanic	Line Worker
Watchmaker	Installer-Repairer
Electrician	Baker
Miner	Cook
Oil Burner Installer	Bricklayer
Roofer	Cable Splicer
Parts Clerk	Plumber

Noticing the Cues in Your Child

Some of the same cues that were suggested for relating to data interests of your child can be used here as well. In addition, you can pick up hints if your child likes to collect things—tools, stamps, pictures, flowers, and so on. Another way to relate to this area is to provide parts of an old watch or motor to observe—whether the child shows any natural interest. You may want to encourage your child to watch and help you fix a lamp or tinker with the family car. If you have magazines around the house that relate to data or things, encourage your child to read and explore some of the ideas found there. If you have back issues of old magazines, you can let your child cut up some of the pictures to make a scrapbook or collage.

In the middle school or junior high school years, your child's collecting and reading may get more serious—and more costly. You may want to encourage your child to take some exploratory courses, such as industrial arts or home economics, to probe further interests in data or things. Lessons in various musical instruments such as a piano may provide other clues. At a higher level in high school, formal courses in advanced math, chemistry, physics, or earth science should be fostered. Groups such as science clubs, stage crews, explorer scouts, and others should be considered. Summer and part-time work represent another way to explore interest in data or things.

Food preparation occupations are in the Data-Things area. They will continue to be among the fastest-growing of all occupations over the next decade. Your preschool and elementary school age child can be made aware of the work involved in the food preparation process—and not just by cleaning up. Here are some suggestions:

1. Talk about food preparation at mealtime.
2. Make available small cooking units (such as an easy bake oven) for child's play.
3. Buy books with simple recipes for children.
4. Let your child assist in easy food preparation: fixing gelatin, fixing prepared pudding mixes, fixing pans for baking mix.
5. Watch food preparation in commercial establishments or on TV.
6. Talk with cooks, chefs, and bakers about their work.

You should be able to think of other ways of making your child aware of occupational functions and then moving on to more specific exploring activities if your child's interest, attention, and ability support it. Remember, two major things are going on in this developmental process. First, your child is learning more about him/herself. Second, your child is learning more about career options. It is possible that even if your child shows an early interest in, say, food preparation, that interest will not grow beyond a certain point. That's all part of exploring. Perhaps this involvement with food preparation will lead to satisfying leisure activities later in life. The point is that as a parent you can assist this awareness and exploration process in your child's career development better than anyone else. Be assertive about helping your child explore data.

A ten-point checklist at the end of the chapter will help you see how well you are doing.

Conversation Corner

Some questions to talk about at mealtime, while riding in the family automobile, or on a family outing.

1. Why do you think individuals like to work with data?

2. Whom do you know in your neighborhood who works with data?

3. What satisfaction do you think individuals get from working with data?

4. How many occupations dealing primarily with data can you name that are done by friends and relatives?

5. Where are the places of employment for individuals who are in data occupations in your neighborhood or school? What are they?

Data Exploration Checklist

Put a check mark by each activity you have been engaged in as a family. Count one point for each check.

_____ 1. Encourage your child to be aware of working with data (words-numbers-ideas).

_____ 2. Encourage your child to be aware of individuals who work with data.

_____ 3. Encourage your child to be aware of play activities that involve data.

_____ 4. Encourage your child to explore activities (games, hobbies, etc.) that involve working with data.

_____ 5. Encourage your child to explore school subjects (math, science) related to data.

_____ 6. Encourage your child to explore part-time, summer, or volunteer work relating to data.

_____ 7. Encourage your child to explore books, magazines, and television programs about working with data.

_____ 8. Encourage your child to get involved with clubs and extra-curricular activities related to data.

_____ 9. Encourage your child to talk with individuals who work with data.

_____ 10. Encourage your child to explore ways of getting the proper education and training to go into careers involving data.

_____ Total points (checks)

How did you score? Ten points? If so, you are really helping your child become aware of the potential for working with data and knowing more about him/herself. Five points is about average. Three points or less means you should review Chapter 5 and arrange some activities that may provide opportunities for self and career awareness and exploration on the part of your son or daughter.

Keep working at it!

Chapter 6

Exploring The World of Work: People Cues

"A growing number of jobs primarily involve working with people."

"You may be able to pick up cues if your child likes to play with other children rather than play alone."

Now that you have been introduced to the Data-People-Things system and have seen how it works with data, it is going to be easier to follow the people and things cues. In this chapter, we will help you think about occupations involving working with people and how your child may be giving you some cues you may not have recognized. First, what do we mean by *people* work?

People Work Defined

People work is working with human beings or with animals when they are given care and consideration similar to that given human beings.

Simply put, people work is working with humans or animals.

The same hierarchy that was used with data is used here to describe worker functions ranging from simple to complex (DOT):

High (Complex)	0 Mentoring:	Dealing with individuals in terms of their total personality to advise or counsel them on problems by applying principles of law, science, medicine, religion, or other professions.
	1 Negotiating:	Exchanging ideas, information, and opinions with others to make policies, plan programs, and/or arrive jointly at decisions, conclusions, or solutions.

	2 Instructing:	Teaching subject matter to others, or training others (including animals) through explaining, demonstrating, or supervising practice; using knowledge gained through specialized training, such as in medicine, law, or engineering, to make recommendations.
	3 Supervising:	Determining or explaining work to others, encouraging them to get along well with each other and to do their best work.
	4 Diverting:	Amusing others.
Average	5 Persuading:	Influencing others in favor of a product, service, or opinion.
	6 Speaking-Signaling:	Talking with and/or signaling people to give or exchange information. Includes assigning tasks or giving directions to helpers or assistants.
	7 Serving:	Attending to the requests or needs of people or animals. Carrying out the wishes of people, either expressed or understood without being expressed. Immediate response is involved.
Low (Simple)	8 Taking Instructions-Helping:	Helping applies to "nonlearning" helpers. Routine—no variety of responsibility is involved in this function.
	9 No Significant Relationship	

Remember, these are some of the worker's functions, carried out directly on the job. Each level indicates the degree of occupationally significant relationship with people. You may notice some of these levels of functioning in your child's school work, club involvement, summer or part-time employment, or chores around the home, as well as in a host of leisure activities. They are important clues to look for in your child's career development. Encourage those that seem appropriate.

More workers are involved today in rendering services (teaching, cooking, managing, and so on) than in producing goods (manufacturing, mining, farming). Figure 2 shows this gradual change over the last thirty years, and further predictions appear in Chapter 9. This increase in service-producing industries implies a growing number of jobs that primarily involve working with people in some occupationally significant way. A key factor is to understand that working *around* people is not as important in the hierarchy as the *complexity* of the tasks involving people.

Some estimates indicate that about 10 percent or more of all jobs are involved primarily with people rather than with data or things. These jobs include concessions attendant, hostess, security guard, bartender, and orderly. Currently, schools do not put much emphasis on people-related skills, so you may have to keep a special eye out for opportunities to encourage people-related skills in your child.

Figure 2

Industries providing services offer more jobs than those providing goods

Goods producing
  Manufacturing
  Agriculture
  Contract
    construction
  Mining

Service producing
  Trade
  Government
  Services
  Transportation
    and public utilities
  Finance,
    insurance and
    real estate

Workers (in millions) 1/

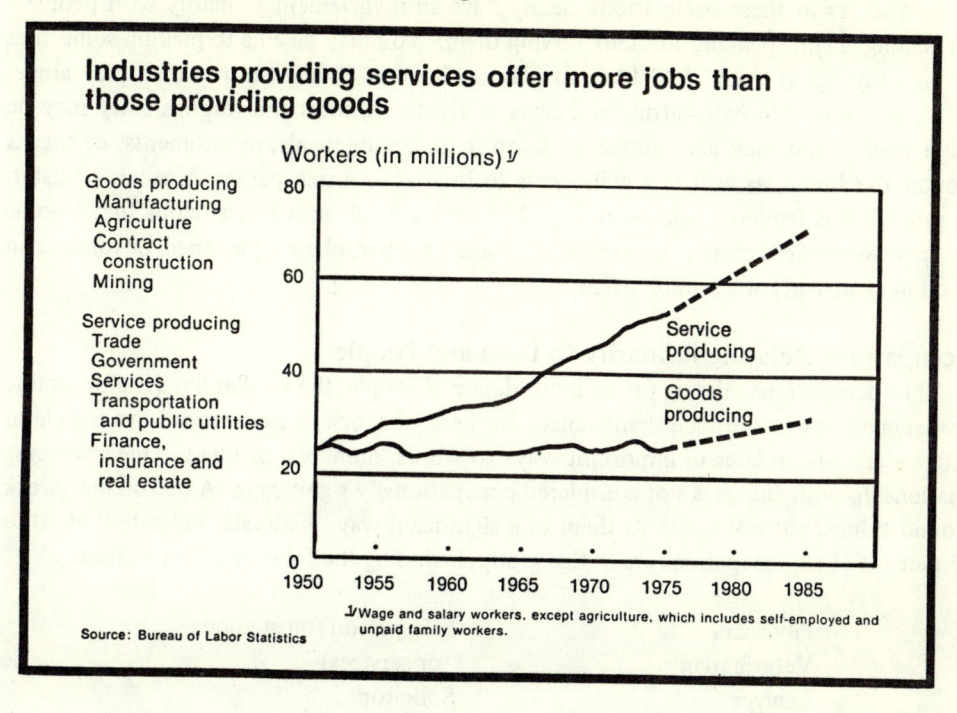

[Line graph showing Service producing rising from ~25 million in 1950 to ~70 million by 1985, and Goods producing remaining relatively flat around 25-30 million from 1950 to 1985, with dashed projections after 1975]

1/ Wage and salary workers, except agriculture, which includes self-employed and unpaid family workers.

Source: Bureau of Labor Statistics

Occupations Relating Primarily to People

In the following occupations, the individual is primarily involved in working with human beings or animals in an occupationally significant way. There is no significant working relationship with data or things.

        Concessions Attendant
        Hostess
        Security Guard
        Lifeguard
        Waiter/Waitress
        Bartender
        Practical Nurse
        House Parent
        Nurse's Aide
        Orderly

Noticing the Cues in Your Child

Workers in these occupations clearly have an involvement primarily with people—persuading them, speaking to them, serving them. You may be able to pick up some cues by an early age if your child likes to play with other children rather than play alone. Later, an interest in baby-sitting and signs of trustworthiness and responsibility may be other cues. You may also notice an interest in serving meals, refreshments, or snacks around the house, as well as a willingness to look after a sick parent, brother, or sister. In general, this tendency will be reflected in such school activities as clubs that emphasize people-oriented events—sponsoring a pancake supper, planning a dance, or running an election campaign for a school office.

Occupations Relating Primarily to Data and People

In occupations relating primarily to data *and* people, the worker has a major double involvement of occupational significance. In these jobs, one relates primarily to people or animals and also relates in important ways to words, numbers, or ideas. One's working relationship with things is not considered occupationally significant. A person may work around things, but not relate to them in a significant way. Estimates indicate that 20 to 25 percent of all occupations are in this group, including the following illustrations:

Physician	Salesperson (most goods or services)
Veterinarian	
Lawyer	Solicitor
Case Worker/Social Worker	Medical Assistant
School Principal	Teacher Aide
Manager	Bookmobile Driver
Supervisor	Medical Secretary
Dietitian	Teller
Bank Cashier	Hotel/Post Office Clerk
Funeral Director	Receptionist
Teacher (most subjects)	Library Assistant
Reporter	Nurse
Police Officer	Dental Assistant
	Cashier-Checker

It is easy to see from even a quick glance that many well-known occupations are included in this list. A person in one of these occupations may perform rather complex worker functions, often requiring long periods of schooling and mastery of complex tasks. These also are among the occupations with the most prestige. Figure 3 shows the importance of trade-sales work in our economy. Sales work is a major area of People-Data employment.

Figure 3

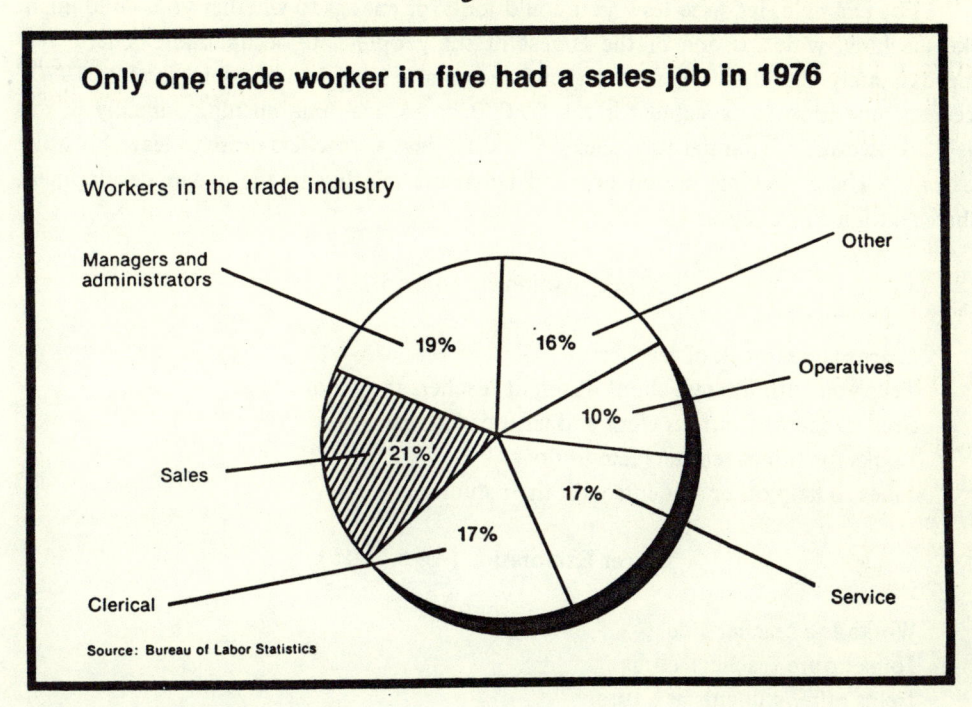

Only one trade worker in five had a sales job in 1976

Workers in the trade industry

- Managers and administrators — 19%
- Other — 16%
- Operatives — 10%
- Service — 17%
- Clerical — 17%
- Sales — 21%

Source: Bureau of Labor Statistics

Twenty-two percent of total employment in *all* industries is in wholesale and retail sales.

Noticing the Cues in Your Child

What are the cues you can look for here? Some suggestions in the previous chapter on data have the same implications here: the desire to play, explore, or work with words, numbers, or ideas, especially as these may relate to human beings or animals. You can see these early in your child's development. Signs include a lasting love of animals, keeping pets around the house, a genuine caring for not only their own pets but others' animals as well. The same cues apply to liking other children:

1. Does your child strike up a conversation easily?
2. Does your child like to be with other children?
3. Does your child like to take friends along on trips?
4. Does your child like to play people games?
5. Does your child have a sincere interest in others?

For example, let's see how you could look for cues as to whether your child might like teaching, which is one of the largest of the People-Data occupations. There were approximately 2,500,000 elementary and secondary school teachers in the late 1970s. Keen competition is expected for the 80,000 or so positions opening annually in this field. However, substantial vacancies occur each year as teachers retire or leave for other reasons. These cues are action oriented behaviors relating to the career development phases outlined in Chapter 1.

Career Awareness (Ages 5-10)

Learns about work of teachers
Tells you with interest about different teachers in school
Sees teachers in various work and leisure settings
Looks for things teachers like to do
Likes to help other students with their studies

Career Exploration (Ages 11-15)

Works as a teacher aide
Joins future teachers' clubs
Helps other students as a tutor
Watches by choice TV programs and movies about teachers
Likes to instruct in civic and religious groups

Career Preparation (Ages 16-22)

Instructs in a summer camp
Works as a part-time recreation aide
Coaches little league teams
Serves as a peer counselor
Volunteers to grade papers for math teachers

You can encourage the activities on this list by supporting the natural awareness, exploration, and preparation process. Give strong encouragement to your child to probe his/her people interests and abilities thoroughly and, in so doing, to get a better understanding of the worker functions for some of the major people occupations.

Conversation Corner

Some questions to talk about at mealtime, in the family automobile, or on a family outing:

1. If you had a chance, would you rather work alone or with one or more persons? Why?
2. Why do individuals like to work with people?
3. What satisfactions are gained from working with people?
4. How many of your friends or relatives work in people-type jobs?
5. Where are some of the people occupations in your neighborhood?

People Exploration Checklist

Put a check mark by each activity you have been engaged in as a family. Count one point for each check.

_____ 1. Encourage your child to be aware of working with people (human beings or animals).

_____ 2. Encourage your child to be aware of individuals who work with people.

_____ 3. Encourage your child to be aware of play activities that involve people.

_____ 4. Encourage your child to explore activities (games, hobbies, etc.) that involve people.

_____ 5. Encourage your child to explore school subjects (distributive education, psychology) related to people.

_____ 6. Encourage your child to explore part-time, summer, or volunteer work relating to people.

_____ 7. Encourage your child to explore books, magazines, television programs about working with people.

_____ 8. Encourage your child to talk with individuals who work with people.

_____ 9. Encourage your child to get involved with clubs and extracurricular activities involved with people.

_____ 10. Encourage your child to explore ways of getting the proper education and training to go into careers involving people.

_____ Total points (checks)

How did you score? Ten points? If so, you are really helping your child become aware of the potential for working with people and knowing more about him/herself. Five is about average. Three or less is low—review Chapter 6 and arrange some activities that may provide opportunities for self and career awareness on the part of your son and daughter.

Keep working at it!

Chapter 7

Exploring The World of Work: Things Cues

"About 20 percent of all occupations require workers to deal mainly with things."

"Girls show just as much interest in things as boys."

By now, you should have gotten the hang of the Data-People-Things concept. It is an easy and convenient way to look at oneself and the world of work. This chapter deals with the *things* concept. You should find it possible to relate to *things* occupations and the way your child may demonstrate some interest and ability regarding *things* activities.

Things Work Defined

Things work involves lifeless objects as distinguished from people or animals, such as substances or materials, machines, tools, equipment, or products. They can be touched or handled and have such characteristics as shape, form, weight, texture, and so on.

Remember, an orientation toward things relates to your child's interests, aptitudes, and achievement—the total self—as well as to a way of looking at jobs in the world of work. Chapter 10 will help you learn more about ways to improve your child's self-understanding.

Keep in mind that girls will probably show just as much interest in things as boys. Sex-role stereotypes that have kept women out of the occupations that relate to this worker function are disappearing, and there is some evidence that girls, especially at an early age, demonstrate better eye-hand coordination, manual dexterity, and manipulative skills than boys. As a parent, you can help provide an opportunity for early awareness of such tendencies by making available play tool kits, rubber hammers, plastic toy tools, erector sets, and the like to *both* your son and your daughter; the results may surprise you!

Here are the worker function levels of the *things* hierarchy (DOT).

High
(Complex)

0 Setting Up: Adjusting machines or equipment by replacing or altering tools, jigs, fixtures, and attachments to prepare them to perform their functions, change their performance, or restore their proper functioning if they break down. This group includes workers who set up one or a number of machines for other workers or who set up and personally operate a variety of machines.

1 Precision Working: Using parts of the body, usually with tools or work aids, to work, guide, or place objects or materials in such a way that rigid standards for the product or process will be met. Considerable judgment on the part of the precision worker is required in selecting the right tools, objects, or material and correctly applying the tool to the task.

2 Operating-Controlling: Starting, stopping, controlling, and adjusting the progress of machines or equipment designed to manufactur and/or process objects or materials. Operating involves setting up the machine and adjusting it or the material as the work progresses. Controlling equipment involves watching gauges, dials, etc., and turning valves and other devices to control such factors as temperature, pressure, flow of liquids, speed of pumps, and reactions of materials. Frequent adjustments of the equipment may be needed.

3 Driving-Operating: Starting, stopping, and controlling the actions of machines or equipment which must be steered or guided to manufacture, process, and/or move things or people. Involves such activities as watching gauges and dials; estimating distances, and determining speed and direction of other objects; turning cranks and wheels; pushing clutches or brakes; and pushing or pulling gear lifts or levers. Includes such machines as cranes, conveyor systems, tractors, paving machines, hoisting machines, and equipment for loading large industrial furnaces. Does not include machines powered by hand such as hand trucks and dollies, or power-assisted machines like electric wheelbarrows or electric hand trucks.

Average	4 Manipulating:	Using tools, special devices, or parts of the body to work, move, guide, or place objects or materials. Involves the use of some judgment with regard to the degree of accuracy needed and the selecting the proper tool, object, or material, but such judgments are usually not difficult to make.
	5 Tending:	Starting, stopping, and watching the operation of machines and equipment. Involves adjusting materials or controls of the machine, such as changing guides, adjusting timers and temperature gauges, turning valves to allow flow of materials, and flipping switches in response to lights. Little judgment is involved in making these adjustments.
	6 Feeding-Offbearing:	Throwing, dumping, putting, or feeding materials into or removing them from machines or equipment which may be automatic or may be tended or operated by other workers.
Low (Simple)	7 Handling:	Using parts of the body, hand tools, and/or special devices to work, move, or carry objects or materials. Permits little or no judgment in meeting standards or in selecting the proper tool, object, or material.
	8 No Significant Relationship	

Remember, these are some of the worker functions carried out directly on the job. Each level indicates the degree of occupationally significant relationship with things for an occupation. You may notice some of these levels of functioning in your child's school work, club involvement, summer or part-time employment, or chores around the home, or in a host of leisure activities. They are important cues to look for in your child's career development.

Even though the emphasis of the nation's economy is now more on providing services, significant numbers of persons are involved in the production of goods; particularly in agriculture, mining, manufacturing, and construction. Jobs in these industries are primarily involved with things. Take manufacturing, for example; 23 percent of employment in *all* industries is in manufacturing. As Figure 4 shows, 70 percent of this employment is carried out by blue-collar workers.

About 20 percent of all occupations require workers to deal mainly with things. These jobs include dump-truck driver, greenskeeper, meatcutter, and upholsterer. At present, schools do not emphasize many of the *things* jobs, so parents and the community must provide some knowledge of these occupations to children and youth. You will need to be especially sensitive to cues your son or daughter may give you about *things* activities.

Figure 4

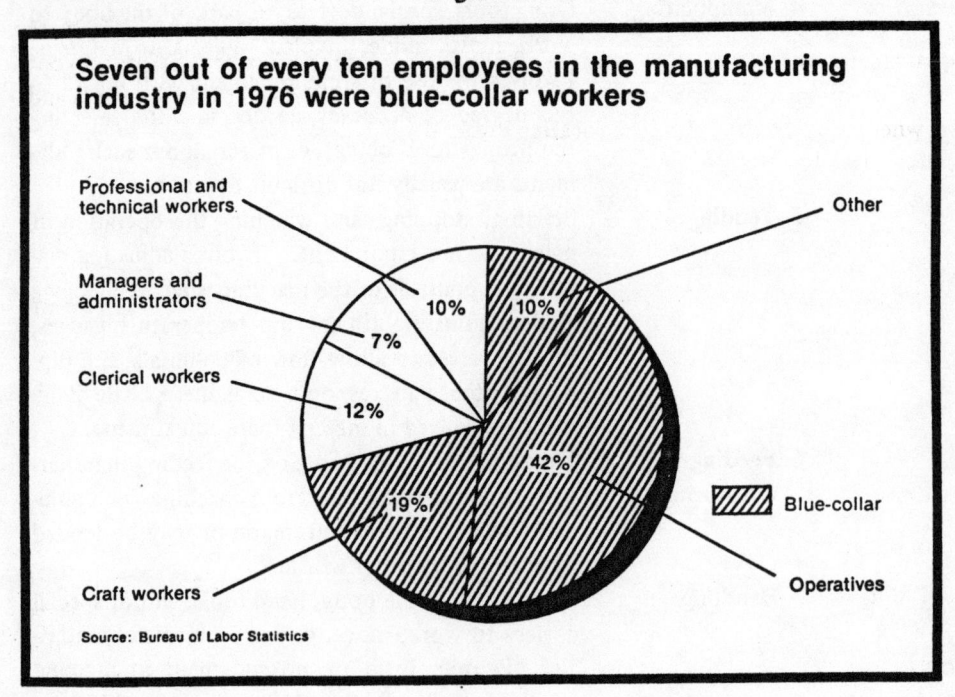

Seven out of every ten employees in the manufacturing industry in 1976 were blue-collar workers

- Professional and technical workers: 10%
- Other: 10%
- Managers and administrators: 7%
- Clerical workers: 12%
- Craft workers: 19%
- Operatives: 42%
- Blue-collar

Source: Bureau of Labor Statistics

Occupations Relating Primarily to Things

In the following occupations, the person is essentially involved in working directly with things in an occupationally significant way. There is no significant relationship with data or people. Some illustrations of these jobs are:

Greenskeeper	Tire Recapper
Bulldozer Operator	Bindery Worker
Operating Engineer	Firefighter
Dump-Truck Driver	Baker's Helper
Tractor-Trailer Driver	Cook's Helper
Milk Truck Driver	Deckhand
Meatcutter	Material Handler
Pantry Person	Miner's Helper
Hand Presser	Tree Pruner
Janitor	Park Worker
Auto-Mechanic Helper	Nursery Worker
Appliance Repairperson	General Laborer
Upholsterer	Arc Welder
Cement Mason	Construction Worker

These occupations obviously require direct involvement with machines, tools, equipment, or products. They are mainly in manufacturing or construction. Since these occupations are not as visible as teaching or selling, it will take some keen effort on your part as a parent to find out whether your son or daughter has some of these talents and knows where they can be expressed vocationally.

Occupations Relating to Data-People-Things

Chapter 5 provided an extended list of Data-Things occupations, and you may want to refer to that section and apply it here. A few occupations, however, relate primarily to People-Things and Data-People-Things, but the number and percentage is small. Here are some examples:

Mill Supervisor	Telephone Operator
Chef	Central Office Operator
Garage Supervisor	Service Station Attendant
Cosmetologist	

As you can tell, most of these jobs involve a direct relationship with people, but have some technical or Things orientation as well. There are only a few since this is somewhat of a rare combination. The more frequent combinations can be noted in the other lists in Chapters 5 and 6.

Noticing the Cues in Your Child

What are some of the cues you can look for in determining whether your child has a natural or developed tendency toward Things? Look for a desire to play, explore, or work with tools, equipment, machines—some refer to such activities as "working with one's hands." An interest in seeing what "makes things tick" is a good cue to interest in this area. Wanting to put broken toys back together is another. Preference may be noted for building-type toys such as tinker toys, erector sets, Lincoln logs, building blocks, and so on.

Later in mid-childhood these cues may take on more precise form as your child's manual dexterity and eye-hand coordination improve. In late childhood, the signs may be helping with home repair projects, asking and learning more about hand tools, and operating simple machines. Curiosity about the operation of clocks, radios, televisions, mixers, and other home appliances may also increase. In junior and senior high school, specific courses may be explored such as industrial arts, home economics, trade and industrial education, agricultural education, or horticulture. Part-time jobs may be located or encouraged to further probe interests and abilities. These and other similar experiences will help give some feeling of understanding of your child's natural or developed interests in the direction of Things, or in carrying out the worker functions related to Things.

An Occupational Example

From the table below it can be seen that the construction industry is one of the more stable areas of work in the goods production sector. One of the largest occupational groups in construction is *operating engineers*—machine operators who work around all kinds of construction sites. They operate cranes, bulldozers, truck excavators, paving machines, and similar equipment. There were nearly 600,000 operating engineers in 1976, according to U.S. Department of Labor estimates. The occupation is expected to grow faster than the average in the construction industry, and job opportunities are expected to be plentiful. Union wages in large metropolitan areas were at $9.00 or more per hour in 1977.

Figure 5

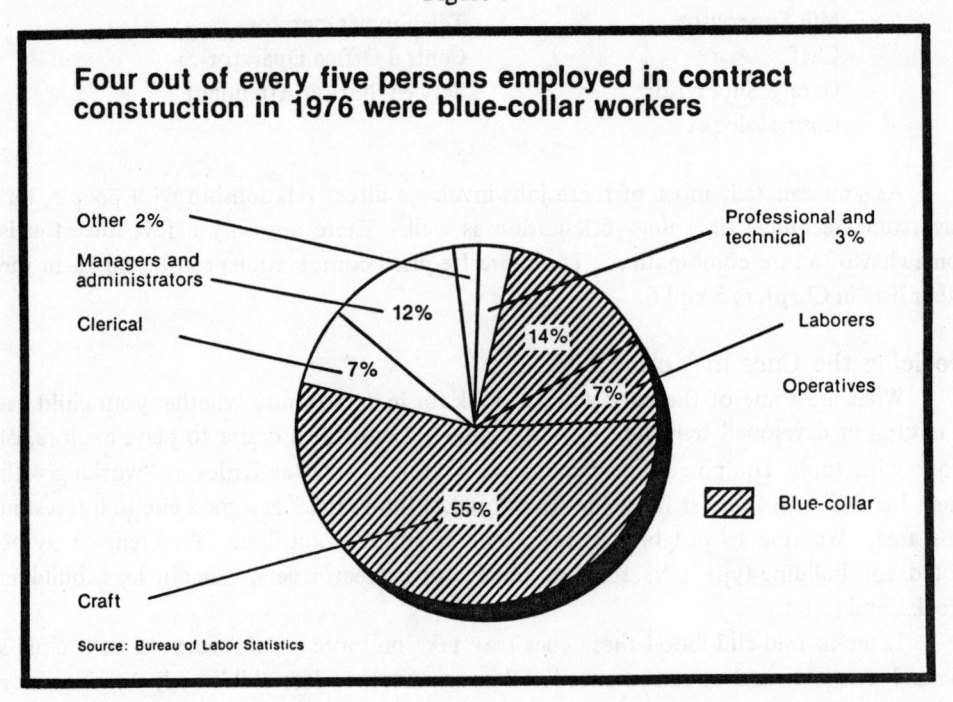

Four out of every five persons employed in contract construction in 1976 were blue-collar workers

- Other 2%
- Managers and administrators
- Clerical 7%
- 12%
- 14%
- 7%
- 55%
- Craft
- Professional and technical 3%
- Laborers
- Operatives
- Blue-collar

Source: Bureau of Labor Statistics

The following cues at each stage indicate that a child might like an occupation such as operating engineer. These cues are action oriented behaviors relating to the career development phases outlined in Chapter 1.

Career Awareness (Ages 5-10)
Learns about production work
Tells about seeing individuals working at a construction site
Develops a respect for individuals who work with their hands
Wants to operate toys such as dump trucks; puts together pulleys; or plans and operates a model railroad
Assists in repairing and putting together items around the home such as bicycles, tricycles, and toasters

Career Exploration (Ages 11-15)
Takes summer exploratory course in building trades
Spends a day on a construction site in a school "shadowing experience"
Volunteers to work at a local garage after school
Shows initiative around the house in fixing broken appliances
Buys a tool set with allowance money
Likes to read magazines such as *Popular Science* and *Popular Mechanics*

Career Preparation (Ages 16-22)
Takes industrial arts in school; likes construction work
Spends summer vacation working as a laborer on a construction site
Works after school in a large machinery repair shop
Tinkers with cars and motors in spare time
Studies apprenticeship programs

Obviously, this is only a partial list of possible cues that outline the child's natural awareness, exploration, and preparation process. Some children will gravitate to these activities on their own, while others will need some encouragement from parents to see just what and how deep their interest, aptitudes, and abilities may be. If you can help your son or daughter through a sequence of events similar to the ones above, it may not solve all his/her career planning problems, but it will surely aid in the developmental process.

Conversation Corner

Some questions to talk about at mealtime, in the family automobile, or on a family outing.

1. Why do you think individuals like to work with things?

2. Why do you think some individuals like to work with the production of goods rather than services?

3. What satisfactions are gained from working with things?

4. How many things occupations can you name that are done by friends and relatives?

5. Where are some of the things occupations in your neighborhood or school? What are they?

Things Exploration Checklist

Put a checkmark by the following activities in which you have been engaged as a family. Count one point for each check.

_____ 1. Encourage your child to be aware of working with things—tools, machines, equipment, or products.

_____ 2. Encourage your child to be aware of individuals who work with things.

_____ 3. Encourage your child to be aware of play activities with things.

_____ 4. Encourage your child to explore activities (games, hobbies, etc.) that involve working with things.

_____ 5. Encourage your child to explore school subjects (science, industrial arts) related to things.

_____ 6. Encourage your child to explore part-time, summer, or volunteer work relating to things.

_____ 7. Encourage your child to explore books, magazines, and television programs about working with things.

_____ 8. Encourage your child to talk with individuals who work with things.

_____ 9. Encourage your child to get involved with clubs and extracurricular activities involved with things.

_____ 10. Encourage your child to explore ways of getting the proper education and training to go into careers involving things.

_____ Total points (checks)

How did you score? Ten points? If so, you are really helping your child become aware of the potential for working with things and knowing more about him/herself. Five points is about average. Three points or less means you should review Chapter 7 and arrange some activities that may provide opportunities for self and career awareness on the part of your son or daughter.

Keep working at it!

Chapter 8

Taking Part in Your Child's Career Planning Process

"Career planning is a process."

"Career planning is influenced by both facts and feelings."

"Career planning is a product of experiences."

This chapter is aimed at putting you, the parent, in the driver's seat in the career planning process. Career planning is a journey over the hills and through the valleys of experience. The goal of this tour or journey is not to isolate your child's career development so that you can control the outcomes, but rather to provide guideposts that can aid in the full exploration of available options at appropriate times.

The *first guidepost* on this tour is that career development and career planning are really *processes*—not events or points in time. This means that the crucial thing is contributing to your child's career development *over time*, not just during occasional peak experiences or pressure-packed decisions about what classes to take in the ninth grade. The process is better supported by regular conversation at the table, or meaningful discussions about the work of family and friends, or increased involvement and intensity in work done around the home.

The *second guidepost* on the tour is that the process is influenced by *both facts and feelings*. Most of the content that contributes to this process is *informational*, such as how much pay a carpenter receives, how long it takes to become an accountant, or what makes up the work of a medical technologist. Such information can be learned. The process also takes into account *feelings* about work and workers, such as respect for work, interest in what people do on their jobs, and recognition of the fact that people do many different kinds of work that contribute to our society. In short, your child will learn about the world of work and about him/herself by gathering some factual information as well as by forming some attitudes and outlooks toward the entire process. You will influence much of this kind of learning by your attitude toward work and workers as well as by the natural flow of information you provide your child.

Let's take an example of how this works. The formation of sex-role stereotypes begins in the preschool years. Children learn sex-roles through play activities and expression of family views as well as from the world around them. You can help create a feeling of openness toward a variety of play activities through the purchase of nonsexist games, books, and toys. As your child hears references in conversation to "women's work" or "men's work" or just "work," he or she will form attitudes. Your child will begin to establish a self-concept of what is right for himself or herself and what would be approved by the family. Girls who think and talk only of being teachers, nurses, or stenographers have different self-concepts from those who consider being mechanics, physicians, or real estate brokers. The boy who thinks about being a nurse, stenographer, or cook probably comes from a family that has encouraged him to think with respect toward all kinds of work available to him.

The *third guidepost* on the tour is that *we are all products of our experiences*. A commercial company uses the expression "you never choose the career you never heard of"—a cliche, to be sure, but an accurate one. If your child never learns to play the piano, he/she will never become a professional piano performer. If he/she has never heard of a landscape architect, it becomes an unlikely career choice. If the work of a plasterer is unknown, then it certainly won't be pursued as a career choice. On the positive side, if you arrange for a volunteer job at a summer camp, a whole host of jobs in camping and teaching open up. If you take your child to work with you and introduce him/her to the people with whom you work, this opens up a whole new set of opportunities. If you compile lists of new kinds of workers you have seen on your vacation, it can reinforce some of the experiences that might slip by unnoticed.

In brief, remember:

1. Career planning is a *process*.
2. Career planning is influenced by *facts and feelings*.
3. Career planning is a *product of experiences*.

Helping in Stages

With the three guideposts just discussed in mind, let's take a look at how they relate to the various stages of your child's early years. We have selected a three-stage process and listed several concepts to emphasize during each period. These concepts are guides in helping your child's progress through the career development phases outlined in Chapter 1. Various researchers arrange these stages in different ways and with different terms, but the general principles are similar to those that follow.

Awareness (Ages 5-10)

Create opportunities to learn about workers and what they do.

Create opportunities to learn about work of family and friends.
Create awareness through books, magazines, television, and radio, which introduce workers to your child.
Create opportunities to gain further respect for workers and what they do.
Create opportunities to talk about careers at mealtime, in the car, and on family outings.
Create opportunities to learn about various leisure-time activities.
Create opportunities to learn about self in relation to workers.

Exploration (Ages 11-15)

Provide ways to begin to assume responsibility for career planning.
Provide opportunities to acquire further knowledge of workers, work settings, and lifestyles.
Provide opportunities to learn about educational and vocational resources.
Provide opportunities to try out new courses in junior high or middle school.
Provide opportunities to begin thinking about the career decision-making process.
Provide ways to explore self through expanded leisure activities.
Provide more in-depth opportunities to learn about self in relation to work and workers.
Provide opportunities for career exploration through field trips, volunteer work, part-time and summer employment, and career shadowing experiences.

Preparation (Ages 16-22)

Encourage continued tryout of classes and clubs in school.
Encourage formation of tentative career goals.
Encourage acquisition of knowledge of various educational and vocational paths.
Encourage continued refinement of career decision-making process.
Encourage increased knowledge of and experience in occupational and work settings.
Encourage awareness of a preferred lifestyle.
Encourage continued efforts to understand self in relation to work and work settings.
Encourage commitment with tentativeness in a changing world.

Even if you have all these stages and concepts in mind, it will take some assertive action on your part to make it all happen. You, as a parent, will need to assume leadership in creating a climate assuring your child's timely mastery of these concepts for optimum career development.

Exploring through Leisure

Leisure activities can be an important part of the career development process. Many activities that start out as leisure pursuits can lead to potential career areas, or at least to satisfaction in nonworking hours. Maybe it would be best to define leisure activities in order to provide a common understanding of what we mean.

Leisure activities are relatively self-determined activities that are available due to having discretionary income, time, and social behavior. They may be any one or a combination of volunteer, intellectual, creative, or physical activities.

Leisure Activities and Careers

Leisure is becoming increasingly important in American life. Shorter work weeks and work lives, more opportunities for sports and hobbies, and more money and time for recreational activities all contribute to the growth of leisure activities.

Leisure-time activities contribute to personal development in many ways. Through such activities as running for student council, playing golf, sewing a new garment, or playing bass in a band, skills that may be useful throughout life are developed. Such experiences help crystallize ideas about interests and abilities and aid in making career and other major lifetime decisions.

Leisure-time activities may also serve a useful purpose by leading directly to useful and productive careers. For example, skill and knowledge acquired playing tennis may lead directly to a career operating a sporting goods shop, teaching others how to play the sport, or working as a wholesale representative for a sporting goods manufacturer. Sewing a new shirt or blouse may lead to work as a tailor or seamstress, a job in fashion design or fabric merchandising, or a career in teaching sewing and other home economics skills.

The lists that follow show some of the kinds of leisure activities open to most high school and college students and provide examples of careers to which they may lead. In every case, the list of career fields is suggestive, not comprehensive. Also, as many of these fields have only a limited number of jobs, competition is keen for positions in many career areas. Perhaps the most obvious example is the competition for careers in professional athletics. Competition for other types of jobs may be somewhat less rigorous, but it is there nonetheless. Despite the competition, jobs or opportunities to start a business do exist and some people create careers in crowded fields every year.

Careers in some leisure-related fields, of course, may offer less than lifetime jobs, and career planning must include both immediate prospects and long-range job implications. Examples are the singer whose voice may fade long before the age of normal retirement and the professional athlete whose active participation may, at best, end in his/her early thirties.

For some persons, leisure activities and related jobs may suggest opportunities for part-time work built around a compatible main job. These include such jobs as church organist, summer camp worker, or free-lance writer or artist. In all fields, special opportunities exist in management-type jobs, such as the dancer who operates a dance studio, the musically inclined person who manages (as contrasted with conducting) a symphony orchestra, or the actor who turns to running a summer theater. Here are some examples of leisure activities your child may engage in and a few related occupations.

Music

Composing: Composer, arranger, music critic, record company employee
Dancing: Professional dancer, choreographer, dance teacher
Instrumental Music: Director, performer, instrumental instructor, music group manager
Singing: Choir director, entertainer, voice teacher, music teacher

Art

Drawing: Artist, cartoonist, art teacher
Glass Blowing: Glass blower, glass company employee, glass salesman
Painting: Painter, painting instructor
Photography: Photographer, illustrator, advertising person
Pottery Making: Potter, kiln operator, ceramic designer
Sculpting: Sculptor, art critic, art gallery employee

Crafts

Baking: Baker, home economist, cooking writer or editor
Cooking: Chef, home economist, dietitian
Embroidery: Craft teacher, craft designer, craft shop operator
Glass Cutting: Laboratory equipment designer, glass designer, shop operator
Macrame: Teacher, professional macrame artist, designer
Needlepoint: Designer, shop operator, craft writer, craft wholesaler
Sewing: Tailor, seamstress, sewing teacher, fabric store operator
Weaving: Professional weaver, teacher, designer, shop owner
Woodcraft: Carver, wood furniture designer, furniture refinisher, cabinet maker, carpenter

Outdoor Activities

Backpacking: Outdoor clothing store operator, camp director, travel guide
Bicycling: Cycle shop operator, bicycle repairperson
Camping: Camp director, camp counselor, youth agency worker
Gardening: Farmer, farm store operator, agronomist, botanist
Horseback Riding: Veterinarian, animal caretaker, animal trainer, blacksmith
Raising Animals: Veterinarian, pet shop operator
Sailing: Marina operator, sailmaker, waterfront director, sailor
Swimming: Pool operator, swimming teacher, recreation worker, waterfront director

Individual and Team Sports

Archery: Teacher, sporting goods salesperson, camp operator

Baseball: Player, coach, teacher, camp director
Basketball: Player, coach, teacher, recreation aide
Bowling: Bowling machine repairperson, bowling alley operator, bowling professional
Football: Trainer, professional player, coach, youth agency worker
Hockey: Professional player, coach, teacher, skating rink operator
Skiing: Winter resort operator, ski instructor, ski shop owner
Sports (all): Sports reporter, radio or television announcer, wholesale or retail sporting goods salesperson
Tennis and Golf: Teaching pro, tennis shop operator, golf course superintendent
Track: Sporting goods store operator, outdoor facilities designer, wholesale representative

Out-of School and Community Activities

Boy-Girl Scouts: Scout leader, youth worker, social worker
Boys-Girls Clubs: Teacher, recreation leader, social agency administrator
4-H: Camp operator, teacher, extension agent
Religious Youth Group: Youth worker, minister, rabbi, priest, director of religious education
Tri-Hi-Y, Hi-Y: YMCA-YWCA worker, youth agency worker, recreation department worker

In-School and Extracurricular Activities

Art Club: Artist, designer, photographer, teacher
Choral Club: Singer, music or voice teacher, arranger, music critic
Debate Club: Lawyer, teacher, politician, announcer
Distributive Education Club: Salesperson, store operator, personnel worker
Drama Club: Actor, actress, director, set designer, drama teacher
Fellowship of Christian Athletes: Youth leader, religious worker, teacher
Future Business Leaders of America: Secretary, accountant, clerk, typist, teller
Future Farmers of America: Farmer, extension agent, farm business worker
Health Club: Nurse, physician, medical technician, dentist, orderly
Industrial Cooperative Club: Electrician, mechanic, brick mason, engineer
Newspaper and Yearbook: Reporter, journalist, printer
Photo Club: Photographer, photo shop operator, camera repairperson
Radio Club: Electronics work, radio engineer, electrical engineer, military service, communications worker
Science Club: Engineer, scientist, technician
Student Government: Politician, lawyer, community leader, business manager
Travel Club: Travel agent, airline or railroad agent, salesperson

Part-Time Leisure Interests

The pleasure of leisure activities can be continued throughout a lifetime without actually leading to a career. Not everyone who enjoys basketball will be able to find full-time employment relating to basketball. They may, however, enjoy volunteer coaching or officiating in addition to their wage-earning job. The following examples illustrate how some activities may be pursued as leisure rather than as work, thus contributing to a satisfying life/career style.

Initial Interest:	*Leisure Activity:*
Animal Raising	Organizing local American Kennel Club Group
Baseball	Coaching little league
Bicycling	Taking family bicycle trips
Bowling	Joining company bowling league
Cooking	Entertaining guests for gourmet meals
Drame	Acting in local amateur plays
Flower Growing	Participating in garden club
Sewing	Designing and sewing one's own clothes
Singing	Joining Barber shop quartet or sweet adelines group
Weaving	Teaching weaving at youth center

Exploring at School

School experiences provide special opportunities for your child to do some career exploring. This is especially true in the middle school/junior high school years when he/she is old enough to take part in a variety of activities, yet not subject to the pressure for grades and certain courses that will come later in high school. During these years, both you and your child should be open to a host of new tryout experiences. They can be fun rather than dull or boring. Here are some examples you may want to talk about with your child.

Elective Classes

Elective classes may consist of traditional academic fare—foreign languages, special mathematics, science, and so on. In addition, students should be encouraged to consider such special classes as art or music at either the skill level or the appreciation level. Many schools offer elective courses, with titles such as "Introduction to Vocations," "Careers and You," or "Career Exploration." They may be short, four- to six-week courses or last as long as a full year. No matter what the duration, these can offer an excellent opportunity for a career growth experience. Make every effort to have your child take such a course if available—it should pay handsome dividends.

Prevocational Courses

More and more schools are making prevocational courses available. The more standard ones are industrial arts and home economics. Either of these provides a solid tryout for advanced work in the area or in closely related fields—electricity, electronics, auto mechanics, child care, and commercial food preparation, to name just a few. Other course possibilities are introduction to agriculture, introduction to business, and introduction to distribution. In some cases, your child may be able to take an introductory course in typing for a year or part of a year. This is called "Personal Typing" in some schools. A variety of "mini-courses" in prevocational areas may be as short as a few days to several weeks. Whatever they are called, or whatever the length, be sure your child explores some of these areas if at all possible.

Clubs and Co-Curricular Activities

Almost every school offers a full range of choices among clubs and activities. Many of them relate to the prevocational or regular subjects mentioned above. In addition, the school may sponsor interest groups in chess, backgammon, radio, stage crew, audio-visual, drama, forensics, service groups, Future Farmers of America, Future Teachers of America, and so on. Some schools may make available thirty to forty opportunities like this. In some instances where a skill is involved, a club activity will teach the beginning skill for newcomers and provide opportunities for advanced members to carry out some of the instruction. Clubs of this nature also provide a further exploratory benefit in terms of leadership development. Running for elective office, carrying out the responsibilities of conducting meetings, and seeing projects through to completion provide important clues to an early interest in working with people.

Athletics

Athletics is a rather obvious example for this age group, as many youth are rather definite in their interest along these lines, but your encouragement for a new beginning or a tryout may be all it takes to get started. This is especially true for girls, since their interscholastic programs may just be getting under way in many sections of the country. Girls may need particular support to try out due to the lack of little league or junior programs for them. Another aspect of athletics involves working with teams as managers or trainers or participating in a pep club, cheerleading contingent, or yell group.

Summer School

In larger cities extensive summer school programs are available—and not just for making up failed classes. They provide an opportunity to explore many of the options already mentioned. Summer school may be an especially good time to try out some prevocational courses that do not fit into the regular school year schedule. The same also holds true for courses in public speaking, drama, art, music, and related subjects. There may also be smaller classes and more individualized instruction.

Options Other Than a Four-Year College

Youth and adults alike have increasing numbers of options for education and training at something other than a four-year college or university. Your child may not want to pursue any of these options immediately after high school, but with the increased emphasis on life-long learning, they may appear more attractive at some later time. It is important, however, to know what is available when options are being considered. This is especially true if your child would like to work full-time to do some further occupational exploration and go to school part-time. Detailed information can be followed up by checking into the resources in Chapter 12. Here are just some of the options most widely available:

On-the-Job Training

On-the-job training means that a worker is taught job skills after being hired. In most cases, an experienced worker trains and supervises the beginner. The training may last a few hours or many months. Information is available from employers and local public employment service offices.

Apprenticeships

Apprenticeships combine classroom instruction and on-the-job training. Apprenticeships require two or more years of job experience and instruction. Every apprenticeship is based on a written agreement between the employer and the apprentice. In most apprenticeships, workers are trained for skilled occupations in construction, manufacturing, transportation, and service industries. Information is available from local employers, unions, or public employment service offices.

Vocational Schools

Also called trade schools, vocational schools offer courses in bookkeeping and accounting, secretarial work, television repair, and many other skills. Some trade schools specialize in training such workers as barbers, mechanics, and truck drivers. Courses last from several months to two years. Most vocational schools prepare students to meet any licensing requirements needed to enter a trade or profession. Many schools also award certification to graduates.

There are two main kinds of vocational school, public and proprietary. Public vocational schools are supported by taxes. Proprietary schools are owned by individuals or businesses and operate to make a profit, and they tend to be more expensive than the public schools. Information and accreditation data are available in libraries and schools.

Armed Forces Schools

Armed forces schools provide career education opportunities for people in military service. These opportunities range from on-the-job training and short courses to college and graduate school. In most cases, the training is designed for jobs in military career fields. However, many skills used in military occupations can be applied to civilian jobs. Information is available from local recruiters.

Home Study and Correspondence Schools

Home study and correspondence schools enable people to learn certain job skills at home. Correspondence schools mail study guides, assignments, and examinations to students. The students send the completed work back to the schools for grading. Some schools offer lectures over the radio or on educational television. Home study courses can prepare students for various occupations in business, skilled trades, and many other areas. Information is available from counselors and state accreditation agencies.

Technical Institutes

Advanced, specialized training in such fields as agriculture, data processing, engineering, and medical technology is available at technical institutes. Many graduates of these schools become technicians—that is, workers who assist engineers, scientists, and other highly trained specialists. Most technical institutes have two- or three-year programs, and many are associated with a hospital, university, or other institution. Some technical schools offer short courses similar to those in vocational schools. Information is available from directories in public and school libraries and from counselors.

Community and Junior Colleges

Community and junior colleges provide two years of college-level education and prepare some students to transfer to a four-year college. They train other students for jobs as technicians and for such specialized occupations as nursing, office management, and police work. Most community colleges are financed by local or state taxes. Most junior colleges are privately owned. Information is available in directories in public and school libraries and from counselors.

Points to Ponder

To close this rather long chapter, here are some helpful tips that summarize the major points we have made.

1. Encourage your child to ask and think about the question, "What will I be when I grow up?" In the early years, children's hopes are often expressed in fantasy terms, especially during play. You will hear things such as, "I'm Daddy and I'm Superman, and you're Mommy and you're Wonder Woman." Don't criticize such statements. Your child is exploring who he or she is, and you will understand him or her better if you let your child talk in this way. Provide toys that encourage experimentation through play with many different jobs.
2. Don't discourage your child from planning particular careers at an early age. It is better to ask, "Why does this appeal to you?" than it is to say something like "You wouldn't like to do that" or "That's a terrible job" or "That's completely unrealistic." Until major action decisions have to be made, it is better to let your child think about any possible job choice.
3. Try to help your child think about alternate choices. The question, "If for some reason you couldn't do this, what other things would you want to do?" is a good one to raise. It will help you learn more about your child, and will also help her/him broaden the basis for career decision-making. Talking about your own alternate career choices will also help in this area. For example, discuss jobs you've

had in the past, or changes you might be considering in your present occupation.

4. Try to eliminate sex bias in thinking about your child's future career. Your daughter may very well wish to enter an occupation you think of as "masculine," or your son may want to enter one that you consider "feminine." Don't discourage them from thinking about such occupations. Times are changing, and they will need extra measures of your emotional support. If the child next door discourages your daughter from being a doctor because "girls are nurses," take your daughter to a woman doctor if you can. If you can't, point out women who are in traditionally male jobs; say things like, "A person's sex really doesn't matter; it's ability that counts."

5. Don't hesitate to respond when your child asks, "What do you think I should be when I grow up?" Try to make it clear that it is more important that he/she be happy than become what you would like. However, you can point out particular talents that he/she possesses and discuss the jobs in which these would be helpful.

6. Tell your child about your work. Try to do so in a positive way so that your child will gain respect for you by respecting what you do. Neither encourage nor discourage your child from considering your occupation. The important thing is for your child to see that you, through your work, are making a contribution to society.

7. Encourage your child to ask people about their jobs. Make use of your friends who are in occupations your child is considering. Emphasize to your child that she/he should seek information, not firm advice, from such persons. If your child is particularly interested, ask a friend if your child can visit to see what the job actually involves.

8. Take your child on field trips to see various people at work in factories, offices, automechanic shops, and so on. This is very helpful in letting children acquire a realistic view of a variety of jobs.

9. Help your child explore hobbies and other leisure-time activities that are productive and useful. Sometimes such activities can lead to career choices. Whether they do or not is unimportant. What is important is that they can help your child see himself/herself as one who can accomplish something successfully.

10. Help your child understand how very important her/his school work will be in later job decisions. Show how such subjects as reading, arithmetic, and communications are used in almost all occupations. In short, help your child understand that there are more important reasons for going to school than simply going to school.

11. Encourage your child to engage in part-time work outside the home. If such work is done for pay, you can talk to your child about basic elements in the free enterprise system. Whether or not the work is for pay, it can be valuable in two ways: (1) it can help your child explore career interests and (2) it can help your child discover the sense of accomplishment and pride that can come from work.

12. Encourage your child to visit with teachers and counselors about career plans and hopes. After such visits, talk with your children about what they learned. Feel free to tell them what you think. In doing so, make it clear that you are expressing

your opinion, not telling them what to do with their lives. Don't refuse to discuss such matters with your children just because you don't know the answers.

13. Visit the schools your child attends. If your child has been discussing career plans with a teacher or counselor at school, seek that person out and ask such questions as, "Do you think this career is suitable in view of my child's strengths and weaknesses?" "What are the best schools for pursuing this field of study?" "What is the employment outlook for this career?" You will often learn much and you will certainly help teachers and counselors assist your children more if you are willing to talk to them.

14. Help your child understand that it will be equally important to acquire a set of specific job skills *and* a set of adaptable skills for occupational success. For example, if your child is preparing for a career in journalism, it would be wise to build a broad base of academic subjects that might be used in fields other than journalism.

15. Remember, a college degree is no longer the best or surest route to occupational success. If your child is in high school, encourage him/her to think about all kinds of postsecondary educational opportunities. Try to help your child think about a variety of *kinds* of post-high-school educational opportunities—for example, all-volunteer armed forces, vocational schools, community colleges. Emphasize the wide choice that exists.

The Data-People-Things Game

This game can be played at home, in the car, or on a family outing. It is like the old game of "Twenty Questions." Here is the easy-to-follow format:

1. Start off by selecting a person to begin the game (the youngest, the oldest, etc.).
2. Have the person think of an occupation (writer, waiter, welder).
3. Have the person announce that the occupation is mainly involved with data, people, or things (writer = data; waiter = people; welder = things).
4. Allow players to ask up to 20 questions until the occupation is identified. (Does the person work with tools? Does the person have to be a college graduate?)
5. The game ends when someone guesses the correct answer and then thinks of the next occupation, or when no one thinks of the occupation and the same person thinks of another occupation.

Example:

Players: Mom
Dad
Billy (age 10)
Mary (age 12)

1. Billy, the youngest, starts off.
2. Billy thinks of an occupation: *carpenter*
3. Billy says the occupation is mainly involved with things
4. The questions might go as follows:

Q1 (Dad)	Is the occupation involved with the production of goods?	
A1	Yes.	
Q2 (Mom)	Is the occupation performed mainly by men?	
A2	Yes.	
Q3 (Mary)	Is the occupation mainly inside?	
A3	No.	
Q4 (Mom)	Is the occupation involved with tools?	
A4	Yes.	
Q5 (Dad)	Is the occupation considered a craft or trade?	
A5	Yes.	
Q6 (Mom)	Is the occupation usually learned through apprenticeship?	
A6	Yes.	

Q7 (Mary)	Is the occupation mainly involved with pipes?
A7	No.
Q8 (Mom)	Is the occupation mainly involved with metal?
A8	No.
Q9 (Mary)	Is the occupation mainly involved with wood?
A9	Yes.
Q10 (Mary)	Is the occupation a carpenter?
A10	Yes.

Chapter 9

Forecasting The Labor Market: Trends and Predictions

"Most jobs will be as replacements for existing workers."

"Most women will hold jobs."

"Most jobs will require geographic flexibility."

This chapter will tell you something about the occupational outlook for the next decade. It presents the latest Department of Labor predictions, on which you can make reasonable plans with your child for his/her future career. It is important to remain current and up-to-date in terms of labor market forecasts; you should consult annual or biannual reviews to stay informed.

Recent Job Changes

Over the past quarter century the United States has experienced a very rapid growth in number and kinds of occupations. This has been due to several factors—rapidly growing population, dramatic technological changes, and shifting population locations and tastes. Now that these and other changes have slowed, occupational needs are not so much in futuristic unknown jobs but in replacements of workers who retire or change jobs. See Chart 1. The occupation your child will choose very likely exists today and will be open to him/her as a replacement for a worker who leaves. To be sure, most large companies will have openings. For example, it has been reported that American Telephone and Telegraph (AT&T) alone expects to add 250,000 to 500,000 new employees in the next decade—mostly replacing workers who retire or leave for some other reason.

Chart 1

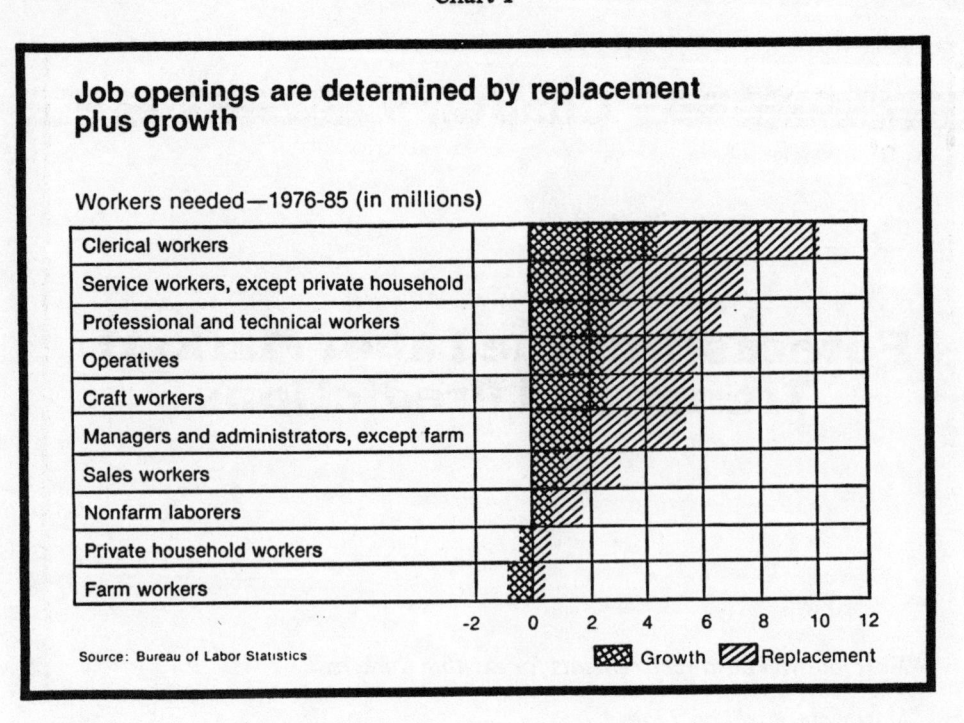

Job openings are determined by replacement plus growth

Workers needed—1976-85 (in millions)

Clerical workers	
Service workers, except private household	
Professional and technical workers	
Operatives	
Craft workers	
Managers and administrators, except farm	
Sales workers	
Nonfarm laborers	
Private household workers	
Farm workers	

-2　0　2　4　6　8　10　12

▨ Growth　▧ Replacement

Source: Bureau of Labor Statistics

Women at Work

Another important factor to keep in mind when studying future job prospects is that 45 to 46 percent of the work force will be made up of women—up from 41 percent in 1977. Six families out of ten will have two wage earners. So if you have a daughter, the likelihood is very great that she will be employed full-time and work for most of her life. Do provide her with the same strong career support you provide for your son because she may need it as much or more than he does (see Chart 2).

Chart 2

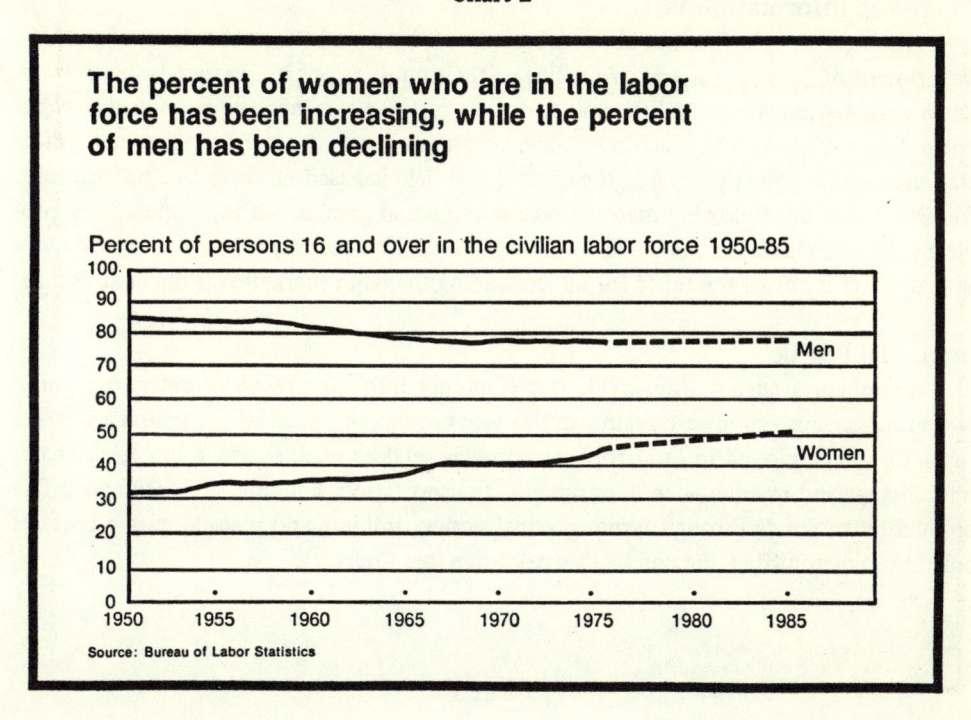

The percent of women who are in the labor force has been increasing, while the percent of men has been declining

Percent of persons 16 and over in the civilian labor force 1950-85

Men

Women

Source: Bureau of Labor Statistics

Where the Jobs Are

Indications are that opportunities will continue to be best in certain parts of the country. The brightest outlook will be in the "Sun Belt"—the South and Southwest. Openings will appear elsewhere, to be sure, but no area has a rosier job future forecast than the Sun Belt states. So your child should be as flexible as possible in terms of geographic preference. The smaller the home-town population and area, the greater the likelihood that a person will have to relocate in order to find a job. Also, the type of occupation will often indicate location: farmers living in the country, oceanographers living near the ocean, and foresters working in the woods. In some situations young persons may even have to accept work they do not particularly want while waiting for a more desirable job or location to open. This may be especially true in some professional fields.

Keep these three things in mind when thinking about the occupational future:

1. Most jobs will be as replacements for existing workers.
2. Most women will hold jobs.
3. Most jobs will require geographic flexibility.

Where the Information Is

The best way to find out about job prospects is to read the publications of the U.S. Department of Labor. The top of the line of their publications in this area is the *Occupational Outlook Handbook*, which comes out every two years, and the periodical *Occupational Outlook Quarterly*. Each resource presents the most accurate and up-to-date information available. Most writing in the commercial field is based on these two publications. We have taken the following material on the industrial profile and the occupational profile by permission from the *1978-79 Occupational Outlook Handbook* to provide you with the best frame of reference for understanding the labor market over the next decade.

Industrial Profile

Economists customarily divide our economy into nine industry categories under two broad groups—goods-producing and service-producing. Most of the nation's workers currently are employed in industries that provide services, such as education, health care, trade, repair and maintenance, government, transportation, banking, and insurance. The production of goods through farming, construction, mining, and manufacturing requires only about one-third of the country's work force (see Chart 3).

Chart 3

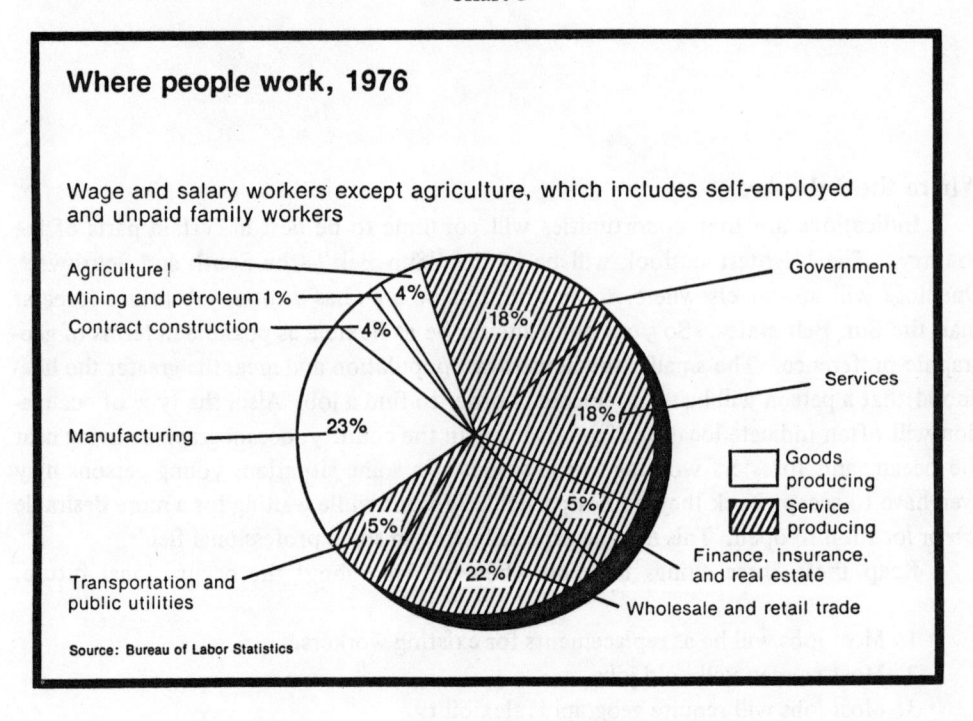

Where people work, 1976

Wage and salary workers except agriculture, which includes self-employed and unpaid family workers

- Agriculture: 4%
- Mining and petroleum: 1%
- Contract construction: 4%
- Manufacturing: 23%
- Transportation and public utilities: 5%
- Wholesale and retail trade: 22%
- Finance, insurance, and real estate: 5%
- Services: 18%
- Government: 18%

Source: Bureau of Labor Statistics

88

Employment in the goods-producing industries has remained relatively constant since World War II, whereas the service-producing industries have expanded rapidly. Among the factors contributing to this rapid growth were the migration from rural to urban areas and the accompanying need for more local government services, and rising incomes and living standards that resulted in a demand for improved health and education services. These factors are expected to continue to cause the demand for services to grow.

Service-Producing Industries

Employment in the service-producing industries is expected to increase from 56.1 million workers in 1976 to 71.0 million in 1985, an increase of 26 percent. Of course, growth rates will vary among the industries within this group (see Chart 4).

Chart 4

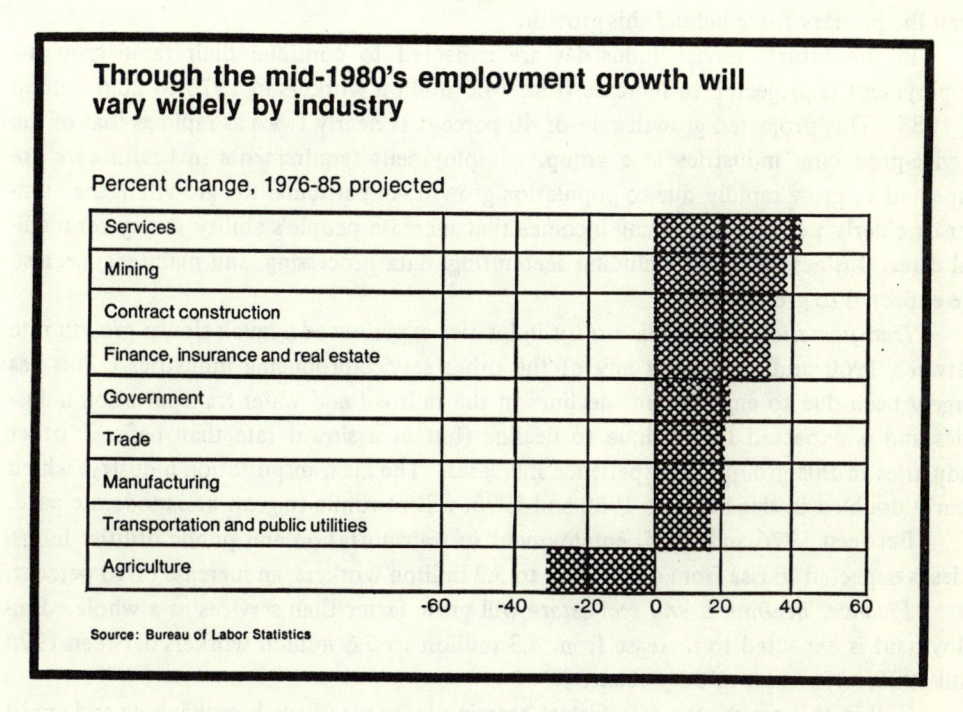

Through the mid-1980's employment growth will vary widely by industry

Percent change, 1976-85 projected

Services	~40
Mining	~40
Contract construction	~30
Finance, insurance and real estate	~27
Government	~22
Trade	~20
Manufacturing	~15
Transportation and public utilities	~12
Agriculture	~-15

Source: Bureau of Labor Statistics

Trade, the largest of the service industries, is expected to grow by about 20 percent between 1976 and 1985, from 17.7 million to 21.3 million workers.

Both wholesale and retail trade have increased as population has grown and as rising incomes have enabled people to buy a greater number and variety of goods. Retail trade has grown more rapidly than wholesale trade as the expansion of the suburbs has created a demand for more shopping centers. Although self-service is expected to become more prevalent, employment in retail trade nonetheless will continue to grow faster than in wholesale trade.

Government has been the second fastest growing service industry. Employment in state and local governments doubled between 1960 and 1976. Growth has been greatest in agencies providing education, health, sanitation, welfare, and police and fire protection. Federal government employment has increased only 20 percent during the same period.

Between 1976 and 1985, employment in government is expected to rise 22 percent, from 14.9 million to 18.3 million workers. This growth rate is less than that expected for services as a whole. Although state and local governments will continue to be the major source of jobs, the budget problems many local governments now face are expected to retard the expansion of some government programs.

Service industries have been the fastest growing group in the service-producing category, nearly doubling in employment between 1960 and 1976. The growing need for health care, maintenance and repair, advertising, and commercial cleaning services has been the primary force behind this growth.

In the future, service industries are expected to continue their rapid growth—employment is projected to increase from 14.6 million workers in 1976 to 20.6 million in 1985. This projected growth rate of 40 percent is nearly twice as rapid as that of the service-producing industries as a group. Employment requirements in health care are expected to grow rapidly due to population growth—in particular the growth in the number of elderly persons—and rising incomes that increase people's ability to pay for medical care. Business services, including accounting, data processing, and maintenance, also are expected to grow rapidly.

Transportation and public utility industries experienced a much slower growth rate between 1960 and 1976 than any of the other service-producing industries. This has largely been due to employment declines in the railroad and water transportation industries and is expected to continue to decline (but at a slower rate than before); other industries in this group will experience increases. The air transportation industry, which nearly doubled in size between 1960 and 1976, will continue to grow at a moderate pace.

Between 1976 and 1985, employment in transportation and public utilities industries is expected to rise from 4.5 million to 5.2 million workers, an increase of 16 percent.

Finance, insurance, and real estate will grow faster than services as a whole. Employment is expected to increase from 4.3 million to 5.6 million workers between 1976 and 1985, an increase of 30 percent.

Within this group, the two fastest growing industries have been banking and credit agencies. Employment in banking nearly doubled between 1960 and 1976, reflecting a growing population that increasingly pays its bills by check. Employment requirements also grew as banks began to provide more service, particularly the bank credit cards, and remained open longer hours. Population growth also meant an increased demand for the services of finance companies, savings and loan associations, and other credit agencies. These trends are expected to continue through the mid-1980s.

Goods-Producing Industries

Employment in the goods-producing industries—agriculture, mining, construction, and manufacturing—has changed very little since 1960. Significant gains in productivity resulting from automated production, improved machinery, and other technological breakthroughs have permitted large increases in output without additional workers. Between 1976 and 1985, employment in goods-production industries is expected to increase by about 17 percent, from 26.6 million to 31.1 million workers.

Growth rates will vary from industry to industry within this group. Employment in agriculture, which has long been declining, stabilized at about 3.5 million workers between 1970 and 1975, but dropped again to 3.3 million in 1976. Since the 1950s, the trend toward fewer but larger farms and the use of more and better machinery has reduced the need for farmers and farm workers. So too has the development of improved hybrid crops. Recently, for example, a hybrid tomato was developed that has a harder skin and can be machine harvested.

Although employment on farms has declined, rapid mechanization combined with better fertilizers, feeds, pesticides, and hybrids have created large increases in output. The worldwide demand for food is rising rapidly as population increases, but production is expected to continue to rise without reversing the employment decline in agriculture. Between 1976 and 1985, employment is expected to drop about 29 percent, from 3.3 million to 2.3 million workers.

Mining, once declining in employment, increased abruptly between 1970 and 1976, experiencing a 26 percent growth rate during this period and matching the growth rate of the fastest growing industry group, services. Most of this growth was a direct result of our need for additional energy. Employment in the oil and gas extraction industry rose 33 percent between 1970 and 1976, and is expected to rise another 70 percent by 1985. Coal, the most commonly used alternative energy source, has been and will continue to be in great demand.

Employment in mining is expected to grow 39 percent between 1976 and 1985, from 0.8 to 1.1 million workers.

Contract construction, which grew fairly rapidly between 1960 and 1968, stagnated between 1968 and 1976. The earlier growth, which reflected an increasing need for houses, apartment and office buildings, highways, and shopping centers, was dampened by the economic downturn that began in the late 1960s.

Buildings that had been vacant are now filling up, however, and as our economy recovers, employment in construction is expected to increase, rising by 38 percent between 1976 and 1985, or from 3.6 million to 4.9 million workers.

Manufacturing employment, also adversely affected by the economic conditions of the early 1970s, is expected to grow from 18.9 million to 22.8 million between 1976 and 1985, an increase of 20 percent.

Manufacturing is divided into two broad categories, durable goods manufacturing and nondurable goods manufacturing. Employment in durable goods manufacturing is expected to increase by about 25 percent, from 11.0 million to 13.8 million workers, while employment in nondurable goods manufacturing is expected to increase by only 13 percent, from 7.9 million to 9.0 million workers.

Growth rates will vary among individual industries within each of these categories. In nondurable goods industries, for example, employment in tobacco manufacturing is expected to decline, while a moderate rise in employment is projected for the synthetic fiber industry. Among durable goods manufacturing industries, medical instrument manufacturing is expected to undergo a rapid employment increase; motor vehicle manufacturing will employ about the same number of workers in 1985 as it did in 1976.

Occupational Profile

Customarily, occupations also are divided into several groups. White-collar workers are those in professional and technical, clerical, sales, and managerial jobs. Blue-collar workers are those in craft, operative, and laborer jobs. Service workers and farm workers constitute separate groups. Chart 5 illustrates the occupational profile in 1976.

Chart 5

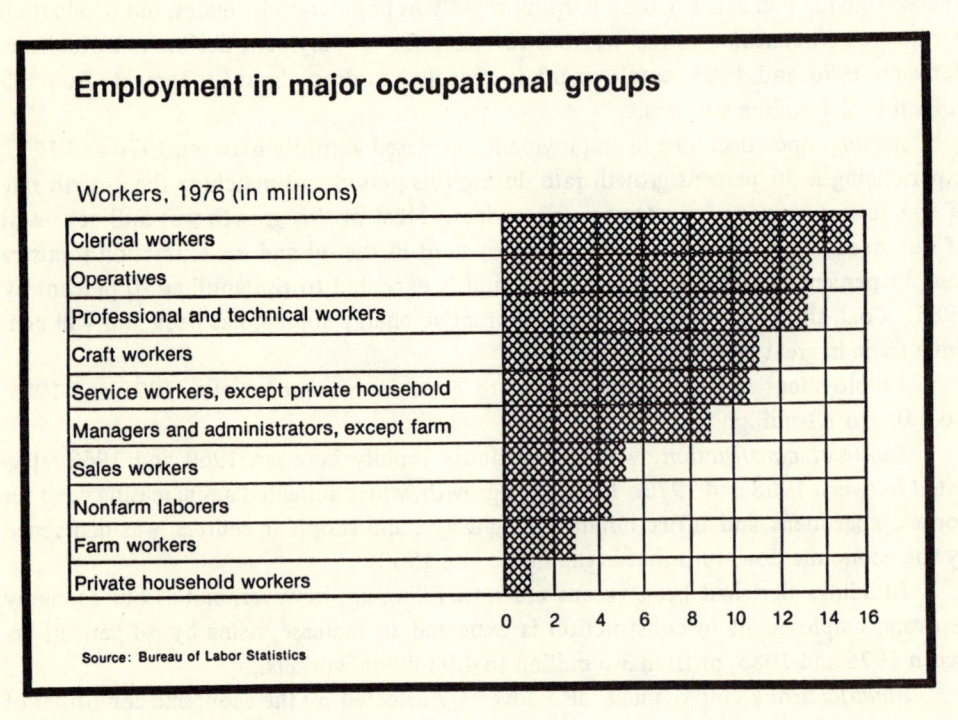

Employment in major occupational groups

Workers, 1976 (in millions)

Occupation	0	2	4	6	8	10	12	14	16
Clerical workers									
Operatives									
Professional and technical workers									
Craft workers									
Service workers, except private household									
Managers and administrators, except farm									
Sales workers									
Nonfarm laborers									
Farm workers									
Private household workers									

Source: Bureau of Labor Statistics

Growth rates among these groups have differed markedly, as shown in Chart 6. Once a small proportion of the total labor force, white-collar workers have steadily increased in importance until they now represent about half of the total. The number of service workers also has risen rapidly, while the blue-collar work force has grown only slowly and the number of farm workers has declined.

Chart 6

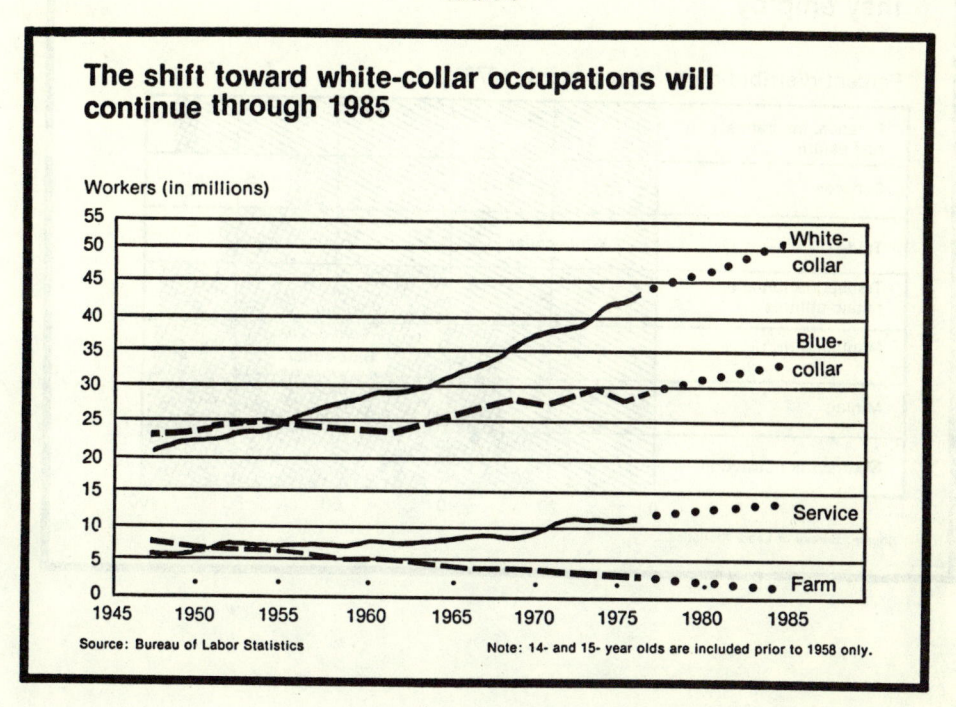

The shift toward white-collar occupations will continue through 1985

Workers (in millions)

Source: Bureau of Labor Statistics   Note: 14- and 15- year olds are included prior to 1958 only.

Most of these changes in occupational employment have been due to variations in the growth rates of industries. Every industry group has a unique occupational pattern (see Chart 6). Construction, for example, employs mostly blue-collar workers, while finance, insurance, and real estate is predominantly a white-collar industry group. Growth in the construction industry would result in an increase in employment of blue-collar workers. The same would be true for growth in mining, manufacturing, or transportation —industries that also employ mostly blue-collar workers. The magnitude of the change would depend on both the rate of growth and the size of the industry.

Chart 7

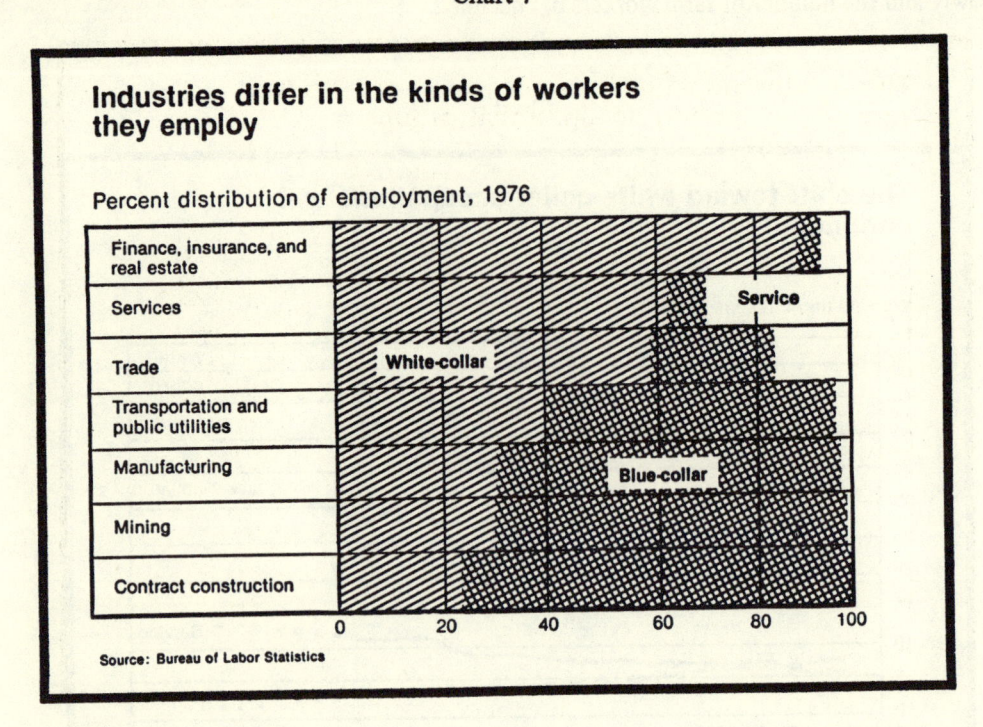

Industries differ in the kinds of workers they employ

Percent distribution of employment, 1976

Industry	White-collar	Blue-collar	Service
Finance, insurance, and real estate			
Services			
Trade			
Transportation and public utilities			
Manufacturing			
Mining			
Contract construction			

Source: Bureau of Labor Statistics

The following sections describe the changes that are expected to occur among the broad occupational groups between 1976 and 1985 (see also Chart 7).

Professional and technical workers include a wide range of workers, many of them highly trained. Among this group are scientists and engineers, medical practitioners, teachers, entertainers, pilots, and accountants. Employment in this group is expected to grow by about 18 percent between 1976 and 1985, rising from 13.3 million to 15.8 million workers.

Greater efforts in energy production, transportation, and environmental protection will contribute to a growing demand for scientists, engineers, and technicians. The medical professions can be expected to grow as the health services industry expands. The demand for professional workers to develop and utilize computer resources also is projected to grow rapidly.

Some occupations will offer less favorable job prospects, in many cases because the supply of workers exceeds the available openings. Teachers will continue to face competition, as will artists and entertainers, airline pilots, and oceanographers.

Through the mid-1980's employment growth will vary widely among occupational groups

Percent change in employment, 1976-85

Clerical workers	~29
Service workers, except private household	~23
Craft workers	~20
Managers and administrators, except farm	~21
Professional and technical workers	~18
Operatives	~12
Sales workers	~14
Nonfarm laborers	~9
Private household workers	~-15
Farm workers	~-28

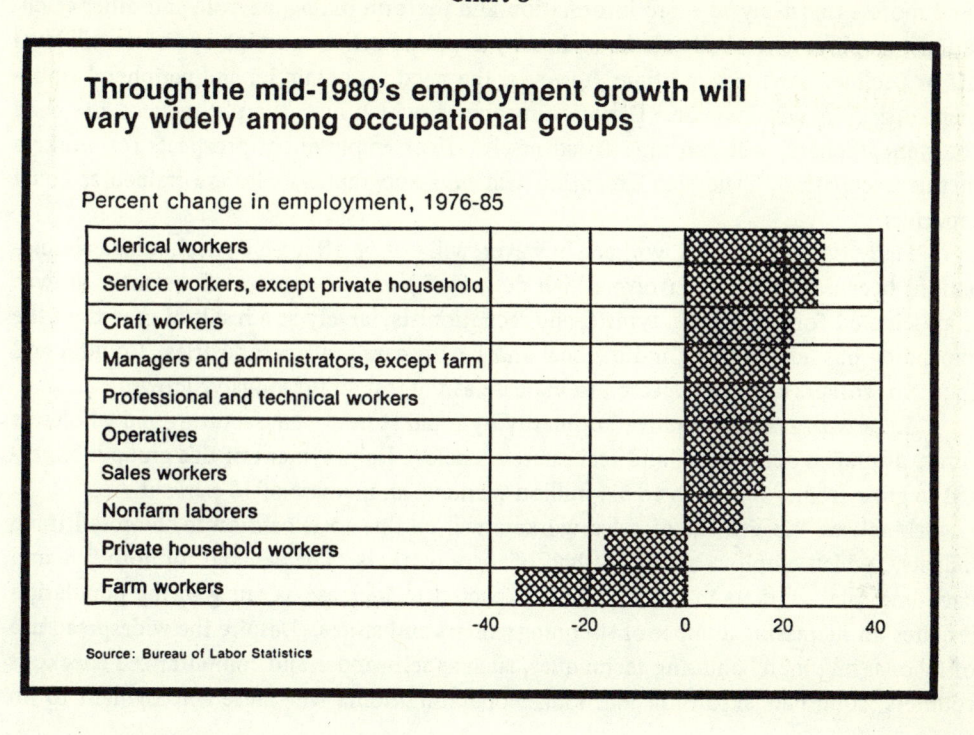

Source: Bureau of Labor Statistics

Managers and administrators include workers such as corporate executives, school and health services administrators, department store managers, and self-employed business operators. This group is expected to grow from 9.3 million to 11.3 million workers, an increase of 21 percent. The rapidly expanding service industries are expected to offer more jobs for managers than the slowly growing manufacturing industries.

Changes in business size and organization have resulted in differing trends for self-employed and salaried managers. The number of self-employed managers will continue to decline as many areas of business are increasingly dominated by large corporations and chain operations. Some kinds of small businesses, such as quick-service groceries and fast-food restaurants, still will provide opportunities for self-employment, however. The demand for salaried managers will continue to grow rapidly as firms increasingly depend on trained management specialists, particularly in highly technical areas of operation.

Clerical workers constitute both the largest and the fastest growing occupational group. Employment in these occupations is expected to grow about 29 percent between 1976 and 1985, rising from 15.6 million to 20.0 million workers.

New developments in computers, office machines, and dictating equipment will greatly affect employment in many occupations within this group. As computers are used more extensively to store information and perform billing, payroll, and other calculations, employment of file clerks and many types of office machine operators will level off or decline. At the same time, however, the need for computer and peripheral equipment operators will increase. Dictation machines, which have sharply reduced the need for stenographers, will continue to adversely affect employment prospects for workers in this occupation. The sole exception will be stenographers who are trained as court reporters.

Many types of clerical workers, however, will not be affected by technological innovations because their jobs involve a high degree of personal contact. Substantial growth is anticipated for secretaries, typists, and receptionists, largely as a result of growth in the expanding business services and medical and health care services industries. Counter and fountain workers also are expected to increase as the restaurant industry grows.

Sales workers are employed primarily by retail stores, manufacturing and wholesale firms, insurance companies, and real estate agencies. Employment of this group is expected to grow from 5.5 million to 6.4 million workers, an increase of 17 percent.

Much of the growth of sales workers will be due to expansion in the retail trade industry, which employs about one-half of these workers. The demand for both full- and part-time sales workers in retail trade is expected to increase as our growing population requires an increasing number of shopping centers and stores. Despite the widespread use of labor-saving merchandising techniques, such as self-service and computerized checkout counters, suburban expansion and longer operating hours will cause employment to increase.

Craft workers include a wide variety of highly skilled workers, such as carpenters, tool-and-die makers, instrument makers, all-round machinists, electricians, and automobile mechanics. Between 1976 and 1985, employment of this group is expected to increase 22 percent, from 11.3 million to 13.7 million workers.

Construction workers and mechanics, the two largest occupations within this group, are expected to account for about two-thirds of the employment gain for craft workers, and blue-collar worker supervisors and metalcraft workers for most of the remainder.

Nearly all construction trades are expected to grow, but particularly rapid increases are anticipated for heavy equipment operators, plumbers, ironworkers, roofers, and cement masons. Among mechanics and repairers, the most rapid increases will be for workers who repair computers, office machines, air conditioners, and industrial machinery.

In contrast, a continuation of the long-run employment decline in the railroad industry will lead to the decline of some craft occupations concentrated in that industry, such as railroad and car shop repairers. Because of advances in printing technology, very little growth is anticipated in printing crafts.

Operatives are the largest blue-collar group, including workers such as assemblers, packers, truck and bus drivers, and many types of machine operators. Employment of operatives is tied closely to the production of goods, because the majority of these workers are employed in manufacturing industries. The projected slow growth of manufacturing, along with improved production processes, will hold down the demand for these workers. Textile operatives, such as spinners, knitters, and weavers, are expected to decline due to increasing use of machinery in the textile industry.

Outside of manufacturing, employment of most transportation operatives, such as truckdrivers and bus drivers, will increase as the transportation industry grows. An exception will be brake and switch operators; these occupations are expected to decline along with the railroad industry.

Employment of operatives is expected to rise from 13.4 million to 15.6 million workers between 1976 and 1985, an increase of 17 percent.

Laborers (except farm) include workers such as garbage collectors, construction laborers, freight and stock handlers, and equipment washers. Employment in this group is expected to grow only slowly as machinery increasingly replaces manual labor in construction and manufacturing, the two largest employers of these workers. Power-driven equipment, such as forklift trucks, cranes, and hoists, will handle more and more material in factories, loading docks and warehouses. Other machines will do excavating, ditch digging, and similar work. Between 1976 and 1985, employment of laborers is expected to increase 11 percent from 4.3 million to 4.8 million workers.

Service workers include a wide range of workers—firefighters, janitors, cosmetologists, private household workers, and bartenders are a few examples. These workers, most of whom are employed in the service-producing industries, make up one of the fastest growing occupational groups.

Some of the main factors that are expected to increase the need for these workers are the rising demand for medical care; the greater need for commercial cleaning and protective services; and the more frequent use of restaurants, beauty salons, and leisure services as incomes rise. The employment of private household workers, however, will continue to decline despite a rising demand for their services, because low wages and the strenuous nature of the work make this occupation unattractive to many people.

Employment of service workers is expected to increase 23 percent between 1976 and 1985, from 12.0 million to 14.8 million workers.

Farm workers include farmers and farm operators, as well as farm laborers. Employment of these workers has declined for decades as farm productivity has increased as a result of the trend toward fewer but larger farms, the use of more and better machinery, and the development of new feeds, fertilizers, and pesticides. Between 1976 and 1985, the number of farm workers is expected to decline 34 percent, from 2.8 million to 1.9 million workers.

The Job Outlook

Finally, this chapter closes with the latest word on the job outlook for the next decade. This section lists 281 of the most significant occupations in the nation with the number of workers in each area, the expected number of openings annually over the next ten years, and a brief description of the prospects for each. The material is adapted from the spring 1978 issue of the *Occupational Outlook Quarterly* and used here by permission. It is the best brief guide available in terms of specific job forecasts for the near future.

The Job Outlook in Brief
Based on *The Occupational Outlook Handbook, 1978-79 Edition*

Occupation	Estimated employment 1976	Average annual openings 1976-85	Employment prospects
INDUSTRIAL PRODUCTION AND RELATED OCCUPATIONS			
Foundry occupations			
Patternmakers	18,000	900	Employment expected to grow about as fast as average. Increased use of metal patterns will partially offset tremendous increase in foundry production. Job openings are sensitive to economic changes.
Molders	53,000	1,900	Employment expected to increase about as fast as average. Although large demand likely for metal castings, laborsaving innovations will moderate employment growth.
Coremakers	22,000	1,000	Employment expected to increase only about as fast as average as growing use of machine coremaking limits the need for additional workers.
Machining occupations			
All-round machinist	405,000	20,000	Employment expected to increase about as fast as average due to growing demand for machined metal parts. Many openings likely in maintenance shops of manufacturing plants.
Instrument makers	6,000	300	Employment expected to grow about as fast as average in response to the need for new and custom made instruments. Laborsaving innovations may limit growth somewhat.
Machine tool operators	508,000	22,000	Employment expected to increase about as fast as average as metalworking industries expand. Although advances in machine tools may affect some jobs, opportunities should be plentiful.
Setup workers	60,000	3,500	Employment expected to increase about as fast as average as demand for machined goods grows. Automatically controlled machine tools may limit need for additional workers.
Tool-and-die makers	183,000	9,000	Employment expected to increase about as fast as average as need for tools and dies continues. However, advances in tool-making processes may limit growth.
Printing occupations			
Compositors	152,000	3,600	Employment expected to decline as trend to high-speed phototypesetting and typesetting computers continues. Replacement needs will create some openings. Best prospects for graduates of posthigh school programs in printing technology.

Occupation	Estimated employment 1976	Average annual openings 1976-85	Employment prospects
Lithographers	29,000	1,900	Employment expected to increase faster than average in response to continued growth of offset printing. Best job prospects for graduates of posthigh school programs in printing technology.
Photoengravers	10,000	100	Employment expected to decline as firms switch from letterpress to offset printing. Job opportunities will be scarce.
Electrotypers and stereotypers	4,000	60	Employment expected to decline due to greater use of offset printing and other laborsaving equipment. Job opportunities will be scarce.
Printing press operators and assistants	145,000	5,100	Employment expected to increase more slowly than average as faster and more efficient presses limit growth. Applicants will face competition for jobs.
Bookbinders and bindery workers	80,000	3,400	Employment expected to increase more slowly than average due to increasing mechanization of bindery operations.

Other industrial production and related occupations

Occupation	Estimated employment 1976	Average annual openings 1976-85	Employment prospects
Assemblers	1,100,000	70,000	Employment expected to increase faster than average due to growing demand for consumer products and industrial machinery and equipment. Since most jobs are in durable goods industries, however, economic changes and national defense spending often affect job opportunities.
Automobile painters	32,000	1,300	Employment expected to increase about as fast as average due to growing number of vehicles damaged in traffic accidents. Job opportunities are best in heavily populated areas.
Blacksmiths	10,000	100	Employment expected to decline as blacksmiths are replaced by welders and machines in large shops. Slight increase in employment of farriers due to growing popularity of horseracing and recreational horseback riding.
Blue-collar worker supervisors	1,445,000	79,000	Employment expected to increase about as fast as average. Large part of increase will be due to expansion of nonmanufacturing industries. Because competition for supervisory jobs is keen, the best opportunities are for workers with leadership ability and some college.
Boilermaking occupations	34,000	3,800	Employment expected to increase much faster than average due to construction of many new electric powerplants and expansion of chemical, petroleum, steel, and shipbuilding industries. Jobs are sensitive to economic changes.
Boiler tenders	73,000	1,500	Employment expected to decline as more boilers are equipped with automatic controls. However, some openings will arise due to replacement needs.

Occupation	Estimated employment 1976	Average annual openings 1976-85	Employment prospects
Electroplaters	36,000	1,300	Employment expected to grow more slowly than average as increasing use of automated plating equipment restricts growth. Favorable job opportunities should exist.
Forge shop occupations	71,000	2,700	Although forge shop production should expand considerably, slower than average employment growth expected as improved forging techniques and equipment allow greater output per worker. Most job openings due to replacement needs.
Furniture upholsterers	27,000	1,100	Little change in employment expected as people buy new, inexpensive furniture instead of reupholstering the old. Most job openings limited to replacement needs.
Inspectors (manufacturing)	692,000	52,000	Employment expected to grow faster than average as amount of industrial machinery and equipment increases and manufactured goods become more complex. Some industries that employ inspectors are sensitive to business conditions.
Millwrights	96,000	3,600	Employment expected to increase about as fast as average due to construction of new plants, improvements in existing plants, and installation and maintenance of increasingly complex machinery.
Motion picture projectionists	16,500	1,200	Little change in employment expected. Limited growth in number of theaters and use of laborsaving equipment will restrict openings thus creating keen competition for jobs.
Ophthalmic laboratory technicians	22,000	1,500	Employment expected to grow faster than average as demand for eyeglasses rises due to population growth and greater awareness of need for proper eye care.
Photographic laboratory occupations	35,000	2,400	Employment expected to grow faster than average due to increasing use of photography in business, government, and research and development activities and rising popularity of amateur photography.
Power truck operators	360,000	14,600	Employment expected to increase about as fast as average as more firms use power trucks in place of hand labor. Job opportunities dependent upon demand for manufactured goods.
Production painters	104,000	6,900	Employment expected to grow about as fast as average. Although manufacturing output is rising rapidly, increased use of automatic painting processes and other laborsaving innovations will moderate demand for painters.
Stationary engineers	194,000	7,400	Despite increased use of large boilers and auxiliary equipment, employment expected to change little because of trend to more powerful and more centralized equipment. Many openings will arise annually due to replacement needs.

Occupation	Estimated employment 1976	Average annual openings 1976-85	Employment prospects
Waste water treatment plant operators	100,000	10,400	Employment expected to grow much faster than average as new treatment plants are built and existing ones are expanded to cope more effectively with water pollution.
Welders	660,000	33,800	Employment expected to grow faster than average due to expansion of metalworking industries and greater use of welding. Very good opportunities except during economic downturns.

OFFICE OCCUPATIONS

Clerical occupations

Occupation	Estimated employment 1976	Average annual openings 1976-85	Employment prospects
Bookkeeping workers	1,700,000	95,000	Employment expected to grow more slowly than average due to increasing use of bookkeeping machines and electronic computers. Due to high replacement needs, job opportunities are expected to be numerous.
Cashiers	1,250,000	92,000	Plentiful job opportunities expected as employment grows faster than average and replacement needs remain high. However, widespread adoption of automatic checkout systems could slow future growth.
Collection workers	64,000	4,400	Employment expected to grow faster than average as increasing use of credit results in a greater number of delinquent accounts. Good job opportunities for aggressive and personable people, particularly in collection agencies and retail trade firms.
File clerks	270,000	16,500	Employment expected to grow about as fast as average as business expansion creates a need for more and better recordkeeping. Jobseekers with typing and other secretarial skills should have the best opportunities.
Hotel front office clerks	62,000	3,300	Employment expected to grow more slowly than average as more hotel and motel chains use computerized reservation systems. Most openings will result from replacement needs.
Office machine operators	163,000	7,700	Employment expected to grow more slowly than average as centralized and computerized recordkeeping and processing systems spread. Most openings will result from replacement needs.
Postal clerks	270,000	3,700	Employment expected to decline due to falling mail volume and increasing automation of mail processing. Many openings will result from replacement needs.
Receptionists	500,000	38,000	Employment expected to grow faster than average as business, personal, and professional services expand. Good job opportunities for full- and part-time work.

Occupation	Estimated employment 1976	Average annual openings 1976-85	Employment prospects
Secretaries and stenographers	3,500,000	295,000	Skilled persons seeking secretarial and shorthand reporter positions should find numerous opportunities. Part-time secretarial jobs also should remain plentiful. However, increasing use of dictation machines will limit opportunities for office stenographers.
Shipping and receiving clerks	440,000	23,000	Employment expected to rise about as fast as average as business expansion results in a greater volume of goods to be distributed.
Statistical clerks	337,000	21,000	Employment expected to grow about as fast as average as need for collection and processing of data increases. Knowledge of computers may be helpful for some jobs.
Stock clerks	490,000	25,000	Employment expected to increase about as fast as average. Use of computers for inventory control may limit growth somewhat. Some competition for jobs likely.
Typists	1,000,000	63,000	Employment expected to grow about as fast as average as business expansion increases the amount of paperwork. Demand should be strong, particularly for typists capable of handling a variety of office duties.

Computer and related occupations

Occupation	Estimated employment 1976	Average annual openings 1976-85	Employment prospects
Computer operating personnel	565,000	8,500	Employment of console and peripheral equipment operators expected to rise about as fast as average as use of computers expands. Employment of keypunch operators expected to decline, however, due to more efficient direct data entry techniques.
Programmers	230,000	9,700	Employment expected to grow faster than average as computer usage expands, particularly in accounting and business management firms. Brightest prospects for college graduates with degree in computer science or related field.
Systems analysts	160,000	7,600	Employment expected to grow faster than average as computer capabilities are increased and computers are used to solve a greater variety of problems. Excellent prospects for graduates of computer-related curriculums.

Banking occupations

Occupation	Estimated employment 1976	Average annual openings 1976-85	Employment prospects
Bank clerks	456,000	36,000	Employment expected to grow faster than average as banking services expand. Job opportunities should be good, especially for persons trained in computer usage.
Bank officers and managers	319,000	28,000	Employment expected to increase faster than average as rising costs of new technology and services require more officers to provide sound management. Good opportunities for college graduates as management trainees.

Occupation	Estimated employment 1976	Average annual openings 1976-85	Employment prospects
Bank tellers	310,000	21,000	Employment expected to grow faster than average. High replacement needs and expansion of bank services should create good opportunities for jobs.
Insurance occupations			
Actuaries	9,000	500	Employment expected to rise faster than average as volume of insurance sales increases. However, a large number of qualified applicants may create keen competition for jobs.
Claim representatives	155,000	7,700	Employment expected to grow about as fast as average due to increasing insurance claims.
Underwriters, insurance agents, and brokers	490,000	27,500	Employment expected to grow about as fast as average as insurance sales continue to expand. Favorable opportunities for agents and brokers who are ambitious and enjoy saleswork.
Administrative and related occupations			
Accountants	865,000	51,500	Employment expected to increase about as fast as average as managers rely more on accounting information to make business decisions. College graduates will be in greater demand than applicants who lack this training.
Advertising workers	180,000	N.A.*	Employment expected to increase faster than average as advertising expenditures rise. Best opportunities in retail advertising. Jobs are strongly affected by general business conditions.
Buyers	109,000	5,700	Slower than average employment growth expected as chain stores increasingly rely on centralized buying. Keen competition anticipated because merchandising attracts large numbers of college graduates.
City managers	3,000	250	Employment expected to grow faster than average. But, competition will be keen, even for persons with graduate degrees in public administration.
College student personnel workers	57,000	N.A.*	Competition for jobs expected as tighter budgets in both public and private colleges and universities limit employment growth. Some additional workers may be needed in junior and community colleges.
Credit managers	53,000	2,500	Employment expected to grow more slowly than average as use of credit by businesses and consumers continues to increase. Best prospects in metropolitan areas.
Hotel managers and assistants	137,000	7,000	Employment expected to grow more slowly than average. Some openings will result as additional hotels and motels are built and chain and franchise operations spread. Best opportunities for persons with degrees in hotel administration.

*Not Available

Occupation	Estimated employment 1976	Average annual openings 1976-85	Employment prospects
Industrial traffic managers	21,000	N.A.*	Employment expected to grow about as fast as average due to emphasis on reducing cost of receiving raw materials and distributing finished products. Best opportunities for college graduates with majors in traffic management or transportation.
Lawyers	396,000	23,400	Employment expected to grow faster than average in response to increased business activity and population. However, keen competition likely for salaried positions. Best prospects for establishing new practices will be in small towns and expanding suburbs, although starting a practice will remain a risky and expensive venture.
Marketing research workers	'25,000	N.A.*	Employment expected to grow much faster than average as demand for new products stimulates marketing activities. Best opportunities for applicants with graduate training in marketing research or statistics.
Personnel and labor relations workers	335,000	23,000	Employment expected to grow faster than average as new standards for employment practices in areas of occupational safety and health, equal employment opportunity, and pensions stimulate demand. Best opportunities with State and local governments.
Public relations workers	115,000	8,300	Employment expected to grow faster than average as corporations, associations, and other large organizations expand public relations efforts to gain public support and approval. Competition for jobs likely to be keen, however, especially during economic downturns.
Purchasing agents	192,000	13,800	Employment expected to increase faster than average as businesses try to reduce purchasing costs. Excellent job opportunities, especially for persons with master's degrees in business administration.
Urban planners	16,000	1,100	Employment expected to grow faster than average as Federal support for State and local community development, urban restoration, and land use planning programs increases.

SERVICE OCCUPATIONS

Cleaning and related occupations

Building custodians	2,100,000	160,000	Employment expected to grow about as fast as average as rising number of office buildings, hospitals, and apartment houses increases demand for maintenance services. Good opportunities for full-time, part-time, and evening work.
Hotel housekeepers and assistants	17,000	1,100	Employment expected to grow more slowly than average. Best opportunities in newly built hotels and motels.

*Not Available

Occupation	Estimated employment 1976	Average annual openings 1976-85	Employment prospects
Pest controllers	27,000	N.A.*	Employment expected to grow faster than average in effort to control rapidly reproducing pest population.

Food service occupations

Occupation	Estimated employment 1976	Average annual openings 1976-85	Employment prospects
Bartenders	261,000	17,800	Employment expected to increase about as fast as average as many new restaurants, hotels, and bars open. Most favorable opportunities in States that have recently liberalized their drinking laws.
Cooks and chefs	1,065,000	79,000	Employment expected to increase faster than average as population grows and people spend more money on eating out. Most starting jobs available in small restaurants, school cafeterias, and other eating places where food preparation is simple.
Dining room attendants and dishwashers	442,000	22,400	Plentiful job openings expected due to high turnover and substantial employment growth. Many opportunities for students in part-time jobs.
Food counter workers	421,000	33,000	Employment expected to grow faster than average due to increasing business in eating places. Job openings will be plentiful.
Meatcutters	215,000	4,900	Employment expected to decline as practice of cutting and wrapping meat for several stores at one location limits growth.
Waiters and waitresses	1,260,000	71,000	Employment expected to grow about as fast as average as restaurant business increases. Job openings should be plentiful.

Personal service occupations

Occupation	Estimated employment 1976	Average annual openings 1976-85	Employment prospects
Barbers	124,000	8,100	Employment expected to change little with most openings resulting from replacement needs. Better opportunities for hairstylists than for conventional barbers.
Bellhops and bell captains	16,600	600	Little change in employment expected as increasing popularity of economy motels limits growth. Best opportunities in motels, small hotels, and resort areas open only part of the year.
Cosmetologists	534,000	30,000	Employment expected to grow about as fast as average in response to rising demand for beauty shop services. Good opportunities for both newcomers and experienced cosmetologists, including those seeking part-time work.
Funeral directors and embalmers	45,000	2,200	Little employment change expected since existing funeral homes and their employees should be able to meet any additional demand for funeral services.

*Not Available

Occupation	Estimated employment 1976	Average annual openings 1976-85	Employment prospects

Private household service occupations

Private household workers	1,125,000	53,000	Despite expected decline in employment, replacement needs will create many job openings. Job opportunities for domestic workers will be plentiful.

Protective and related service

Correction officers	90,000	8,900	Employment expected to increase about as fast as average as number of persons in correctional facilities increases. Also, replacement needs will create a substantial number of job openings.
FBI special agents	8,600	N.A.*	Employment expected to rise as FBI responsibilities grow. Traditionally low turnover rate.
Firefighters	210,000	8,300	Employment expected to increase about as fast as average as need for fire protection grows and professionals replace volunteers. Keen competition for jobs in urban areas; better opportunities in smaller communities.
Guards	500,000	63,000	Employment expected to grow faster than average due to increased concern over crime and vandalism. Best opportunities in guard and security agencies and in night-shift jobs.
Police officers	500,000	32,500	Employment expected to rise faster than average as law enforcement becomes a higher priority. Good prospects for applicants with college training in law enforcement.
State police officers	48,000	1,900	Employment expected to grow about as fast as average primarily due to demand for officers to work in highway patrol.
Construction inspectors (government)	22,000	2,300	Employment expected to grow faster than average as safe construction of new housing and commercial buildings is emphasized. Best opportunities for college graduates and persons experienced as carpenters, electricians, or plumbers.
Health and regulatory inspectors (government)	115,000	7,900	Employment expected to grow faster than average as a result of public concern for improved quality and safety of consumer products. Employment of health inspectors likely to grow more rapidly than that of regulatory inspectors.
Occupational safety and health workers	28,000	N.A.*	Employment expected to grow faster than average as new safety and health programs are started and existing ones upgraded and/or expanded. Best prospects for graduates of curriculums related to occupational safety and health.

*Not Available

Occupation	Estimated employment 1976	Average annual openings 1976-85	Employment prospects
Other service occupations			
Mail carriers	250,000	5,300	Little change in employment due to anticipated cutbacks in frequency of mail deliveries. Some openings will result due to replacement needs. These openings will be concentrated in metropolitan areas.
Telephone operators	340,000	11,600	Employment expected to decline due to increased direct dialing and technological improvements. Many openings will result from replacement needs.
EDUCATION AND RELATED OCCUPATIONS			
Teaching occupations			
Kindergarten and elementary school teachers	1,364,000	70,000	Competition for jobs expected as enrollments continue to decline until early 1980's. Reentrants will face increasing competition from new graduates.
Secondary school teachers	1,111,000	13,000	Keen competition expected due to declining enrollments coupled with large increases in supply of teachers. More favorable opportunities will exist for persons qualified to teach vocational subjects, mathematics, and the natural and physical sciences.
College and university teachers	593,000[4]	17,000	Despite expected employment growth, applicants will face keen competition for jobs. Best opportunities in public colleges and universities. Persons who do not have a Ph.D. will find it increasingly difficult to secure a teaching position.
Teacher aides	320,000	29,000	Employment expected to rise much faster than average as more aides are hired to lessen teachers' clerical duties.
Library occupations			
Librarians	128,000	8,000	Although employment expected to grow, field is likely to be somewhat competitive. Best prospects in school and public libraries away from large east and west coast cities.
Library technicians and assistants	143,000	8,300	Employment expected to grow faster than average. Public and college and university libraries will offer the best job opportunities.
SALES OCCUPATIONS			
Automobile parts counter workers	75,000	4,200	Employment expected to grow faster than average due to increasing demand for new accessories and replacement parts.
Automobile sales workers	130,000	9,000	Employment expected to grow faster than average as demand for automobiles increases. Job openings may fluctuate, however, because sales are affected by changing economic conditions and consumer preferences.

Occupation	Estimated employment 1976	Average annual openings 1976-85	Employment prospects
Automobile service advisors	24,000	1,000	Employment expected to grow about as fast as average as automobiles increase in number and complexity. Most job openings in large dealerships in heavily populated areas.
Gasoline service station attendants	420,000	14,800	Employment expected to increase more slowly than average as trends toward cars with better gas mileage and self-service gas stations limit growth. Nevertheless, replacement needs will create many job openings.
Manufacturers sales workers	362,000	17,600	Employment expected to grow about as fast as average because of rising demand for technical products and resulting need for trained sales workers.
Models	8,300	N.A.*	Employment expected to grow faster than average due to rising advertising expenditures and greater sales of clothing and accessories. Nevertheless, because occupation is so small and the glamour of modeling attracts many persons, competition for openings should be keen.
Real estate agents and brokers	450,000	45,500	Employment expected to rise faster than average in response to growing demand for housing and other properties. However, field is highly competitive. Best prospects for college graduates and transfers from other sales jobs.
Retail trade sales workers	2,725,000	155,000	Employment expected to grow more slowly than average; however, high turnover should create excellent opportunities for full-time, part-time, and temporary work.
Route drivers	200,000	3,400	Employment expected to change little, but several thousand openings will result annually from replacement needs. Best opportunities for applicants who have sales experience and good driving records and who are seeking wholesale routes.
Securities sales workers	90,000	5,500	Employment expected to grow about as fast as average as investment in securities continues to increase. Favorable job opportunities likely except during periods of economic downturn.
Travel agents	15,000	1,400	Although employment expected to grow faster than average, competition for jobs will be keen. Because travel expenditures often depend on business conditions, job opportunities are very sensitive to economic changes.
Wholesale trade sales workers	808,000	41,000	Employment expected to grow about as fast as average, as wholesalers sell wider variety of products and improve customer services. Good opportunities for persons with product knowledge and sales ability.

*Not Available

Occupation	Estimated employment 1976	Average annual openings 1976-85	Employment prospects

CONSTRUCTION OCCUPATIONS

Occupation	Estimated employment 1976	Average annual openings 1976-85	Employment prospects
Bricklayers, stonemasons, and marble setters	175,000	7,500	Employment expected to grow about as fast as average as new homes, factories, offices, and other structures are built. Job openings should be plentiful except during economic downturns.
Carpenters	1,010,000	67,000	Employment expected to grow about as fast as average due to increasing construction of new structures and alteration and maintenance of old ones. Plentiful job opportunities except during economic downturns.
Cement masons and terrazzo workers	71,000	7,500	Employment expected to increase much faster than average due to growing construction activity and greater use of concrete as a building material. Job opportunities should be favorable.
Construction laborers	715,000	40,000	Employment expected to grow about as fast as average due to increasing construction activity. Job openings should be plentiful except during economic downturns.
Drywall installers and finishers	45,000	N.A.*	Employment expected to grow much faster than average as drywall is increasingly used in place of plaster. Most job openings will be in metropolitan areas.
Electricians (construction)	260,000	13,700	Employment expected to increase faster than average as more electricians are needed to install electrical fixtures and wiring in new and renovated buildings.
Elevator constructors	20,000	N.A.*	Employment expected to increase faster than average as number of high-rise apartments and commercial buildings grows.
Floor covering installers	85,000	3,200	Employment expected to increase about as fast as average due to expanding construction activity and widespread use of resilient floor coverings and carpeting. Best opportunities for persons able to install carpeting and resilient flooring.
Glaziers	10,000	600	Employment expected to increase faster than average as popularity of glass in building design continues. Greatest opportunities in metropolitan areas.
Insulation workers	30,000	2,900	Employment expected to grow much faster than average as energy saving insulation is installed in homes and businesses. Best opportunities in metropolitan areas.
Ironworkers	71,000	6,500	Employment expected to increase much faster than average for all occupations due to growing use of structural steel. Job opportunities are more abundant during early spring.

*Not Available

Occupation	Estimated employment 1976	Average annual openings 1976-85	Employment prospects
Lathers	20,000	N.A.*	Employment expected to grow about as fast as average due to increased need for lathers to construct some of the more expensive new buildings and to renovate older buildings.
Operating engineers	585,000	41,000	Employment expected to grow faster than average as construction of more factories, mass transit systems, office buildings, and other structures increases demand for operating engineers. Job opportunities should be plentiful.
Painters	410,000	27,000	Employment of painters expected to grow about as fast as average due to need to paint new structures and repaint existing ones.
Paperhangers	15,000	2,400	Employment of paperhangers expected to grow much faster than average as popularity of wallpaper and vinyl wallcovering rises.
Plasterers	24,000	900	Little change in employment expected as drywall materials are used in place of plaster. Some openings will result from replacement needs.
Plumbers and pipefitters	385,000	30,000	Employment expected to grow faster than average as larger proportion of homes have air-conditioning equipment, solar heating devices, and appliances such as washing machines and kitchen waste-disposal equipment.
Roofers	90,000	6,300	Employment expected to grow faster than average due to new construction and need to repair existing roofs. Demand for dampproofing and waterproofing also will stimulate need for more roofers. Jobs will be easiest to find in warm weather months.
Sheet-metal workers	65,000	2,600	Employment expected to increase about as fast as average due to need for air-conditioning and heating ducts and other sheet-metal products in homes, stores, offices, and other buildings.
Tilesetters	36,000	1,800	Employment expected to increase about as fast as average due to trend toward two or more tile bathrooms in houses and apartments.

OCCUPATIONS IN TRANSPORTATION ACTIVITIES

Air transportation occupations

Occupation	Estimated employment 1976	Average annual openings 1976-85	Employment prospects
Air traffic controllers	21,000	1,100	Although employment expected to grow faster than average, applicants may face keen competition for available jobs. Best opportunities for college graduates with experience as controllers, pilots, or navigators.
Airplane mechanics	110,000	5,200	Employment expected to grow faster than average, but opportunities in various areas of aviation may differ. Good opportunities in general aviation; keen competition for airline jobs; opportunities in Federal Government dependent upon defense spending.

*Not Available

Occupation	Estimated employment 1976	Average annual openings 1976-85	Employment prospects
Airplane pilots	83,000	4,100	Employment expected to grow faster than average, but applicants are likely to face keen competition for available jobs. Best opportunities for recent college graduates with flying experience.
Flight attendants	42,000	6,000	Employment expected to grow much faster than average as the number of airline passengers increases. However, competition for jobs should be keen.
Reservation, ticket, and passenger agents	51,000	2,900	Employment expected to grow faster than average as airline travel increases. Nevertheless, popularity of airline jobs will result in keen competition.
Merchant marine occupations			
Merchant marine officers	13,300	600	Employment expected to grow more slowly than average as size of Nation's fleet remains fairly constant. Best opportunities for graduates of maritime-union training programs.
Merchant marine sailors	33,200	400	Employment expected to decline as smaller crews operate new ships. Keen competition likely for those openings created by replacement needs.
Railroad occupations			
Brake operators	65,000	1,700	Little change in employment expected as laborsaving innovations in freight hauling moderate growth. Some openings will result from replacement needs.
Conductors	35,900	2,200	Employment expected to grow more slowly than average as technological advances increase freight hauling efficiency. Most openings due to replacement needs.
Locomotive engineers	33,300	2,400	Despite expected increase in demand for railroad services, slower than average employment growth likely as larger and better designed freight cars improve freight hauling efficiency. Most openings due to replacement needs.
Shop trades	72,600	800	Employment expected to decline as shop efficiency increases and railroad cars are more easily maintained. Openings limited to replacement needs.
Signal department workers	11,500	400	Employment expected to change little as new signal systems require less maintenance. Some openings will arise due to replacement needs.
Station agents	7,000	N.A.*	Employment expected to decline as centrally located stations handle more customer orders and billings and as mobile agents service smaller stations.

*Not Available

Occupation	Estimated employment 1976	Average annual openings 1976-85	Employment prospects
Telegraphers, telephoners, and tower operators	10,200	N.A.*	Employment expected to decline due to wider use of mechanized yard operations, centralized traffic control, and automatic signaling. Limited number of openings will arise due to replacement needs.
Track workers	56,200	800	Employment expected to change little due to use of laborsaving machines and installation of improved track control systems requiring less track. Most openings will be due to replacement needs.

Driving occupations

Occupation	Estimated employment 1976	Average annual openings 1976-85	Employment prospects
Intercity busdrivers	25,000	1,400	Employment expected to grow about as fast as average due to moderate increase in bus travel. Keen competition likely for job openings.
Local transit busdrivers	81,000	5,100	Employment expected to grow about as fast as average due to improved local bus service in many cities.
Local truckdrivers	1,600,000	73,000	Employment expected to increase faster than average due to growth in amount of freight to be distributed. Best opportunities for applicants with good driving records.
Long distance truckdrivers	467,000	15,400	Employment expected to grow more slowly than average. Stiff competition is likely for available jobs in this high-paying occupation.
Parking attendants	38,000	2,500	Employment expected to grow more slowly than average as trend to self-parking systems continues. High turnover rate, however, will create many job opportunities, especially in large commercial parking facilities in urban areas.
Taxicab drivers	94,000	4,200	Although employment expected to change little, high turnover should create numerous job opportunities.

SCIENTIFIC AND TECHNICAL OCCUPATIONS

Conservation occupations

Occupation	Estimated employment 1976	Average annual openings 1976-85	Employment prospects
Foresters	25,000	1,100	Employment expected to grow about as fast as average as environmental concern and need for forest products increase. However, applicants likely to face keen competition for jobs.
Forestry technicians	11,000	600	Employment expected to grow faster than average as use of technology in forest industry increases. Even applicants with specialized postsecondary school training may face competition, however.
Range managers	3,000	200	Employment expected to grow faster than average. Good employment prospects likely as use of rangelands for grazing, recreation, and wildlife habitats increases.

*Not Available

Occupation	Estimated employment 1976	Average annual openings 1976-85	Employment prospects
Soil conservationists	7,500	400	Employment expected to increase as fast as average as organizations try to preserve farmland values and comply with recent conservation and antipollution laws. However, competition may be keen.

Engineers

Occupation	Estimated employment 1976	Average annual openings 1976-85	Employment prospects
Engineers	1,133,000 [6]	56,500 [6]	Employment expected to grow slightly faster than average. Good employment opportunities for engineering graduates in most specialties. Some openings also available to graduates in related fields.
Aerospace engineers	50,000	1,500	Employment expected to grow more slowly than average due to limited increase in Federal expenditures on space and defense programs.
Agricultural engineers	12,000	600	Employment expected to grow faster than average, in response to increasing demand for agricultural products, modernization of farm operations, and increasing emphasis on conservation of resources.
Biomedical engineers	3,000	150	Employment expected to grow faster than average but actual number of openings will be small. Increased research funds could create new jobs in instrumentation and systems for delivery of health services.
Ceramic engineers	12,000	600	Employment expected to grow faster than average as a result of need to develop and improve ceramic materials for nuclear energy, electronics, defense, and medical science.
Chemical engineers	53,000	2,100	Employment expected to grow about as fast as average. Growing complexity and automation of chemical processes will require additional chemical engineers to design, build, and maintain plants and equipment.
Civil engineers	155,000	8,900	Employment expected to increase about as fast as average as result of growing need for housing, industrial buildings, electric power generating plants, and transportation systems. Work related to environmental pollution and energy self-sufficiency also will create openings.
Electrical engineers	300,000	12,800	Employment expected to increase about as fast as average due to growing demand for computers, communications equipment, military electronics, and electrical and electronic consumer goods. Increased research and development in power generation also should create many openings.
Industrial engineers	200,000	10,500	Employment expected to grow faster than average due to industry growth, increasing complexity of industrial operations, expansion of automated processes, and greater emphasis on scientific management and safety engineering.

Occupation	Estimated employment 1976	Average annual openings 1976-85	Employment prospects
Mechanical engineers	200,000	9,300	Employment expected to increase about as fast as average due to growing demand for industrial machinery and machine tools. Need to develop new energy systems and to solve environmental pollution problems also will create openings.
Metallurgical engineers	17,000	900	Employment expected to grow faster than average due to need to develop new metals and alloys, adapt current ones to new needs, solve problems associated with efficient use of nuclear energy, and develop new ways of recycling solid waste materials.
Mining engineers	6,000	600	Employment expected to grow faster than average due to efforts to attain energy self-sufficiency and to develop more technologically advanced mining systems.
Petroleum engineers	20,000	1,300	Employment expected to grow faster than average as demand for petroleum and natural gas requires increased drilling and more sophisticated recovery methods.

Environmental scientists

Occupation	Estimated employment 1976	Average annual openings 1976-85	Employment prospects
Geologists	34,000	2,300	Employment expected to grow faster than average as domestic mineral exploration increases. Good opportunities for persons with degrees in geology or related scientific fields.
Geophysicists	12,000	800	Employment expected to grow faster than average as petroleum and mining companies need additional geophysicists who are able to use sophisticated electronic techniques in exploration activities. Very good opportunities for graduates in geophysics or related areas.
Meteorologists	5,500	200	Employment expected to increase about as fast as average. Favorable opportunities, particularly with weather consulting firms and radio and television stations.
Oceanographers	2,700	150	Although employment expected to grow about as fast as average, competition for openings is likely. Best opportunities for persons who have Ph.D.'s; those who have less education may be limited to research assistant and technician jobs.

Life science occupations

Occupation	Estimated employment 1976	Average annual openings 1976-85	Employment prospects
Biochemists	12,700	600	Employment expected to grow about as fast as average due to increase in funds for biochemical research and development. Favorable opportunities for advanced degree holders.
Life scientists	205,000	12,000	Employment expected to grow faster than average due to increasing expenditures for medical research and environmental protection. Good opportunities for persons with advanced degrees.

Occupation	Estimated employment 1976	Average annual openings 1976-85	Employment prospects
Soil scientists	2,500	80	Some employment growth expected as concern for pollution and destruction of our soil resources increases. Applicants may face competition for job openings.

Mathematics occupations

Mathematicians	38,000	1,000	Slower than average employment growth is expected to lead to keen competition for jobs, especially for academic positions. Opportunities expected to be best for advanced degree holders in applied mathematics seeking jobs in government and private industry.
Statisticians	24,000	1,500	Employment expected to grow faster than average as use of statistics expands into new areas. Persons combining knowledge of statistics with a field of application, such as economics, may expect favorable job opportunities.

Physical scientists

Astronomers	2,000	40	Limited employment growth expected as only slight increases in funds for basic research in astronomy are expected. Competition for jobs is likely to be keen.
Chemists	148,000	6,300	Employment expected to grow about as fast as average as a result of increasing demand for new products and rising concern about energy shortages, pollution control, and health care. Except for positions in colleges and universities, good opportunities should exist.
Food scientists	7,000	300	Employment expected to grow about as fast as average due to increasing demand for food scientists in research and development, quality control, and production. Favorable opportunities for persons with food science degrees.
Physicists	48,000	1,100	Although employment will grow more slowly than average, generally favorable job opportunities are expected for persons with advanced degrees in physics. However, persons seeking college and university positions, as well as graduates with only a bachelor's degree, will face keen competition.

Other scientific and technical occupations

Broadcast technicians	22,500	N.A.*	Employment expected to increase about as fast as average as new radio and television stations are licensed. Job competition is keen in this small occupation, however, and prospects are best in smaller cities.
Drafters	320,000	16,500	Employment expected to grow faster than average as a result of increasing complexity of designs of modern products and processes. Best prospects for graduates with associate degrees in drafting.

*Not Available

Occupation	Estimated employment 1976	Average annual openings 1976-85	Employment prospects
Engineering and science technicians	586,000	29,000	Employment expected to grow faster than average as more technicians will be needed to support the growing number of engineers and scientists. Favorable job opportunities, particularly for graduates of postsecondary school training programs.
Surveyors	52,000	3,500	Employment expected to grow faster than average. Best prospects for persons with postsecondary school training. Few job opportunities during economic downturns.

MECHANICS AND REPAIRERS

Telephone craft occupations

Occupation	Estimated employment 1976	Average annual openings 1976-85	Employment prospects
Central office craft occupations	135,000	5,000	Employment expected to increase about as fast as average as many new telephone systems are installed and maintained. Most job openings will be in metropolitan areas.
Central office equipment installers	20,000	N.A.*	Employment expected to decline as most new central office equipment is manufactured in components that come partially assembled.
Line installers and cable splicers	54,000	600	Little change in employment as new technological improvements limit growth. Job openings may be found more easily in small cities.
Telephone and PBX installers and repairers	110,000	4,000	Employment expected to increase about as fast as average due to growing demand for telephones and PBX and CENTREX systems.

Other mechanics and repairers

Occupation	Estimated employment 1976	Average annual openings 1976-85	Employment prospects
Air-conditioning, refrigeration, and heating mechanics	175,000	17,400	Employment expected to increase much faster than average. Most openings will be for air-conditioning and refrigeration mechanics.
Appliance repairers	144,000	7,000	Employment expected to grow about as fast as average due to increasing use of appliances as population and incomes rise.
Automobile body repairers	174,000	6,000	Employment expected to increase about as fast as average due to rising number of vehicles damaged in traffic accidents.
Automobile mechanics	790,000	32,000	Employment expected to increase about as fast as average due to growing number of automobiles. Job opportunities will be plentiful.
Boat-engine mechanics	15,000	800	Employment expected to grow about as fast as average due to increasing number of boats. Job opportunities particularly favorable for mechanics with knowledge of electricity and electronics.
Bowling-pin-machine mechanics	5,800	N.A.*	Employment expected to increase more slowly than average due to limited growth in number of bowling facilities.

*Not Available

Occupation	Estimated employment 1976	Average annual openings 1976-85	Employment prospects
Business machine repairers	58,000	3,400	Employment expected to grow faster than average as more machines are used to handle increasing volume of paperwork. Employment prospects will be good.
Computer service technicians	50,000	5,200	Employment expected to grow much faster than average as more computer equipment is used. Most openings will occur in metropolitan areas.
Diesel mechanics	100,000	5,000	Employment expected to grow faster than average as use of diesel engines expands.
Electric sign repairers	10,000	N.A.*	Employment expected to increase as fast as average due to need to maintain growing number of electric signs.
Farm equipment mechanics	66,000	4,000	Employment expected to increase about as fast as average as more technically advanced farm equipment requires greater maintenance. Best opportunities for persons familiar with farms and farm machinery.
Industrial machinery repairers	320,000	30,000	Employment expected to increase much faster than average as more repairers will be needed to maintain growing amount of machinery used in manufacturing, coal mining, oil exploration, and other industries.
Instrument repairers	75,000	N.A.*	Employment expected to grow about as fast as average as use of technically sophisticated instruments for measurement, analysis, and control increases. Job opportunities should be favorable.
Jewelers	19,000	1,300	Employment expected to grow more slowly than average as improved production methods enable jewelry factories to meet expected increase in demand for jewelry. Best opportunities for persons trained in jewelry construction, design, and repair.
Locksmiths	10,000	N.A.*	Employment expected to grow faster than average as public becomes more security conscious. Favorable opportunities for persons able to install and service electronic security systems.
Maintenance electricians	300,000	15,900	Employment expected to increase about as fast as average in response to increased use of electrical and electronic equipment in industry.
Motorcycle mechanics	12,000	N.A.*	Employment expected to grow much faster than average due to rising number of motorcycles. Best opportunities in larger dealerships.
Piano and organ tuners and repairers	8,000	650	Little change in employment expected as number of pianos and organs is limited by competition from other forms of entertainment and recreation. Opportunities will be best in piano and organ dealerships and large repair shops.

*Not Available

Occupation	Estimated employment 1976	Average annual openings 1976-85	Employment prospects
Shoe repairers	25,000	1,800	Despite little change in employment, job prospects should be very good. Opportunities should be especially good for experienced repairers who wish to open their own shops.
Television and radio service technicians	114,000	6,700	Employment expected to grow faster than average as number of home entertainment products increases. Greater use of electronic products such as closed-circuit television, two-way radios, calculators, and home appliances also will lead to job openings.
Truck mechanics and bus mechanics	145,000	6,900	Employment of truck mechanics expected to grow about as fast as average due to increasing use of trucks for transporting freight. Employment of bus mechanics expected to increase more slowly than average.
Vending machine mechanics	25,000	N.A.*	Although some growth will result from greater number of vending machines, employment expected to increase more slowly than average.
Watch repairers	21,000	1,500	Although employment expected to grow more slowly than average, trained workers should find jobs readily available. Opportunities should be good for persons trained in repairing electronic watches.

HEALTH OCCUPATIONS

Dental occupations

Occupation	Estimated employment 1976	Average annual openings 1976-85	Employment prospects
Dentists	112,000	4,800	Employment expected to grow about as fast as average due to population growth, increased awareness of importance of dental care, and expansion of prepayment arrangements. Opportunities should be very good.
Dental assistants	135,000	13,500	Employment expected to grow much faster than average as dentists increasingly use assistants in their practice. Very good opportunities for full- and part-time jobs, especially for graduates of approved programs.
Dental hygienists	27,000	5,100	Employment expected to grow much faster than average because of expanding population and growing awareness of importance of regular dental care. Opportunities for jobs should be good.
Dental laboratory technicians	42,000	3,700	Employment expected to grow faster than average due to expansion of dental prepayment plans and increasing number of older persons who require dentures. Favorable opportunities for graduates of approved programs.

*Not Available

Occupation	Estimated employment 1976	Average annual openings 1976-85	Employment prospects

Medical practitioners

Chiropractors	18,000	1,600	New chiropractors may have difficulty establishing a practice due to dramatic increases in number of chiropractic graduates. Best opportunities in small towns and areas with few practitioners.
Optometrists	19,700	1,500	Employment expected to grow about as fast as average due to increase in population and greater recognition of importance of good vision. Employment prospects will be favorable.
Physicians and osteopathic physicians	375,000	21,800	Employment outlook expected to be very favorable. New physicians should have little difficulty in establishing new practices.
Podiatrists	7,500	500	Employment expected to grow about as fast as average as expanding population demands more health services. Opportunities for graduates to establish new practices or to enter salaried positions should be favorable.
Veterinarians	30,500	1,800	Employment expected to grow faster than average because of growth in number of pets and increase in veterinary research. Opportunities should be favorable.

Medical technologist, technician and assistant occupations

Electrocardiograph technicians	12,000	700	Employment expected to grow faster than average as greater reliance placed on electrocardiographs to diagnose heart diseases and their use increases in physical examinations of older patients.
Electroencephalographic technologists and technicians	4,300	300	Employment expected to grow faster than average due to increased use of EEG's in surgery and in diagnosing and monitoring patients with brain disease.
Emergency medical technicians	287,000	37,000	Employment expected to grow much faster than average due to increasing public awareness of need for better emergency medical services.
Medical laboratory workers	240,000	20,000	Employment expected to grow faster than average as physicians make wider use of laboratory facilities. Job opportunities should be favorable.
Medical records technicians and clerks	57,000	9,000	Employment expected to grow much faster than average as the number of health insurance, Medicare, and Medicaid claims increases the need for more complete medical records. Favorable opportunities for those with specialized training.

Occupation	Estimated employment 1976	Average annual openings 1976-85	Employment prospects
Operating room technicians	30,000	2,100	Employment expected to increase faster than average as technicians assume more of the routine nursing tasks in operating rooms. Good opportunities, especially for graduates of 2-year community and junior college programs.
Optometric assistants	11,800	700	Employment expected to grow faster than average due to greater demand for eye care services. Job opportunities for persons who have completed a formal training program should be excellent.
Radiologic (X-ray) technologists	80,000	6,300	Employment expected to expand faster than average as X-ray equipment is increasingly used to diagnose and treat diseases. Applicants may face competition for jobs.
Respiratory therapy workers	36,000	4,700	Employment expected to grow much faster than average due to new applications of respiratory therapy in treating diseases. Job opportunities should be good.

Nursing occupations

Occupation	Estimated employment 1976	Average annual openings 1976-85	Employment prospects
Registered nurses	960,000	83,000	Employment expected to grow faster than average. Favorable opportunities, especially in some southern States and many inner-city locations. Nurses may find competition for higher paying jobs and for jobs in some urban areas with large nursing-training facilities.
Licensed practical nurses	460,000	53,000	Employment expected to grow much faster than average as population grows and health insurance plans expand. Job prospects are very good.
Nursing aides, orderlies, and attendants	1,000,000	83,000	Employment expected to grow faster than average due to increased demand for medical care. Most job openings will be in nursing homes, convalescent homes, and other long-term care facilities.

Therapy and rehabilitation occupations

Occupation	Estimated employment 1976	Average annual openings 1976-85	Employment prospects
Occupational therapists	10,600	1,300	Employment expected to grow much faster than average due to public interest in rehabilitation of disabled persons and growth of established occupational therapy programs. Prospects should be favorable.
Occupational therapy assistants	8,900	1,200	Employment expected to grow much faster than average due to increased need for assistants in health care institutions. Opportunities should be very good, especially for graduates of approved programs.
Physical therapists	25,000	2,100	Employment expected to grow faster than average because of increased public recognition of importance of rehabilitation. Very good employment opportunities, particularly in suburban and rural areas.

Occupation	Estimated employment 1976	Average annual openings 1976-85	Employment prospects
Physical therapist assistants and aides	12,500	1,100	Employment expected to grow faster than average due to expanding physical therapy services. Job opportunities for graduates of approved programs should be excellent.
Speech pathologists and audiologists	38,000	2,900	Employment expected to increase faster than average due to growing public concern over speech and hearing disorders. Holders of bachelor's degrees will face considerable competition for jobs.

Other health occupations

Occupation	Estimated employment 1976	Average annual openings 1976-85	Employment prospects
Dietitians	45,000	2,800	Employment expected to grow about as fast as average in response to increasing concern for proper nutrition and food management. Good full- and part-time opportunities for holders of bachelor's degrees and persons with specialized training.
Dispensing opticians	14,500	1,300	Employment expected to increase faster than average as population grows and demand for eyeglasses rises. Opportunities will be particularly favorable for persons with associate degrees in opticianry.
Health service administrators	160,000	16,000	Employment expected to grow much faster than average as quantity of patient services increases and health services management becomes more complex.
Medical record administrators	12,300	1,000	Employment expected to grow faster than average due to increasing use of health facilities as more people are covered by health insurance. Good opportunities for graduates of approved programs.
Pharmacists	120,000	8,900	Employment expected to grow about as fast as average due to establishment of new community pharmacies and increasing use of pharmacists in health facilities. Favorable prospects for pharmacy school graduates.

SOCIAL SCIENTISTS

Occupation	Estimated employment 1976	Average annual openings 1976-85	Employment prospects
Anthropologists	3,500	200	Employment expected to increase about as fast as average. Most new jobs will be in nonacademic areas. Even persons with Ph.D's in anthropology can expect keen competition for jobs.
Economists	115,000	6,400	Employment expected to grow faster than average. Master's and Ph.D degree holders may face keen competition for college and university positions but can expect good opportunities in nonacademic areas. Persons with bachelor's degrees likely to face keen competition.
Geographers	10,000	600	Employment expected to grow faster than average. Advanced degree holders face good prospects in the nonacademic job market, but all bachelor's degree holders will face competition.

Occupation	Estimated employment 1976	Average annual openings 1976-85	Employment prospects
Historians	22,500	900	Employment to grow more slowly than average. Keen competition expected, particularly for academic positions. Persons with training in historical specialties such as historic preservation and business history have best opportunities.
Political scientists	14,000	400	Employment expected to increase more slowly than average. Keen competition likely for all graduates. Best opportunities for Ph.D's trained in statistical research, American Government, public administration, or policy science.
Psychologists	90,000	5,600	Employment expected to grow faster than average. Ph.D's likely to face increasing competition, particularly for academic positions. Best prospects for Ph.D's trained in applied areas, such as clinical counseling and industrial psychology. Keen competition for persons below Ph.D level.
Sociologists	19,000	800	Employment expected to grow more slowly than average. Ph.D's may expect competition, particularly for academic positions. Best opportunities for Ph.D's trained in statistical research techniques. Very keen competition below Ph.D level.

SOCIAL SERVICE OCCUPATIONS

Counseling occupations

School counselors	43,000	1,500	Employment expected to grow more slowly than average as declining school enrollment coupled with financial constraints limit growth.
Employment counselors	6,400	N.A.*	Applicants with master's degrees or experience in related fields are expected to face some competition in both public and private employment agencies.
Rehabilitation counselors	19,000	N.A.*	Employment growth dependent upon government funding for rehabilitation agencies. Some openings expected in private companies to help in equal employment opportunity efforts.
College career planning and placement counselors	3,900	N.A.*	Employment expected to grow, especially in junior and community colleges, as many of these schools currently do not have career planning or placement offices. Also, expanding services available to minority, low-income, and handicapped students should increase demand.

Clergy

Protestant ministers	190,000	N.A.*	Increasing competition for ministers to serve individual congregations as trend toward merger and unity among denominations reduces demand. Some ministers will find work in youth, family relations, and welfare programs and as chaplains in hospitals, universities, or the Armed Forces.

*Not Available

Occupation	Estimated employment 1976	Average annual openings 1976-85	Employment prospects
Rabbis	4,000	N.A.*	Reform rabbis may face some competition for available positions, and Orthodox clergy expected to encounter very keen competition. Conservative rabbis should have good opportunities.
Roman Catholic priests	59,000	N.A.*	Growing number of priests needed as supply of seminary graduates fails to keep pace with increasing Catholic population. Priests may find opportunities not only in established parishes but also in social work, religious radio, newspapers, and television and missionary work.

Other social service occupations

Occupation	Estimated employment 1976	Average annual openings 1976-85	Employment prospects
Cooperative extension service workers	16,000	600	Employment expected to increase more slowly than average. Need for persons capable of relaying advances in farming practices from researchers to farmers will lead to some growth.
Home economists	141,000	6,100	Although little employment growth expected, many jobs will arise because of replacement needs. Keen competition likely for most jobs, especially high school teaching positions. However, advanced degree holders may find good prospects in college and university teaching.
Homemaker-home health aides	70,000	37,000	Employment expected to increase much faster than average due to growing public awareness of availability of home care services and probable changes in Federal legislation. Job opportunities should be plentiful.
Park, recreation, and leisure workers	85,000	N.A.*	Need for trained workers expected to grow significantly as physical fitness and recreation become increasingly important. Best prospects for persons with at least a bachelor's degree. Many opportunities for part-time and summer work.
Social service aides	100,000	7,500	Employment expected to grow faster than average as social welfare programs expand and aides perform tasks formerly handled by professional personnel. Many opportunities for part-time work.
Social workers	330,000	25,000	Employment expected to increase faster than average due to expansion of health services, passage of social welfare legislation, and potential development of national health insurance. Best opportunities for graduates of master's and Ph.D. degree programs in social work.

ART, DESIGN, AND COMMUNICATIONS-RELATED OCCUPATIONS

Performing artists

Occupation	Estimated employment 1976	Average annual openings 1976-85	Employment prospects
Actors and actresses	13,000	600	Employment expected to grow about as fast as average. Overcrowding in this field will persist. Persons finding jobs may be limited to part-time work only.

*Not Available

Occupation	Estimated employment 1976	Average annual openings 1976-85	Employment prospects
Dancers	8,000	500	Although employment expected to grow about as fast as average, applicants are likely to face keen competition for openings. Teaching offers best opportunities.
Musicians	127,000	7,200	Employment expected to grow about as fast as average. However, job competition will be keen except for the most highly-skilled performers.
Singers	23,000	1,200	Although employment growth is expected to be about as fast as average, competition for long-term jobs likely to be keen. Some opportunities for part-time and short-term jobs in opera and concert stage, movies, theater, nightclubs, and television commercials.

Design occupations

Occupation	Estimated employment 1976	Average annual openings 1976-85	Employment prospects
Architects	49,000	3,100	Employment expected to rise about as fast as average. Competition for jobs likely. Prospects are best in the South and States without architectural schools.
Commercial artists	67,000	3,600	Employment expected to increase about as fast as average as more artists are needed in areas of visual advertising, such as television graphics and packaging displays, and industrial design. However, even talented and well-trained persons may face competition.
Display workers	36,000	1,900	Employment expected to grow more slowly than average as increased specialization of job duties limits need for more workers. Opportunities will be concentrated in large stores located in metropolitan areas.
Floral designers	37,000	3,300	Expected increases in sale of flowers and floral arrangements will cause employment to grow faster than average. Employment openings are sensitive to economic fluctuations.
Industrial designers	12,000	500	Slower than average employment growth expected as trend away from frequent redesign of household products, automobiles, and industrial equipment continues. Best opportunities for college graduates with degrees in industrial design.
Interior designers	37,000	1,900	Increasing use of design services in business establishments and homes expected to cause employment to grow about as fast as average. Competition for jobs likely, however. Best opportunities for talented college graduates in interior design and graduates of professional interior design schools.
Landscape architects	13,000	900	Employment expected to grow faster than average due to increases in new construction, and city and regional environmental planning. Few jobs available during economic downturns.

Occupation	Estimated employment 1976	Average annual openings 1976-85	Employment prospects
Photographers	85,000	3,700	Employment expected to grow more slowly than average. Portrait and commercial photographers likely to face keen competition. Best opportunities in areas such as law enforcement and scientific and medical research photography.

Communications-related occupations

Occupation	Estimated employment 1976	Average annual openings 1976-85	Employment prospects
Interpreters	175	N.A.*	Very stiff competition for limited number of openings. People with linguistic abilities may find some opportunities as translators.
Newspaper reporters	40,500	2,100	Slower than average employment growth and rising number of journalism graduates expected to create keen competition for openings. Best opportunities for bright and energetic persons who have exceptional writing ability on newspapers in small towns and suburbs.
Radio and television announcers	26,000	1,300	Employment expected to increase faster than average as new radio and television stations are licensed. Great attraction of broadcasting field will lead to keen competition for openings, however.
Technical writers	22,000	N.A.*	Employment expected to grow about as fast as average due to need for effective communication of scientific and technical information and research results. Best opportunities for persons with both writing ability and scientific or technical background.

*Not Available

Chapter 10

The Other Data: Standardized Tests, Extracurricular Activities

"Tests are not foolproof and are best interpreted in combination with other observations and evaluations."

"Teacher grades are the most accurate predictors of future learning."

"Non-test data can help you help your child in career planning."

Whereas Chapters 5, 6, and 7 related to job activities in career and career exploration, this chapter deals with data related to the individual, learning objectives, and their measurement. Much of the first part of this chapter is adapted from an address by the late Distinguished Professor George E. Hill of Ohio University. His address, "Standards for Test Users," was delivered at the Michigan School Testing Conference, University of Michigan, Ann Arbor, 1968.

Our point of view regarding the uses of standardized tests in schools and other learning settings is based on assumptions regarding the purposes of all learning activities. Mastering basic skills (reading, writing, basic science, mathematics, and communication) is, of course, necessary for all successful careers. Children should be encouraged to achieve in these basic skills and you, as parents, can help them understand how these skills are related to the work people do. These skills, commonly called "basics," provide the foundation tools, but as important as they are, healthy personal and career development also require meeting the following eight needs:

1. Children need to mature in their understanding of themselves, to grow up in the habit of self-examination and self-understanding, which makes rational the

life of feeling, the life of the spirit, which is the real heart of humane human existence.
2. Children need to mature in their sense of responsibility for themselves, to develop a sense of self-regard which puts pride and a feeling of concern for others behind their management of their own personal resources and the use of these for socially constructive ends.
3. Children need to mature in their understanding of human relations, of how human beings can best live together in our complicated society. The end sought in this development of understanding is, of course, to be found in a fourth learning.
4. Children need to mature in their skill in human relations, in learning the art of harmonious relations with the many others in their lives.
5. Children need to learn—and this learning starts much earlier than most schools recognize—the significance of education in the life of modern man, the relation between education and employment, and the respect for gainful employment which will enable them to move gradually toward becoming productive workers in the American economy.
6. Children need to mature in their ability to make decisions, to solve problems, to meet the multiple exigencies of life with reasonable skill in the use of their intellectual and emotional resources.
7. Children need to mature in their ability to meet changing conditions and to adapt to the necessity for change in both their personal and their vocational lives. "Learning how to keep on learning," as some have put it, is one of the most important of the learnings fostered by our schools.
8. Finally, children need to mature in their sense of values, the ideals that pull their behavior toward goals of improved human relations, the conscience which guides their daily decisions.

These eight learnings apply with equal relevance to education in kindergarten and in graduate school. Life is going to be productive, and it is going to be satisfying only if the learner begins early in life to achieve these learnings and keeps on maturing with respect to them into adulthood. Of course, it is recognized that explicit attention to such educational ends as are suggested by these learnings will differ in the primary grades as against the secondary school and college. The intellectual content of maturing in these learnings will become broader and deeper as the processes of growing up move along. But let it be noted that far more seekers of the Ph.D. fail because of immaturity with respect to one or more of these eight learnings than because of intellectual incompetence.

Tests

Careful observation and monitoring by parents of the progress children are making in meeting these eight needs should help shape these basics for parent-child discussions about career likes and dislikes. These childhood needs also relate to important and realistic understanding of the "other data"—measures of achievement, aptitude, ability, and interests. These measurement data are collected in schools through the use of standardized tests and teacher-made tests, as well as teacher evaluation in the form of grades.

Any parent reading this book has undoubtedly taken a standardized test in school, in the armed services, or when applying for a job, a license, or a certificate of some type. A standardized test is one that has been given to a large, representative sample of persons in exactly the same way to determine the range of scores that can be expected of the general population. With a distribution of the range of scores, an individual score can be compared with others. Parents should be cautioned that many factors influence a test score, including how one feels at the time a test is taken, the conditions under which a test is given, and appropriateness of the test for a particular individual. Tests are not foolproof and are best interpreted in combination with other observations and evaluations. Before a parent jumps to conclusions about a child's test score, it would be wise to consult the child's teacher or counselor. Tests should assist in self-understanding above all else.

The following types of tests are most commonly used in schools:

1. *Achievement Tests* are usually given to children at several grade levels to find out how much has been learned in specific areas, such as English, math, science, and foreign languages.

2. *Aptitude Tests* are most often given at junior and senior high levels to find out a child's potential to develop skills.

3. *Ability Tests* are given at various school levels to determine a child's potential to learn. Sometimes called IQ, intelligence, or mental ability tests, these have come under extreme criticism and some schools no longer use them. If ability test scores are properly used, they can be helpful in understanding a child's school performance. If used improperly, these scores can be very harmful and misleading.

4. *Interest "Tests"* are inventories that help a person more clearly identify his/her interests. These measures can be helpful in identifying careers to investigate and explore. Our Career Sort in Chapter 13 is a kind of interest inventory that can provide leads toward career investigations. These "tests" have no right or wrong answers, only expressed interests. And such measured interests do not imply aptitude or ability.

This general discussion about testing is designed to help a parent look for some of the other sources of data and to suggest that the best way to avoid misuse of test data is to consult a school counselor, school psychologist, or teacher regarding your child's test scores. For the most effective way to understand and help your child through the use of test data, we suggest the following guiding principles:

Principle 1: There is no single best testing method or procedure to be universally recommended. Standardized tests are not better than personal data blanks, for example, in any general sense. Good schools use observation rating scales, inventories, anecdotal records, interviews, questionnaires, autobiographies, and sociometric tests in addition to standardized tests.

Principle 2: The effectiveness of testing is directly related to the extent to which school professional staff members and parents accept active roles. Programs of student testing carried out primarily by school counselors as "service" to the faculty are inefficient, incomplete, and insufficient. This principle applies to participation both in collection and in use of appraisal data. While the need to participate in collection and the need to participate in the use of test data cannot be said to be exactly the same for all professional staff members, some need is present in both areas for all, if maximally productive programs are to result. Test data are student and parent property, and parents have a right of access to data and its interpretation.

Principle 3: To aim for complete understanding of students is both futile and foolish. It is futile because it can never be accomplished, and it is foolish because it is unnecessary. The "pot of gold" at the end of the rainbow of student testing is not complete understanding but increased understanding—not attainment of insight but reduction of ignorance. Parents need enough understanding to formulate positive means of helping their children, but their need for understanding is limited by their means and opportunity for being of help.

Principle 4: Understanding and helping your children should be concurrent and sequential. As we seek to understand children, we are able to help them more; as we help students, we understand them better. To attempt to compartmentalize these two functions is to render each less than optimally productive. The ultimate goal in using tests is to help your child to greater self-understanding.

Principle 5: Test data should involve both the study of children and the study of their environments. To consider only the child independent of the environment is to place far too much confidence in his/her ability to help himself/herself. To concentrate primarily on environmental factors is to deny children the right to develop independence. The endless controversies that have arisen over the nature/nurture question will probably never be completely resolved in terms of scientific knowledge, but they must be resolved at least on a philosophical basis by each person who wishes to help his/her child.

Principle 6: Testing is not required in the same amount or to the same degree or necessarily at the same time for all children. The use of data other than standardized tests has been greatly reduced because of failure to recognize this principle. To say that some children require more extensive testing than others is not to say that some are more worthwhile than others, but simply that all do not require the same amount of attention.

Other Data: Grades and Extracurricular Activities

As important as test data are in helping children and youth to understand their interests, aptitudes, achievement potential, and personal characteristics, nontest data can help you help your child in career planning in many important ways.

Important data come from teacher grades and report cards. In spite of the questions parents and children may have about grades, research has shown that grades are the most accurate predictors of future learning. A pattern of high grades over a period of time—in the language arts, for example—is a good cue to the potential of your child in a variety of careers requiring language and writing skills. The same is true in other subject areas taught to your child.

Many sources of "other data" require you as a parent to become skilled in observing your child's activities at play and at work. If your child reads a great deal, you can get career interest cues from the type of reading he/she does. Reading science fiction may indicate that a child has a bent toward science, is interested in futuristic things, and likes creative ideas.

Observing and learning from your child's activities in sports, music, drama, art, and dance can be a beginning point from which you can help your child explore the career implications of the activity. The examples illustrated in Chapters 5, 6, 7 can be used in conversation with your child, or in pointing toward the investigation of career areas related to their activities.

Your child's interest and participation in achievement clubs, magazine drives, mock political campaigns, and the like provide a good source of data about possible career interests, leadership potential, and ability to work with people. The initiatives your child takes in a paper route, in baby-sitting, in scouts, YMCA, YWCA, and other clubs are also good career building data. If your child likes to perform volunteer jobs on the playground, at school, around the house, or in the community, you should consider such activities as potentially important career development data.

Remember, data can come from observing your child's behavior and participation in activities. Our research and observations lead us to believe that boys and girls learn and develop attitudes in the environment where most of their time is spent. For your child, this place is probably in and around home. Your interest can best be shown to your child when you are alert to the other observational data, when you show an interest in your child's activities, and when you reinforce or reward him/her in ways that build feelings of worthiness (Chapter 2). You can also use this data as a starting point for further career exploration.

Other Data Test

Now let's test your understanding of some of the basic concepts in the use of other data. Check *True* or *False* for each item.

		True	False
1.	Tests are more important than other data in learning about your child.	____	____
2.	An interest test will tell a person what he/she is capable of doing.	____	____
3.	Achievement tests tell what a person has learned.	____	____
4.	Aptitude tests can help tell what skills a person can develop.	____	____
5.	Tests are not foolproof and should be used with caution.	____	____
6.	There is one single best test for all factors to be considered in career planning.	____	____
7.	Tests can lead to better self-understanding.	____	____
8.	Standardized test data are based on scores of a large- representative sample of persons.	____	____
9.	Some nontest data can be helpful in self-appraisal.	____	____
10.	You can understand and help your child's career plans better if you observe patterns rather than interpret a single test score.	____	____

Check your answers on the next page and score your test.

```
 10  = Perfect
8 - 9 = Good
  7  = Fair
1 - 6 = Reread Chapter 10
```

Answers to *Other Data Test*

1. False
2. False
3. True
4. True
5. True
6. False
7. True
8. True
9. True
10. True

Chapter 11

The Other People: Counselors, Teachers, Role Models

"A positive parent-counselor relationship must be developed if the child is to be successful in career planning."

"Children can relate better to careers if they can see people at work and talk with them about what they do."

"The other people who can be helpful in your child's career planning extend far beyond the home and school."

Ideally, education has as its chief aim the maximum development of each individual. Within the past three decades, the scope of American education has been extended outward from the strictly academic to include a concern for the total development of each pupil. Numerous professional and lay groups have pointed out the need for services supplemental to those provided by the classroom teacher through instruction in basic skills. American educators have long realized the restrictive effects of pupil indecision, lack of adequate career goals, emotional maladjustments, and a general unrealistic understanding of themselves, their potential, and their future. And according to the "10th Annual Gallup Poll of Parents' Attitudes Toward Schools," conducted in 1978, parents want more help for their children's career planning.

It now seems apparent to most parents that pupils—talented, average, or otherwise—cannot excel in school or realize their full potential unless they are provided expert assistance in the following areas:
1. Developing a realistic understanding of themselves.
2. Making decisions concerning high school and post-high-school programs based on adequate and accurate information.

3. Making adjustments to the everyday problems of growing up.
4. Discovering and nourishing worthwhile interests.
5. Securing reliable information about available educational and career opportunities.

With the complexities of everyday living added to the overwhelming amount of information needed to assist children in these areas, a typical parent cannot be expected to have all the answers. Parents have increasingly leaned on the schools for support and assistance in helping their children develop to the maximum of their ability. Today, when counselors are increasingly in the schools, the parent should expect understanding, acceptance, and assistance from this professionally trained person.

Because the school counselor and the parent have a mutual concern for the individual development of the child, it is mandatory that a positive parent-counselor relationship be developed if the child is to be successful in career planning. If such a relationship is to be developed, neither the parent nor the counselor should regard the other or the child in question as a problem, or each will deal with the other as a problem. And if a person is dealt with as a problem, he or she will probably respond in kind. On the other hand, to see the positive is to see the worth and dignity of each child, each parent, each counselor. The quality of response to be expected from individuals reflects the quality of approach to them. It seems to use that this is basic for the enhancement of good interpersonal relationships. But how do the parent and the counselor view each other? As counselor-parents, permit us to review briefly some characteristics of parents and of counselors.

Parents and Their Frustrations

Parents experience a great deal of frustration in relating to the modern-day school because it is different. Where once there was mainly readin', writin', and 'rithmetic, today there are research papers, units of study, career exploration, and social development.

In spite of the confusions and misunderstandings, parents usually are delighted with each success the child experiences in school. They like to know how their children are getting along, how they are progressing, how well they are achieving—because parents are like that. They love their children—they want them to succeed—and they want to feel they have had a part in providing worthwhile and happy school experiences. But when they have questions about the individual progress of their own children, to whom should they turn in the school setting? To the teacher? Certainly! To the principal? Sometimes! To the school counselor? Without question! This is the logical choice today, because the parents have also read popular journals, study commissions' reports, and the PTA's recommendations that each school provide professional counseling services to every child. But then, what are counselors like? This question is often asked by parents who completed high school twenty or more years ago, or by parents who never had the opportunity their children have today.

Counselors and What They Do

Counselors in the modern school are professionally trained persons employed to help children and their parents with problems related to schools, jobs, friends, family, career planning, and personal matters. Children mature at various rates and differ in ability, emotional development, motivation, and social skills, and counselors are prepared to help pupils and their parents understand these differences. At times, parents find that they are so close to their own children that they are unable to see them as they really are. Counselors are prepared to share with parents things about their children that they may not have noticed at home, but that show up through school activities.

Research has indicated that children's progress in school is a fairly predictable matter. Counselors are in a position to help parents learn what to expect from their children so they can plan accordingly. In our society each citizen is expected to become self-supportive and earn an honorable living through a satisfying career. To choose wisely among the many career opportunities, the child must know much about personal and educational requirements as well as occupational opportunities. Such knowledge is acquired gradually over the years. Counselors should not encourage children to make premature career choices, but they can help children and their parents acquire necessary information. In good schools, professional counselors are prepared to provide parents with helpful information about their children, including information from test scores and other data collected for school cumulative records (see Chapter 10).

Professional counselors will respect as confidential the information they receive from parents, but by the same token, their ethics require that they must handle with equal respect the information they obtain from each child. Finally, professional school counselors, like teachers and parents, are interested in the welfare of all children under their charge, and all must cooperate through positive relationships if children are to be the benefactors of their efforts. You should get acquainted with your child's school counselor as one of the important people who can help you and your child.

Other Important People

The foregoing suggestions with regard to the parents' role in working with school counselors also apply to a host of other resource people, listed next. The ways they can help will depend on the initiatives you, as a parent, take in working with them.

Classroom Teachers

Teachers are a potential first-hand source of help in your child's career development and planning. Teachers observe your child daily and are in an excellent position to see your child grow over time. Subject-matter teachers can estimate your child's potential to achieve in various school subjects (English, math, language arts, sciences). They also can evaluate your child's Data-People-Things interests. Teachers are in a good position to observe how your child relates to others, how he/she seems to take leadership responsibilities, and how well he/she organizes his/her time. They can recommend club and special interests activities that supplement academic studies and offer your child experiences valuable to career development.

Vocational-Technical Teachers

Vocational-technical teachers can be especially important in helping you facilitate your child's career planning. Agricultural education teachers can help your child explore and learn about the school's "ag program" and can help you and your child gain knowledge about skills needed in farming, agribusiness, food processing, marketing, farm mechanics, conservation, and horticulture. They can also help your child learn how to become a member of the Future Farmers of America or school clubs that help children develop leadership qualities and learn about the world of work in agriculture.

Business Education-Teachers

Business education teachers also know and can provide expert information about careers and courses of study in bookkeeping, office practice, typing, and shorthand. They can also explain opportunities for study and work in careers in data processing, computer programming, and office management. Your child can learn about the Future Business Leaders of America club and the opportunities to develop career-related skills in club activities.

Distributive Education Teachers

Distributive education teachers teach, supervise, and maintain community contacts with retail businesses, sales and advertising agencies, distributing and marketing enterprises. They can help you and your child learn about on-the-job training opportunities and about careers in retail and wholesale trades, insurance, real estate, finance, buying, transporting, marketing research, and management. These teachers also sponsor the school's Distributive Education Club of America and can provide information about club activities to your child.

Home Economics Teachers

Home economics teachers have specific knowledge about careers in child care, child development, homemaking, home management, sewing, cooking, consumer education, and a host of other home-related careers. "Home Ec" teachers sponsor the Future Homemakers of America club, which provides many career learning opportunities.

Trade and Industrial Teachers

Trade and industrial teachers are expert tradespersons and teachers in a wide variety of industrial areas, including carpentry, drafting, bricklaying, plumbing, printing, cosmetology, electronics, mechanics, law enforcement, mining, and appliance and auto repair. "T and I" teachers sponsor the school's Vocational Industrial Club of America and can help you and your child learn about the career learning activities they offer. Teachers from various trades can explain apprenticeship programs and trade union polities; they are important "other people" in cooperative education, work-study release programs, and on-the-job training. Likewise, these teachers can help your child explore and learn about the variety of skill trades and industrial programs offered by the school and how such programs can lead directly to jobs or to advanced technical training.

Extension Agents

Extension agents can be located through county Extension Offices. They can help with information and contacts in virtually every kind of career area.

Other Teachers and Coaches

Physical education and health teachers and coaching and recreation leaders can give expert advice in their fields of work. Parents should consult them about sports and other physical activity opportunities and on leisure activities and career planning.

Parents' Supervisors

Parents' job supervisors, job managers ("bosses"), and other special people in your employment family also can be important sources of information and guidance for your child's career planning. Other family members, friends, and neighbors in various areas of work tend to take pride in helping you and your children understand their work and careers. Successful young school graduates and youth club representatives are additional helpful sources. Often young peers of your child can be identified as sources of information and as growing career models.

The value of the "other people" who can help rests in: (1) their ability to serve as accurate sources of information; (2) your involvement as a parent; and (3) their utilization as wholesome, successful, and knowledgeable models for your child. Remember, children can relate better to careers if they can see people at work and talk with them about what they do and how they got to their present career level. Modeling is vitally important in your child's understanding and reality testing of a career. Just as you, a parent, will want to exemplify the best career model for your child, you will want to choose carefully the other people you ask to help your child learn about careers.

The other people who can be helpful in your child's career planning extend far beyond the home and school. Parents should encourage and help their children to meet and even work with a variety of career models. Most communities have a host of persons working in the Data-People-Things occupations who would be pleased to talk with, share, or even work with youth interested in their careers. In Chapter 8 we suggested ways to explore careers. In Chapter 12 we will provide a variety of resources leading to people data. After playing the Career Sort game in Chapter 13, you can follow up your child's major interests by identifying people and organizations who can help give a clearer picture of a specific career. By helping your child identify people in careers of interest, you can help your child interview, observe, and get to know more about the real life of a person in a particular career. Parents should be prepared to go beyond close friends and relatives in their use of resource people.

A good way to begin utilizing the "other people" resources is to fill in the "Other People" Resources List below.

"Other People" Resources List

Fill in the blanks below with potential career help persons for your child. If you can list ten leads, you are on the way to utilizing many other people available in your community.

	Name	Occupation	Address	Phone
1.				
2.				
3.				
4.				
5.				
6.				
7.				
8.				
9.				
10.				

Chapter 12

The Other Things: Resources for Further Information

In this era of do-it-yourself and self-help approaches, it is appropriate to provide a lengthy listing of "other things"—resources beyond this book. This will permit you as a parent to probe in depth or casually a number of references that address general or special career development concerns. There are, of course, many more than we can list here. We have culled through the hundreds of resources available and selected those we felt would be of greatest help to you as parents. Most should be in your local public library, school library, or career resource center. The paperbacks will be found at most book stores or quality newsstands.

In addition to the sources listed here, many brief guides and pamphlets for general use are available from businesses such as the New York Life Insurance Company, Prudential Insurance, and General Electric. These brochures often are available through your local contacts. Don't discount their value just because they are free or may be used as public relations devices by the firms involved. "Free" does not mean bad, and "expensive" does not mean good. Evaluation should be based on quality, not cost.

Another valuable source is the wealth of material made available from the various agencies in the U.S. Department of Labor (Washington, DC 20210) and their counterparts in the fifty states. For example, if your child is getting ready to do some job hunting, the Employment and Training Administration's *Merchandising Your Job Talents* has some good hints—and it's free. From the Bureau of Labor Statistics comes the biannual *Occupational Outlook Handbook*. It is clearly the number-one source of occupational information in the United States. Drop by the local office of your State Public Employment Service and look over the many other helpful publications on display there.

General Career Planning

A Directory of Cooperative Education: Its Philosophy and Operation in Participating Colleges in the United States and Canada, volume IV, 1975. Cooperative Education Association, Drexel University, Philadelphia, PA 19104, $7.00.

    Discusses the basic concepts of cooperative education and provides information on postsecondary institutions that meet certain standards in offering cooperative education programs.

A "Starter" File of Free Occupational Literature (revised), 1975. By L. Goodman and A. Gurett, B'nai B'rith Career and Counseling Services, 1640 Rhode Island Ave., NW, Washington, DC 20036, $1.50.

    Contains 117 career pamphlets that can be used to explore 1,000 careers and to organize a cost-free, selective occupational library.

Career Core Competencies: A Cooperative Work Experience Program, 1977. McGraw-Hill, New York, NY.

    Discusses such basic skills as decision-making, working at human relations, and finding a job, which are necessary to pursuing a career. Development of these skills is the object of this series of workbooks, which is to be used in career planning, selection, and adjustment. Practical experience is presented through exercises and activities. Specific goals are listed at the beginning of each workbook.

Career Decisions, 1969. American Personnel and Guidance Association, 1607 New Hampshire Ave., NW, Washington, DC 20009, $2.50 for members, 5 copies (minimum order); nonmembers $3.25 (order #72194).

    Helps students, teachers, and parents plan career success in tomorrow's world.

Career for You, 1969. By E. Ferrari, Abingdon Press, Nashville, TN.

    Provides self-evaluation information in addition to information on how to acquire training and experience necessary to pursue various careers.

Career Resource Bibliographies, American Personnel and Guidance Association, 1607 New Hampshire Ave., NW, Washington, DC 20009.

    Consists of bibliographies compiled from INFORM, the newsletter of APGA's National Career Information Center. Current listings of materials available from trade and professional associations, publishers, government sources, educational institutions, and special career information projects:

        Communications and Media, 75c (order #70951)
        Engineering, 75c (order #70953)
        Health and Medicine, 75c (order #70954)
        Agriculture, 75c (order #70955)
        Business Office and Information Processing, 75c (order #70956)
        Public Services, 75c (order #70957)
        Environment, 75c (order #70958)

    Science, 75c (order #70959)
    Education, 75c (order #70960)
    Building and Construction, 75c (order #70961)
    Transportation, 75c (order #70962)
    Social Services, 75c (order #70963)
    Hospitality, Recreation and Personal Services, 75c (order #70964)
    Sales and Distribution, 75c (order #70965)
    Manufacturing and Industry, 75c (order #70965)
    100 Selected Occupations, 75c (#70967)
    Sources of Financial Aid Information, 75c (order #70968)
    Military Services, 75c (order #70969)

Career Resources A to Z: A Student's Guide to Occupational and Educational Information, 1975. Career Guidance Media, P.O. Box 3422, Alexandria, VA 22302, $1.50.

    Contains references to 250 organizations that have prepared information for career exploration.

Career Wheels. American Personnel and Guidance Association, 1607 New Hampshire Ave., NW, Washington, DC 20009.

    Hand-held, 12-inch discs that provide compact career and educational information for high school counselors and students. Students can dial an amazing amount of data including:

    A general description of each career area, its purposes, educational requirements and opportunities.

    Specialties in each area, including required and applied learning.

    Sample curricula in colleges, technical or professional schools for each area.

    Job possibilities and responsibilities in each area:

Social Science, $5 members, $6.25 nonmembers (order #72076)
Humanities, $5 members, $6.25 nonmembers (order #72077)
Natural Science, $5 members, $6.25 nonmembers (order #72078)
Engineering, $5 members, $6.25 nonmembers (order #72079)
Business, $5 members, $6.25 nonmembers (order #72080)
Entire Set of 5 Career Wheels, $20 members, $26 nonmembers (order #P-7200)

Careers for the Homebound: Home Study Opportunities, 1974. President's Committee on Employment of the Handicapped and B'nai B'rith Career and Counseling Services, 1640 Rhode Island Ave., NW, Washington, DC 20036, free.

    A useful reference for helping the homebound attain educational and vocational objectives. In addition, names and addresses of accredited home study schools are provided.

Deciding, 1972. By. H. Gelatt, B. Varenhorst, and R. Carey; College Entrance Examination Board, New York, NY 10019.

Instructional materials for grades 7 through 10, teaching students how to make decisions and assisting them in developing effective decision-making skills.

Decisions and Outcomes, 1973. By H. Gelatt, B. Varenhorst, R. Carey, and G. Miller, College Entrance Examination Board, New York, NY 10019.

Exercises for senior high school students, college students, and adults to teach effective decision-making skills, including examining values, using appropriate information, and converting this information into action.

Exploring Careers through Part-time and Summer Employment, 1977. By C. Lobb, Richards Rosen Press, 29 East 21st Street, New York, NY 10010, $4.98.

Describes people and agencies who can help students locate and secure their first part-time and summer employment in all areas from aerospace to zoos.

Exploring Careers through Volunteerism, 1976. By C. Lobb, Richards Rosen Press, 29 East 21st Street, New York, NY 10010, $4.98.

Discusses changing patterns of education and work along with an overview of career education. Work opportunities, current trends, preparing for a career, opportunities, current trends, preparing for a career, opportunities for women and minorities, and financial assistance are explored.

Free to Choose: Decision-making for Young Men, 1976. By J. Mitchell, Delacorte, New York, NY.

Seeks to make young men aware of the choices they must make and how to decide among alternative courses of action. Demonstrates that stereotypes can be broken to achieve individuality. Bibliographies are included.

Handbook of Job Facts, 1972. Compiled by C. Lang, Science Research Associates, Chicago, IL.

Consists of a detailed chart describing duties, education, training, special qualifications, percentage of men and women employed, advancement potential, earnings, and outlook for 300 occupations; designed to help the job-hunter. For each occupation the chart also has a code number as a guide to additional information that may be found in SRA's Widening Occupational Roles or Occupational Exploration kits.

How to Make a Habit of Success (revised), 1975. By B. Haldane, Acropolis Books, 2400 Seventeenth Street, NW, Washington, DC 20009, $3.50.

Emphasizes identifying and applying one's best talents in the most appropriate direction. Techniques demonstrate how to build on achievements.

How to Select a Private Vocational School, 1974. By G. Pitts, American Personnel and Guidance Association, 1607 New Hampshire Ave., NW, Washington, DC 20009, $3.75

for 5 copies (minimum order); nonmembers $5.00 (order #72202).

    Assists students in the selection of a post-high-school proprietary trade, technical, business, or correspondence school. Deals with such subjects as: which school is best for an individual; the meaning of accreditation; a ten-point checklist in looking at private vocational schools; financial assistance; and other information needed by students in selecting post-high-school vocational training.

It's Your Life, 1975. By J. Pancrazio, Benefic, Westchester, IL.

    Aims at development and improvement of one's psychological health. Cartoons, hypothetical dialogues, and case studies encourage constructive thinking about perceptions, self-knowledge, communication, change, drugs, love, and planning for the future. The importance of all these in making career decisions is emphasized throughout.

Occupational Outlook Handbook. The 1978-79 edition gives descriptions and projections for more than 850 occupations and 30 major industries. Published every two years. Reprints of specific occupations available at minimal cost.

Occupational Outlook Quarterly. Report on new occupational research results and sources of current career materials. Published quarterly. Yearly subscription price, $4.30; single copy, $1.15.

    (Both publications are for sale by the Superintendent of Documents, U.S. Government Printing Office, Washington, DC 20402, and regional offices of the Bureau of Labor Statistics. They are also available for reference at local Employment Security offices, in most public libraries, and in school and college counseling/placement offices.)

Paraprofessions: Careers of the Future and the Present, 1972. By S. Splaver, Julian Messner, 1230 Avenue of the Americas, New York, NY 10020, $5.19.

    Describes the role of paraprofessionals in architecture, urban planning, teaching, library science, engineering, law, medicine, mental health, and forestry.

Solving Your Career Mystery, 1075. By M. Karlin, Richards Rosen Press, 29 East 21st Street, New York, NY 10010, $4.98.

    A complete examination of the world of work, presenting a rational guide to choosing a career by listing all the alternatives; skilled, unskilled, professional, trades, outdoor work, creative work, etc.

Success Core, 1975. Institutional Development Associates, Chicago, IL.

    A workbook designed to facilitate attitudinal adjustment and self-knowledge. The student is encouraged to examine closely and to articulate his or her fears, perceptions, and goals as a pathway to success in career pursuits.

The Art of Developing a Career: A Student's Guide, 1974. By R. Carkhuff and T. Friel,

Human Resource Development Press, Box 863, Dept. M-44, Amherst, MA 01002.

    Examines the phases of career development and then provides step-by-step exercises to take the student through the exploratory, understanding, and action phases of career development. Emphasis is on self-exploration of interests, abilities, and values as well as understanding occupational requirements.

The Counselor and Military Service Opportunities, 1973. By Dean L. Hummel, Houghton Mifflin, Boston, MA.

    A 110-page monograph that describes military service opportunities available in the various branches of service, academies, and National Guard units. List of qualifications, training opportunities, and military service sources are included.

The Joy of Work, 1974. By J. Keefe and S. Stein, Richards Rosen Press, 29 East 21st Street, New York, NY 10010, $4.98.

    Discusses job satisfaction as a consequence of a sound occupational choice. The book's prime target is directing the teenager to find the work that will be rewarding and enjoyable.

The Parent's Role in Career Development, 1967. By D. Knapp and J. Bedford, American Personnel and Guidance Association, 1607 New Hampshire Ave., NW, Washington, DC 20009, $2.25 for 5 copies (minimum order); nonmembers $3.00 (order #72193).

    Describes how parental influence may be wisely used to advance vocational development.

The Three Boxes of Life, 1978. By R. Bolles, Ten Speed Press, P.O. Box 7123, Berkeley, CA 94707, $6.95 paperback.

    Describes three stages of life—education, work, and retirement— and offers practical tools for blending learning, achievement, and leisure during these stages. *The Quick Job-Hunting Map—Beginners Version* is included.

Turn Yourself On—Goal Planning for Success, 1970. By R. Linneman, Richards Rosen Press, 29 East 21st Street, New York, NY 10010, $4.98.

    A careful explanation of the importance of planning for the future and the wisdom of having goals that are realistically as well as carefully planned, then just as carefully worked at.

Up Your Career!, 1975. By D. Dauev, Waveland, Prospect Heights, IL.

    Guides the reader toward the career best suited to his or her needs, abilities, and interests by working through the exercises provided. Topics include finding out about oneself and about available jobs, writing a resume, making career plans, using an employment agency, and recognizing job discrimination. After it has been used as a "how-to" guide, the workbook may be useful as a reference tool.

Vacation Guide for Vocational Decisions, 1977. By M. Roark, Professional Printing Services, First and Berkeley Streets, Radford, VA 24141.

    Discusses the career decision process and outlines a course of action that can be pursued in the summer to help the individual reach tentative career decisions.

What Color Is Your Parachute? 1978. By R. Bolles, Ten Speed Press, P.O. Box 7123, Berkeley, CA 94707, $5.95.

    Step-by-step detail on how to identify what you want to do with the rest of your life, how to locate the job you want, and how to convince an employer that you are right for the job. This new edition includes *The Quick Job-Hunting Map*— 24 pages of exercises to help the job-hunter or career changer.

You and Your Child's Career, 1966. By D. Sinick, B'nai B'rith Vocational Service, 1640 Rhode Island Ave., NW, Washington, DC 20036.

    Helps parents who are concerned with the career development of their children. Discusses how vocational guidance helps young people. Confronts some of the common fallacies in making career plans. Includes a parents' self-rating scale.

Your Attitudes: You Do Best What You are Best Fitted To Do, 1974. By G. Barth, Lothrop, New York, NY.

    Describes 19 special aptitudes and typical jobs that require them. Helps students get a better idea of their aptitudes by asking such questions as "Do you like paperwork?" "Are you skillful with small tools?" and "Can you remember tunes?" Also included are tips on preparing a resume and applying for a job.

Your Career: How to Plan It, Manage It, Change It, 1976. By R. Buskirk, New American Library, 1301 Avenue of the Americas, New York, NY 10019, $1.95.

    Discusses planning your career, performing on the job, advancing in your career, and increasing your productivity by planning, setting goals, and mapping out strategies.

Your Personality and Your Job, 1971. D. Sinick, Science Research Associates, Chicago, IL 60611.

    Discusses the importance of knowing your personality when choosing a job. Helps examine personality qualities, needs, and sources of satisfaction.

Military Service Opportunities

A Woman's World of Exciting Jobs. U.S. Army Recruiting Command, Hampton, VA 23369.

    Describes occupational fields open to women in the Army. Outlines typical jobs and describes the training for each job in an occupational area.

Air Force Academy—Gateway to Aerospace.
>Outlines the admission requirements and how to obtain a nomination to the academy. Describes cadet life and the academic program.

Be a Leader of Men. NAVMC 6943, Headquarters, U.S. Marine Corps, Washington, DC 20380.
>Describes service and benefits as a Marine officer.

It's Your Choice. Department of Defense, Washington, DC 20301.
>A guide to the opportunities open to volunteers for military service. Explains how one may choose the military service program that will serve him/her best. Contains information on enlistment and officer programs in the armed forces.

Life in the U.S. Navy. Bureau of Naval Personnel, Washington, DC 20370.
>Describes life in various careers in the Navy and includes information on occupations performed, career opportunities, and qualifications for enlistment.

Navy Officer Careers Handbook. Bureau of Naval Personnel, Washington, DC 20370.
>Describes how the Navy is organized, officer occupations, qualifications required, avenues to a commission, and paths of professional advancement.

Occupational Opportunities. NAVMC 6657, Headquarters, U.S. Marine Corps, Washington, DC 20380.
>Outlines occupational fields and schools available in the Marine Corps.

The Secret of Getting Ahead. U.S. Army Recruiting Command, Hampton, VA 23369.
>Describes the Selective Service System, the Army Reserve, the National Guard, opportunities in the Regular Army, vocational training programs, the Army graduate specialist program, and the kinds of training one can apply for.

U.S. Naval Academy: A Guide for Counselors and Candidates. Bureau of Naval Personnel, Washington, DC 20370.
>Outlines the steps to becoming a midshipman and tells how to obtain a nomination to the Naval Academy.

Special Help for Women and Girls

CATALYST, 6 East 82nd Street, New York, NY 10028.
>Series of self-guidance publications, prepared specifically for women. The series includes the Career Opportunities Series (27 booklets on specific occupational fields); the Education Opportunities Series (11 booklets on educational opportunities in specific areas); the Self-Guidance Series (two booklets on planning to work and the job campaign). In addition, *CATALYST* publishes the Career

Options Series for Undergraduate Women.

Everything a Woman Needs to Know to Get Paid What She's Worth, 1973. By C. Bird, David McKay, New York, NY, $8.95.
    Offers "tactics" for job-hunting, getting promoted, and so on for women who are concerned about demonstrating their competencies in the labor force.

Growing Up Female in America. By E. Merriam, Doubleday, New York, NY, $7.95 hardcover.
    A collection of autobiographical material about ten American women growing up. Good supplementary source material.

How to Decide: A Guide for Women. By N. Scholz, J. Prince, and G. Miller, Decision-Making Program, College Entrance Examination Board, 888 Seventh Ave., New York, NY 10010, $5.95.
    A how-to workbook that can help women of all ages learn a step-by-step process for making decisions related to their education, career, work, home, and family. The structure leads each woman from an analysis of her own values, through information-gathering, to formulating and implementing her own plan of action.

I Can Be Anything: Careers and Colleges for Young Women (revised), 1978. By J. Mitchell, College Entrance Examination Board, 888 Seventh Ave., New York, NY 10019, $7.95.
    Contains information on traditional and nontraditional jobs, primarily for young women. Brief descriptions of educational requirements about future potential are provided.

Job Ideas for Today's Woman, 1974. By R. Lembeck, Prentice-Hall, Englewood Cliffs, NJ, $6.95.
    Describes over 1,000 jobs that women can consider as part-time work, freelance work, full-time work at home, and as entrepreneur.

Nontraditional Careers for Women, 1973. By S. Splaver, Julian Messner, New York, NY 10020.
    Addresses the contemporary female in commenting on more than 500 jobs now open to women. Without demeaning or excluding occupations previously reserved exclusively for women, thumbnail descriptions of careers and the history of their availability to both sexes are provided. Myriad sources of additional information on specific careers are cited. Includes bibliography.

Other Choices for Becoming a Woman: A Handbook to Help High School Women Make Decisions, 1976. By J. Mitchell, Delacorte, New York, NY.

Straightforward discussion about adult choices high school women must make. Articles cover career, educational, and spiritual choices. Contributors include Margaret Mead, Jean Stapleton, and Dr. Kenneth Hoyt. Bibliographies are included.

Sex in the Marketplace: American Women at Work, 1971. By J. Kreps, Johns Hopkins Press, Baltimore, MD.

Analysis by an economist of the labor-force participation of American women. The underutilization of women is emphasized.

Woman's Work Book, 1975. By K. Abarbanel and G. Siegel, Praeger, 111 Fourth Ave., New York, NY 10003, $4.95.

How-to book on planning a job campaign, launching that campaign, landing a job, and knowing employment rights. Directories of occupational organizations, career-counseling services, educational opportunities, and women's centers are included.

Your Future As a Working Woman, 1975. By G. Stevenson, Richards Rosen Press, 29 East 21st Street, New York, NY 10010, $4.98.

Explains why high school girls need to plan careers and tells them how to make the most of their working years. The author is an editor for *Manpower Magazine*, the U.S. Department of Labor career information magazine.

Special Help for Minority Youth

Black Elite: The New Market for Highly Educated Black Americans. By R. Freeman, commissioned by the Carnegie Commission on Higher Education, McGraw-Hill, 1 South Box 402, Hightstown, NJ 08520, $13.95.

Describes and examines the recent changes in which young black men and women have attained rough economic parity with whites.

Career Development Opportunities for Native Americans, 1978. Bureau of Indian Affairs, U.S. Department of the Interior, Washington, DC, free.

Describes opportunities beyond high school; emphasizing financial aid programs for postsecondary study.

Graduate and Professional School Opportunities for Minority Students, 1975. Educational Testing Service, Princeton, NJ 08540, $3.00.

Provides summaries of graduate and professional schools, including the name of the program, the schook, the address, the person to contact, application fees, required tests, application dates, and data on minority students.

Graduate Fellowships for Black Americans, 1976. National Fellowship Fund, 795 Peachtree St., NE, Atlanta, GA 30308, free.

>Provides a list of graduate fellowships for black Americans pursuing doctoral study in the basic biological and physical sciences, the humanities, and the basic social sciences. Application and selection procedures are detailed.

Making It in College, 1976. By M. Walker and M. Beach, Mason/Charter, 641 Lexington Ave., New York, NY 10022, $8.95.

>Advice for minority students on how to evaluate, select, and get into the college of one's choice. Discusses techniques for improving learning skills and dealing with institutional discrimination.

The Black Collegian. Black Collegiate Services, Inc., 3217 Martin Luther King, Jr. Blvd., New Orleans, LA 70125, subscription rate $10.00 for 2 years (10 issues); $12.00 for 3 years.

>Magazine published five times a year. Articles cover a broad range of interests to the black student, including career information, occupational outlooks, and job opportunities.

Thinking about Graduate School: A Planning Guide for Freshman and Sophomore Mi Minority College Students, 1973. By J. Walker Graduate Record Examination Board, Educational Testing Service, Princeton, NJ.

>Provides an overview of graduate studies, including admission requirements and the cost of financing graduate study. Descriptions of specific subject areas are given.

Winners: Eight Special Young People, 1978. By D. Siegel, Julian Messner, 1230 Avenue of the Americas, New York, NY 10020, $7.29.

>Presents eight young people who are victims of various disabilities telling about their "ups and downs," their struggle for independence and self-reliance.

Special Help for the College Bound

After College. . .Junior. . .Military Service. . .What? The Complete Career Exploration Handbook, 1971. By N. Brown, Grosset and Dunlap, New York, NY.

>Explores traditional approaches and alternatives to career selection and helps identify types of work that complement an individual's interests and skills. Provides tips on obtaining a job in those areas.

Career Development for the College Student, 1976. By P. Dumphy, Carroll Press, 43 Squantum St., Cranston, RI 92920, $4.25.

>Introduction to the realities of the employment marketplace and comprehensive survey of college-level occupations. Techniques in job-seeking, letters of appli-

cation, resumes, selecting an employer, performance on the job, and future career development.

Career Patterns of Liberal Arts Graduates, 1973. By R. Calvert, Carroll Press, 43 Squantum St., Cranston, RI 92920, $10.00.
    Report based on a comprehensive survey of 11,000 alumni from 100 liberal arts colleges. Important information for anyone contemplating a liberal arts college curriculum.

Choosing the College for You, 1976. By R. Ewen. "Concise Guide Series," Watts, New York, NY.
    Handbook designed to help college-bound students find the institution best suited to their unique interests and circumstances. Includes comments by former college students about their problems and how they solved them. Tables provide figures on cost, size, and "level of difficulty" for approximately 450 institutions.

College Planning/Search Book, 1977. American College Testing Program, Iowa City, IA.
    A first-rate step-by-step approach to all you wanted to know about planning for college.

Helpful Hints for Selecting a School or College: Look Out for Yourself! 1977. U.S. Department of Health, Education and Welfare, Office of the Assistant Secretary for Education, Washington, DC 20202, $.08 (order #017-080-01776-8).
    Questions and answers on programs and course offerings, financial aid, and facilities and policies. Sources of additional information are also provided.

HEW Fact Sheet: Five Federal Financial Aid Programs, 1975. U.S. Department of Health, Education and Welfare, Office of Education, Washington, DC 20202, free.
    Describes five programs of student assistance—Basic Educational Opportunity Grants, Supplemental Opportunity Grants, College Work-Study, National Direct Student Loans, and Guaranteed Student Loans. Details are provided on eligibility, application procedures, and amount of grant or loan.

How to Visit Colleges, 1972. American Personnel and Guidance Association, 1607 New Hampshire Ave., NW, Washington, DC 20009, $3.75 for 5 copies (minimum order; order #72189).
    Establishes procedures and guides that students can use in selecting a two- or four-year college suited to their individual needs. Sections on when to visit, questions to ask, and what to do after visiting take the students step by step through the selection of post-high-school education.

Occupational Outlook for College Graduates, 1978-79 edition. U.S. Department of Labor, Bureau of Labor Statistics, Washington, DC, $4.50 (bulletin #1956).

A guide to career opportunities in a board range of occupations for which a college degree is, or is becoming, the usual background for employment. Follows the same format as the *Occupational Outlook Handbook* and details approximately 100 occupations.

PATH: A Career Workbook for Liberal Arts Students, 1975. By H. Figler, Carroll Press, 43 Squantum St., Cranston, RI 92920, $6.25.

Comprehensive exercises to help young people discover their own work values and abilities. Includes lists of possible career fields for college graduates and interim jobs that can build career assets.

The Case Against College, 1975. By C. Bird, David McKay, New York, NY, $9.95.

A ringing attack on many of the myths associated with why young people should go to college; proposes a gap between what everyone expects colleges to do and what they actually can and do deliver.

Vocational School Guides

Comparative Guide to Two-Year Colleges and Career Programs, 1976. By J. Cass and M. Birnbaum, Harper & Row, 10 East 53rd Street, New York, NY 10022, $6.95.

Guide to two-year colleges emphasizing post-secondary terminal/career-oriented programs. Identifies programs and includes information on institutions offering such programs.

Lovejoy's Career and Vocational School Guide, 1973. By C. Lovejoy, Simon and Schuster, Rockefeller Center, 630 Fifth Avenue, New York, NY 10020, $3.95.

Directory of schools and training programs in more than 250 careers, skills, and trades. Information includes where to find training programs, how to prepare for a career while in the armed services, trades that can be learned on-the-job, and special job training for the handicapped.

The National Guidance Handbook: A Guide to Vocational Education Programs, 1975. Science Research Associates, Chicago, IL 60611.

Discusses the expansion of vocational and technical education in recent years and its outcomes. Provides information on how to enroll in a job preparation program and to find employment. Provides descriptions of occupations in 14 career clusters and a discussion of apprenticeships.

Trade and Technical School Directory, 1971. Chronicle Guidance Publications, Moravia, NY 13118.

Provides descriptions of trade and technical schools based on data supplied by the institutions themselves. Includes general information, admissions requirements, costs, and major programs offered.

College and University Guides

Accredited Institutions of Post-Secondary Education 1977-78, 1977. Council on Post-Secondary Accreditation by the American Council on Education, 1 Dupont Circle, Washington, DC 20036.

    A directory of accredited institutions, professionally accredited programs, and candidates for accreditation. The definitive work in the field. Issued annually.

Barron's Educational Series. Barron's Educational Series, Inc., 113 Grossways Park Drive, Woodbury, NY 11797.

    Series of handbooks for the college-bound student. Editions include *Barron's Profiles of American Colleges, Volume One: Descriptions of the Colleges,* $6.95. *Barron's Handbook of College Transfer Information,* $3.95.

Counselor's Comparative Guide to American Colleges, 1977. By James Cass and Max Birnbaum, Harper & Row, New York, NY 10022, $12.50.

    A first-hand look at some of the background issues of interest in selecting a college such as role of students in governance of institutions, nature of community, coed dorms, etc.

Education Directory, Colleges and Universities 1977-78, 1978. National Center for Education Statistics, U.S. Government Printing Office, Washington, DC 20204.

    An annual directory listing all the accredited institutions of higher education in the United States as recognized by the U.S. Commissioner of Education.

Lovejoy's College Guide, 1976. By C. Lovejoy, Simon & Schuster, Rockefeller Center, 630 Fifth Avenue, New York, NY 10020, $5.95.

    Reference covering 3,600 American colleges and universities. Provides information on expenses, financial aid, admissions, curricula, and special programs.

The College Blue Book, 16th edition (five volume set), 1977. Ed. by D. Biesel, Macmillan, 866 Third Avenue, New York, NY 10022.

    Narrative Descriptions volume fully describes over 3,000 colleges in the United States and Canada, including information on costs, admissions procedures, and campus facilities.

The College Handbook, 1977. College Entrance Examination Board, College Board Publication Orders, Box 2815, Princeton, NJ 08540, $8.95.

    Describes 2,878 colleges on the basis of data provided by the colleges. Includes information on curricula, admissions, student life, expenses, and financial aid.

Job Search, Interviewing, Resume Writing

Career Search: A Personal Pursuit, 1976. By E. Chapman, Science Research Associates, Chicago, IL.

>An easy-to-follow, 20-Step system for making career choices. At the end of each chapter is a hypothetical career problem that can be solved from the information in the chapter.

Finding a Job You Feel Good About, 1977. By C. Garrison, W. McCurdy, P. Munson, P. Pavlik, J. Saunders, K. Sims, and D. Telis, Argus Communications, 7440 Natchez Avenue, Niles, IL 60648, $2.50.

>Easy-to-read self-exploration book that helps identify strengths, abilities, interests, and jobs that match an individual's unique personality. A plan of action is suggested in the last chapter.

Finding Your First Job, 1975. C. McDaniels, Time Share, Hartford, CT.

>Step-by-step approach to locating a job when leaving high school. Discusses how to find a job, write a resume, handle an interview, decide on a job, and succeed on the job.

Go Hire Yourself an Employer, 1973. By R. Irish, Doubleday, Anchor Press, New York, NY, $2.95.

>Outlines a nontraditional approach to job-seeking. Includes sections on formulating career objectives, writing a resume, and conducting an interview.

Help Wanted: Case Studies of Classified Ads, 1976. By J. Walsh, M. Johnson, and M. Sugarman, Olympus Plaza, 1670 East Thirteenth South, Salt Lake City, UT 84105, $3.95 paperback.

>Discusses whether or not classified help-wanted ads in daily newspapers are an accurate reflection of local labor market and are of significant use to employers and job-seekers.

How Teenagers Can Get Good Jobs, 1971. By R. Gelinas and P. Gelinas, Richards Rosen Press, 29 East 21st Street, New York, NY 10010, $4.98.

>Discusses attitudes, interests, and personality helpful in securing jobs for this age group.

How to Complete Job Application Forms, 1975. American Personnel and Guidance Association, 1607 New Hampshire Ave., NW, Washington, DC 20009, $3.75 for 5 copies (minimum order); nonmembers $5.00 (order #72212).

>Helps students and job-seekers understand and cope with the problems presented by a typical job application form. The ability to perform this task is often a critical skill that can make or break an applicant.

How to Find and Apply for a Job, 1975. By J. Kushner and H. Kelly, Career Information Series, South-Western, Cincinnati, OH.

  Helps the reader know himself or herself and learn good techniques for seeking and applying for jobs. The techniques presented are recommended by employers and researchers in the field. They begin with preparation of a personal inventory and continue through steps to take after an interview.

How to Get a Job and Keep It, 1975. By D. Goble, Steck-Vaughn, Austin, TX.

  Helps career seekers locate, apply for, keep, and advance in a job by teaching the reader how to present himself well, follow written instructions, fill out standard forms, and earn a promotion. A glossary of terms one might encounter in job-hunting is appended.

How to Get the Job That's Right for You, 1975. By B. Greco, Dow Jones-Irwin, Homewood, IL.

  Emphasizes taking the initiative in your own career development by knowing your abilities and options. Resumes, job interviews, and the possibilities for job changes are discussed. In addition, the author includes a list of resources, including companies, directories, inventories, and forms.

Job Power Now! By B. Haldane, J. Haldane, and L. Martin, Acropolis Books, Washington, DC 20009, $3.95 paperback.

  A young people's job-finding guide, using the latest information from the U.S. Department of Labor. Illustrates, by many examples, how boys and girls can increase their "job power." Describes job search techniques and gives real life examples.

Job Search Pyramid. By C. McDaniels, Garrett Park Press, Garrett Park, MD 20766, $2.00.

  Part of a set of 25 wall charts (17 x 22 inches in size), this one devoted to a five-phase approach to job-searching: planning, preparing, acting, measuring, and finalizing.

Making the Most of Your Job Interview, 1976. New York Life Insurance Company, 51 Madison Ave., New York, NY 10010, free.

  Discusses the research that should go into preparing for a job interview and how to present yourself in an interview. Pointers are given on answering questions and preparing a resume.

Resume Writing, 1976. By B. Bostwick, Capitol Publications, Inc., 2430 Pennsylvania Ave., NW, Washington, DC 20037, $9.95 paperback.

  Comprehensive, step-by-step approach to writing an effective resume. Emphasis is on the importance of communicating personal accomplishments through

through a resume form or style that allows for clear description of career goals.

Tea Leaves: A New Look at Resumes. By R. Bolles, Ten Speed Press, P.O. Box 7123, Berkeley, CA 94707, $0.50.
    Examines effective preparation and use of resumes that will reach the hands of the hiring influence and get you an interview.

The Job Hunter's Manual, 1975. By D. Sweet, Addison-Wesley, Reading, MA.
    Discusses the various phases of job-hunting, self-evaluation, resume writing, record-keeping, and interviewing and provides step-by-step procedures for accomplishing each phase.

The Job You Want—How to Get It, 1975. By W. Blackedge, E. Blackedge, and H. Keily. "Career Information" series, South-Western, Cincinnati, OH.
    Helps job-seekers of all ages determine and attain career goals. Young people are advised of what lies ahead and how to prepare for a career. Experienced people are reminded of ways to present themselves effectively to new employers.

The Resume Workbook: A Personal Career File for Job Applications, 1970. By C. Nutter, Carroll Press, 43 Squantum St., Cranston, RI 92920, $5.00.
    Self-help tool for job-seekers of all ages in all situations. Balances instruction with worksheets for a complete guide to writing a resume.

The Teenager and the Interview, 1971. By J. Keefe, Richards Rosen Press, 29 East 21st Street, New York, NY 10010, $4.98.
    Provides guides for presenting oneself with intelligence and composure for teenagers, many of whom find interviews the most difficult of everyday situations.

What Students Should Know about Interviewing, 1975. General Electric, Recruiting and Entry Level Programs Operation, New York, NY, free.
    Presents tips on how to prepare for an interview, what the interviewer will be looking for, how to act during an interview, and what to expect after the interview.

Who's Hiring Who? By R. Lathrop, Ten Speed Press, P.O. Box 7123, Berkeley, CA 94707, $5.95 paperback.
    Shows the new job-seeker how to cope with today's job market by utilizing job-hunting techniques that produce results. Provides a unique analysis of the job market.

Chapter 13

The Career Sort:
A Game to Help Your Child
Screen Career Interests

In previous chapters in this book you have learned about important feelings (faith, worthiness, and success) in healthy career planning and development. You have learned the SWING steps in career decision-making, and you have learned about Data-People-Things characteristics of occupations and how they are important in comparing a career planner with possible occupations. You have also taken some "tests," played career games, and read about important sources of information. One game you may have played with your family was the Data-People-Things game. Now you are ready to help your child use the Data-People-Things ideas in becoming better informed about specific occupations within classified occupational groupings.

Career Sort Instructions

The Career Sort is a series of career cards found at the end of this chapter. These cards are based on the *Dictionary of Occupational Titles* (DOT), fourth edition, published by the United States Department of Labor, 1977. The occupational group arrangement is a way of classifying the more than 20,000 different jobs listed in the DOT—the jobs that make up the work force in the United States. The Career Sort is a way of: (1) gaining information about job tasks in specific occupations; (2) learning about other closely related occupations; (3) relating interests to various occupational groups; and (4) developing your child's self-understanding.

There are four steps to follow in making the most effective use of the Career Sort.

Step 1. Separate all the cards along the perforated lines and shuffle as you would a deck of cards. Cards should be shuffled with stick figures on top.

Example: Top Side of Card

86

CONSTRUCTION OCCUPATIONS

High

Ave

Low

      Data   People   Things

This side of the card tells the general area of the occupations and the degree (high, average, low) of Data-People-Things characteristics important to the person in the occupational group.

Step 2. Have your child separate the cards into three piles labeled *Like*, *Neutral* or *Undecided*, and *Dislike*, based on his/her first feelings related to the top side of the card.

Step 3. Turn over the *Like* and *Neutral* cards and have your child sort them a second time. This time he/she should put on the *Like* pile of cards a more refined choice based on specific *occupations*, on required general level of education needed (ED), and on school subjects recommended.

Example: Bottom Side of Card

86   *Occupations*: Carpenters; brick and stone masons and tile setters; plumbers, gas fitters, steam fitters; asbestos and insulation workers; floor laying and finishing workers; glaziers; roofers

ED: High school, apprenticeship

School Subjects: Math, mech. drawing, voc. ed.

DOT pp 854-872   OOH pp 252-288

Step 4. This step will lead you to a detailed definition and explanation of the occupational groups your child likes and in which he/she shows an interest.

To make Step 4 really meaningful, you must help your child become a researcher (investigator) of his/her own interests. From Step 3, the more refined *Like* cards (from 5 to 10 are usually chosen, according to our research) should be arranged in a priority order for further research. That is, put the *Like* cards in order of first choice, second choice, and so on. Next, tear out the page at the end of the chapter, labeled *List of Career Likes*, and copy from the Career Sort cards the page numbers from the *Dictionary of Occupational Titles* (DOT) and *Occupational Outlook Handbook* (OOH). Your child is now ready to go to the library, a school councelor's office, a career resource center, or a government employment office to read (research) his/her likes in more detail. Of course, your child's findings will be more meaningful if you discuss the investigation following the research. It is very important, if you want more detailed information, to go to the *Dictionary of Occupational Titles*, which can be found in most libraries, career centers, school counselors' offices, and government employment service agencies.

Career Sort Example

The examples of Construction Occupations, N.E.C., that follow were taken from pp. 854-872 of the (Dictionary of Occupational Titles as listed on the bottom side of Career Sort card 86 (DOT pp. 854-872).

Construction Occupations, DOT

86 CONSTRUCTION OCCUPATIONS, N.E.C.

This division includes craft and noncraft occupations, not elsewhere classified, concerned with building and repairing structures.

860 CARPENTERS AND RELATED OCCUPATIONS

This group includes occupations concerned with fabricating, installing, and repairing structures and structural members made of wood and materials that can be worked like wood such as plastic and fiberglass, using bandsaws, ripsaws, planers, braces, hammers, and other carpentry tools and woodworking machines.

860.381.026 CARPENTER APPRENTICE (const.)

Performs duties as described under APPRENTICE (any ind.).

A worker who learns, according to written or oral contractual agreement, a recognized skilled craft or trade requiring one or more years of on-the-job training through job experience supplemented by related instruction, prior to being considered a qualified skilled worker. High school or vocational school education is often a prerequisite for entry into an apprenticeship program. Provisions of apprenticeship agreement regularly include length of apprenticeship; a progressive scale of wages; work processes to be taught; and amount of instruction in subjects related to the craft or trade, such as characteristics of materials used, physics, mathematics, estimating, and blueprint reading. Apprenticeability of a particular craft or trade is best evidenced by its acceptability for registration as a trade by a state apprenticeship agency or the Federal Bureau of Apprenticeship and Training. Generally, where employees are represented by a union, apprenticeship programs come under the guidance of joint apprenticeship committees composed of representatives of the employers or the employer association and representatives of the employees. These committees may determine need for apprentices in a locality and establish minimum apprenticeship standards of education, experience, and training. In instances where committees do not exist, apprenticeship agreement is made between apprentice and employer, or an employer group. The title, APPRENTICE, is often loosely used as a synonym for beginner, HELPER (any ind.), or TRAINEE (any ind.). This practice is technically incorrect and leads to confusion in determining what is meant. Typical classifications for apprentices are BLACKSMITH APPRENTICE (forging); MACHINIST APPRENTICE (mach. shop); and PLUMBER APPRENTICE (const.).

860.381.022 CARPENTER (const.)

Constructs, erects, installs, and repairs structures and fixtures of wood, plywood, and wallboard, using carpenter's handtools and power tools, and conforming to local building codes: Studies blueprints, sketches, or building plans for information pertaining to type of material required, such as lumber of fiberboard, and dimensions of structure or fixture to be fabricated. Selects specified type of lumber or other materials. Prepares layout, using rule, framing square, and calipers. Marks cutting and assembly lines on materials, using pencil, chalk, and marking gauge. Assembles cut and shaped materials and fastens them together with nails, dowel pins, or glue. Verifies trueness of structure with plumb bob and carpenter's level. Erects framework for structure and lays subflooring. Builds stairs and lays out and installs partitions and cabinet work. Covers subfloor with building paper to keep out moisture and lays hardwood, parquet, and wood-strip-block floors by nailing floors to subfloor or cementing them to mastic or asphalt base. Applies shock-absorbing, sound-deadening, and decorative paneling to ceilings and walls. Fits and installs prefabricated window frames, doors, doorframes, weather stripping, interior and exterior trim, and finish hardware, such as locks, letter drops, and kick plates. Constructs forms and chutes for pouring concrete. Erects scaffolding and ladders for assembling structures above ground level. May weld metal parts to steel structural members. When specializing in particular phase of carpentry is designated according to specialty as COMBINATION WINDOW INSTALLER (const.); LAY-OUT CARPENTER (const.). When specializing in finish carpentry, such as installing interior and exterior trim, building stairs, and laying hardwood floors is designated FINISH CARPENTER (const.). When erecting frame buildings and performing general carpentry work in residential construction is designated HOUSE CARPENTER (const.). May remove and replace sections of structures prior to and after installation of insulating materials and be designated BUILDING-INSULATING CARPENTER (const.; ref. tr.). May perform carpentry work in construction of walk-in freezers and environmental test chambers and be designated CARPENTER, REFRIGERATOR (refrigerat. equip.). Additional titles:

DOOR HANGER (const.); FINISHED HARDWARE ERECTOR (const.); GARAGE DOOR HANGER (const.); HARDWOOD FLOOR INSTALLER (const.); JALOUSIE INSTALLER (const.); STAIR BUILDER (const.); TRIM SETTER (const.); WEATHER STRIPPER (const.); WOOD-SASH-AND-FRAME CARPENTER (const.); WOOD-STRIP-BLOCK FLOOR INSTALLER (const.).

860.131.018 SUPERVISOR, CARPENTERS (const.)

Supervises and coordinates activities of workers engaged in construction, installation, and repair of wooden structures and fixtures: Examines blueprints to determine dimensions of structure. Lays out floor-plan and cabinetwork, using rule, framing square, and calipers. Selects materials and structural units, such as lumber, prefabricated doors and cabinets of wood or plastic, and paneling, and inspects them to insure conformance with provisions of building code and local ordinance. Determines sequence of activities concerned with fabrication, assembly, and erection of structure. Assigns workers to such tasks as cutting material to size, building concrete forms, erecting wooden framework, and laying flooring. Inspects work performed by subcontractors, including ductwork, wiring, and pipe installations, to insure conformance with specifications. Installs doors, builds stairs, and lays hardwood floors. May supervise workers engaged in building timber structures, such as cofferdams, trestles, and supports for concrete forms. May make cost estimates for contracts. Performs other duties as described under SUPERVISOR (any ind.). May be designated according to area of specialization as BOWLING-ALLEY-INSTALLATION SUPERVISOR (const.); COFFERDAM-CONSTRUCTION SUPERVISOR (const.); FORM-BUILDING SUPERVISOR (const.); TIMBERING SUPERVISOR (const.).

The OOH, *Occupational Outlook Handbook* (also usually found in libraries, career centers, school counselors' offices, and government service agencies) will give an up-to-date description of the occupations as well as a discussion of demand, starting salaries, education required, and other important information. The construction occupations information that follows was taken from pp. 252-288 of the *Occupational Outlook Handbook* as designated on the bottom side of card 86 (and as an example under Step 4).

Construction Occupations, OOH

Construction craft workers represent the largest group of skilled workers in the nation's labor force. Altogether, there were 3.3 million employed in 1976—about 3 out of every 10 skilled workers.

The more than two dozen skilled construction trades vary greatly in size. Several major trades—carpenter, painter, operating engineer, plumber, and electrician—each had more than 200,000 workers; carpenters alone numbered more than 1 million, about one-third of all construction craft workers. In contrast, only a few thousand each were employed in trades such as marble setter, terrazzo worker, and stonemason.

What Are the Construction Trades?

Workers in the construction trades build, repair, and modernize homes and all kinds of buildings. They also work on a variety of other structures, including highways, airports, and missile launching pads.

Construction work may be divided into three categories: structural, finishing, and mechanical. In general, each trade falls in one of these categories: *Structural work*: Carpenter, operating engineer (construction machinery operator), bricklayer, iron worker, cement mason, stonemason, and boilermaker. *Finishing work*: Lather, plasterer, marble setter, terrazzo worker, painter, paperhanger, glazier, roofer, floor covering installer, and insulation worker. *Mechanical work*: Plumber, pipefitter, construction electrician, sheet-metal worker, elevator constructor, and millwright.

Most construction trades are described individually later in this chapter. Boilermakers and millwrights are described elsewhere in the *Handbook*.

Figure 6

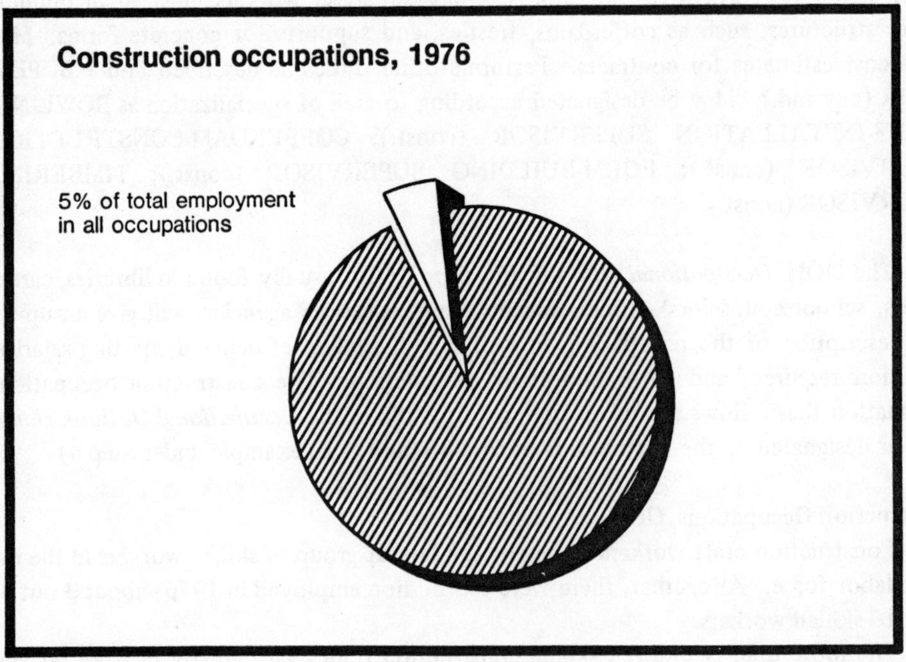

Construction occupations, 1976

5% of total employment in all occupations

Places of Employment

Most jobs are with contractors in the construction industry. The vast majority of construction contractors are small—generally employing fewer than 10 people. A few large contractors, however, employ thousands. Large numbers of construction trade workers are employed in other industries, such as mining and manufacturing, mainly to do maintenance and repair work. Chemical manufacturers, for example, need plumbers and pipefitters to maintain the complex pipe networks in their processing plants. Government agencies employ construction trade workers to maintain highways, buildings, and sanitation systems.

Many construction trade workers are self-employed and contract with homeowners and businesses for small jobs. Self-employment is most common in paperhanging, painting, and floor covering work, but it also is found in other trades.

Employment in the construction trades is distributed geographically in much the same way as the nation's population. Thus, the highest concentration generally is in industrialized and highly populated areas.

Training, Other qualifications, and Advancement

Most training authorities recommend formal apprenticeship training as the best way to acquire the all-round skills in the construction trades. Apprenticeship is a prescribed period of on-the-job training, supplemented by related classroom instruction that is designated to familiarize apprentices with the materials, tools, and principles of their trade. Formal apprenticeship agreements are registered with a state apprenticeship agency or the U.S. Department of Labor's Bureau of Apprenticeship and Training.

Although apprenticeship provides the most thorough training, many people acquire construction skills informally by working as laborers and helpers and observing experienced craft workers. Some acquire skills by attending vocational or trade schools or by taking correspondence school courses.

Apprentices generally must be at least 18 years old and in good physical condition. A high school or vocational school education, or its equivalent, including courses in mathematics and mechanical drawing, is desirable. Courses in construction trades, such as carpentry and electricity, also are recommended. Often, applicants are given tests to determine their aptitudes. For some trades, manual dexterity, mechanical aptitude, and an eye for proper alignment of materials are important.

The formal apprenticeship agreement generally calls for 3 to 4 years of on-the-job training and 144 hours or more of related classroom instruction each year. On the job, most instruction is given by a particular craft worker to whom the apprentice is assigned.

Classroom instruction varies among the construction trades, but usually includes courses such as history of the trade, characteristics of materials, shop mathematics, and basic principles of engineering.

In most communities, the apprenticeship programs are supervised by joint apprenticeship committees composed of local employers and local union representatives. The committee determines the need for apprentices in the community and establishes minimum standards of education, experience, and training. Whenever an employer cannot provide all-round instruction or relatively continuous employment, the committee transfers the apprentice to another employer. Where specialization by contractors is extensive—for instance, in electrical work—customarily the committee rotates apprentices among several contractors at intervals of about 6 months.

In areas where these committees have not been established, the apprenticeship agreement is solely between the apprentice and the employer or employer group. Many people have received valuable training under these programs, but they have some disadvantages. No committee is available to supervise the training offered and settle differences over the terms and conditions of training. What the apprentice learns depends largely on the employer's business prospects and policies. If the employer lacks continuous work or does only a restricted type of work, the apprentice cannot develop all-round skills.

In many localities, craft workers—most commonly electricians and plumbers—are required to have a license to work at their trade. To qualify for these licenses, they must pass an examination to demonstrate a broad knowledge of the job and of state and local regulations.

Construction trades craft workers may advance in a number of ways. Many become supervisors. In most localities, small jobs are run by "working supervisors" who work at the trade along with members of their crews. On larger jobs, the supervisors do only supervisory work. Craft workers also can become estimators for contractors. In these jobs, they estimate material requirements and labor costs to enable the contractor to bid on a particular project. Some craft workers advance to jobs as superintendents on large projects. Others become instructors in trade and vocational schools or sales representatives for building supply companies. A large number of craft workers have become contractors in the homebuilding field.

Starting a small contract construction business is easier than starting a small business in many other industries. Only a moderate financial investment usually is needed, and it is possible to conduct a fairly substantial business from one's home. However, the contract construction field is very competitive, and the rate of business failure is high among small contractors.

Employment Outlook

Employment in the construction trades is expected to increase faster than the average for all occupations through the mid-1980's. In addition to employment growth, many job openings will result each year from the need to replace experienced workers who transfer to other fields of work, retire, or die.

However, since construction activity is sensitive to changes in the nation's economy the number of openings may fluctuate sharply from year to year.

Chart 9

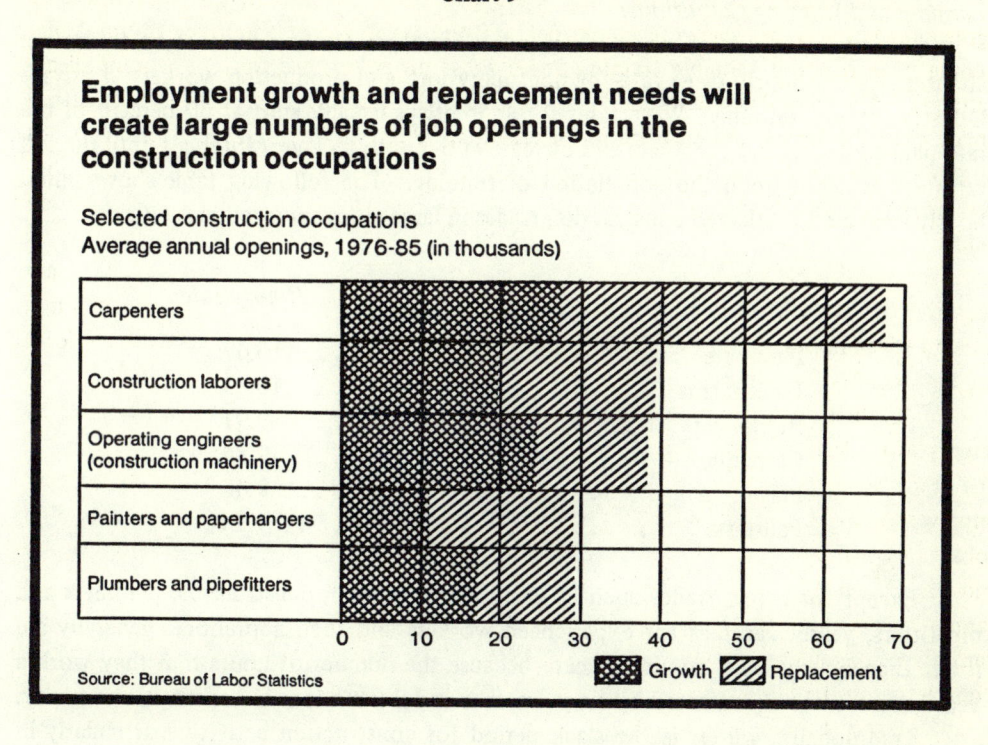

Employment growth and replacement needs will create large numbers of job openings in the construction occupations

Selected construction occupations
Average annual openings, 1976-85 (in thousands)

Occupation	0	10	20	30	40	50	60	70
Carpenters								
Construction laborers								
Operating engineers (construction machinery)								
Painters and paperhangers								
Plumbers and pipefitters								

Source: Bureau of Labor Statistics   Growth   Replacement

Over the long run, construction activity is expected to grow substantially. The anticipated increases in population and households, and the relatively low level of housing construction in the early 1970's are expected to create strong pressure for new housing. Among other factors that will stimulate construction activity are higher levels of personal income and a rise in spending for new industrial plants and equipment. Also, there will be a growing demand for alteration and modernization work on existing structures, as well as for maintenance and repair work on highway systems, dams, bridges, and similar projects.

The increase in employment is not expected to be as great as the expansion in construction activity. Continued technological developments in construction methods, tools and equipment, and materials will raise output per worker. One important development is the growing use of prefabricated units at the job site. For example, preassembled outside walls and partitions can be lifted into place in one operation.

The rates of employment growth will differ among the various construction trades. Employment growth is expected to be fastest for cement masons and for insulation workers. Trades that will have the slowest growth rates are plasterers and sheetmetal workers.

Earnings and Working Conditions:

Average hourly wage rates of unionized workers in the construction trades are about twice the hourly wage rate for nonsupervisory and production workers in private industry, except farming. Wage rates for apprentices usually start at 50 percent of the rate paid to experienced workers and increase at 6-month to 1-year intervals until the full rates are achieved upon the completion of training. The following table shows union hourly averages for selected construction trades in large cities surveyed in 1976.

	Hourly rate
Plumbers	10.47
Electricians	10.33
Bricklayers	9.91
Carpenters	9.84
Plasterers	9.48
Painters	9.24

Except for a few trades such as electricians, elevator constructors, plumbers and pipefitters, yearly earnings for experienced workers and their apprentices generally are lower than hourly rates would indicate because the number of hours that they work a year can be adversely affected by poor weather and fluctuations in construction activity.

Traditionally, winter is the slack period for construction activity, particularly in colder regions. Some workers, such as laborers and roofers, may not work for several months. However, not only cold but also rain may slow—even stop—work on a construction project. Also, because the construction trades are so dependent on one another—particularly on large projects—work delays or strikes in one trade can delay or stop the work of another. The accompanying chart shows that the unemployment rate in the construction industry is about twice that of workers as a whole.

Chart 10

Unemployed rates: Construction and all industries, average 1948-76

Construction	All industries
~11%	~5%

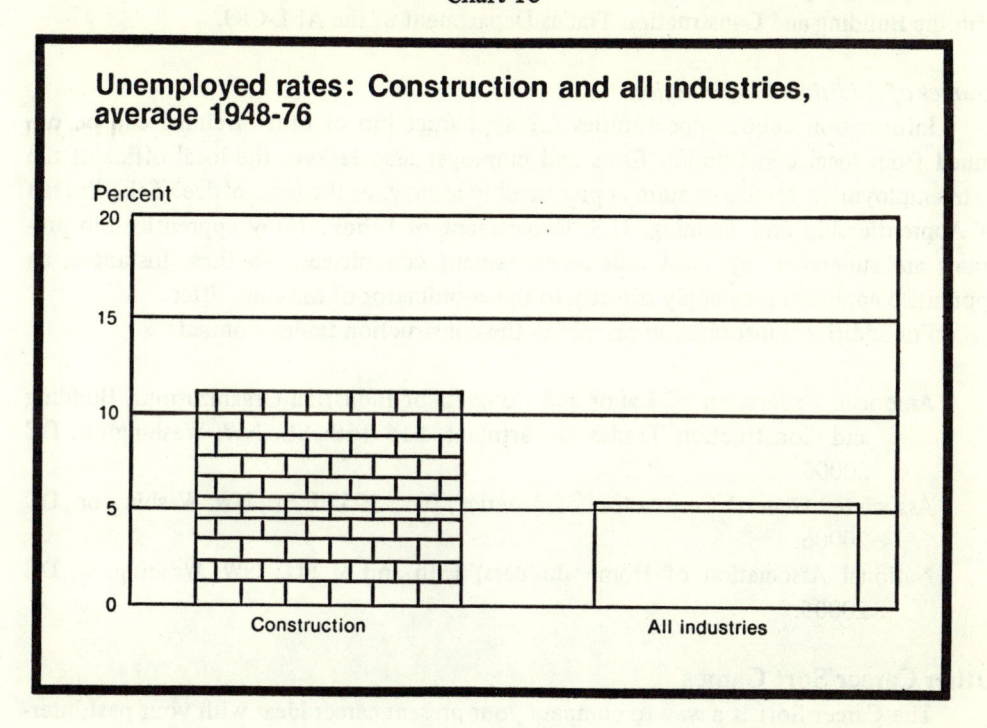

Construction work frequently requires prolonged standing, bending, stooping, and working in cramped quarters. Exposure to weather is common since much of the work is done outdoors or in partially enclosed structures. Many people prefer construction work because it permits them to be outdoors.

Because construction workers may need to work with sharp tools amidst the clutter of materials while standing on temporary scaffolding, and in bad weather, they are more prone to injury than workers in other jobs. Indeed, the construction industry has the highest injury and illness rate of all industries. However, employers increasingly are placing an emphasis on safe working conditions and are stressing safe work habits—practices that reduce the risk of injuries.

The construction trades offer especially good opportunities for young people who are not planning to go to college, but who are willing to spend several years in learning a skilled occupation. Construction workers can find job opportunities in all parts of the country. Their hourly wage rates generally are much higher than those of most other manual workers. As previously noted, construction trade workers with business ability have greater opportunities to open their own businesses than workers in most other skilled occupations.

A large proportion of construction workers are members of trade unions affiliated with the Building and Construction Trades Department of the AFL-CIO.

Sources of Additional Information

Information about opportunities for apprenticeship or other training can be obtained from local construction firms and employer associations, the local office of the state employment service or state apprenticeship agency, or the local office of the Bureau of Apprenticeship and Training, U.S. Department of Labor. Many apprenticeship programs are supervised by local union-management committees. In these instances, an apprentice applicant may apply directly to the coordinator of the committee.

For additional information on jobs in the construction trades, contact:

American Federation of Labor and Congress of Industrial Organizations, Building and Construction Trades Department, 815 16th St., NW, Washington, DC 20006.

Associated General Contractors of America, Inc., 1957 E St., NW, Washington, DC 20006.

National Association of Home Builders, 15th and M Sts., NW, Washington, DC 20005.

Other Career Sort Games

The Career Sort is a way to compare your present career ideas with your past interests, and, if followed through Step 4, it is a way to expand your knowledge about occupations and about yourself.

Children can devise a variety of career games using the Career Sort. Examples are "What's My Career?" played as one person reads the back side of the card while another guesses the occupational group and the degree (high, average, or low) of Data-People-Things involvement in the occupation.

Another example of a card game using the Career Sort is a matching game in which two or more players are dealt eight cards, with the rest of the cards placed top side down. As in gin rummy, the object of the game would be to get a series of three cards with Data, People, or Things with high, average, or low figures. The player having laid down the most series of cards would be the winner, with points assessed against cards in the player's hand—3 for high, 2 for average, and 1 for low figures. The game would end when one player has been assessed 50 points; the winner is the player having the lowest number of total points. At the end of each hand, the person with the lowest number of points has the honor of reading the back side of the cards laid down and earns 5 points to be subtracted from his/her accumulated total.

Numerous other games could be devised. However, the Career Sort is most valuable when parent and child use the cards as outlined earlier, following all four steps, including the follow-up research.

_____
Name

_____
Date

_____
Age

List of Career Likes

Occupation	DOT pp.	OOH pp.

1. _____
2. _____
3. _____
4. _____
5. _____
6. _____
7. _____
8. _____
9. _____
10. _____

Notes: _____

_____

_____

_____

_____

_____

PCQ: Parent Career Quotient a Recap

Place a check mark beside each question you feel deserves a "yes" answer.

_____ 1. Do you provide a good sounding board for your child's dreams, fantasy, and plans for his/her career? (See Chapter 1.)

_____ 2. Do you build on your child's faith in himself/herself and his/her feeling of worth? (See Chapter 2.)

_____ 3. Do you try to provide reinforcement for successful work and leisure experiences and help relate them to career planning? (See Chapter 3.)

_____ 4. Do you help your child learn about the process of career decision-making? (See Chapter 4.)

_____ 5. Do you help your child understand the world of work and himself/herself through *data*? (See Chapter 5.)

_____ 6. Do you help your child understand the world of work and himself/herself through *people*? (See Chapter 6.)

_____ 7. Do you help your child understand the world of work and himself/herself through *things*? (See Chapter 7.)

_____ 8. Do you assist your child in exploring various work and leisure options through school courses, hobbies, reading, part-time and summer jobs, and volunteering? (See Chapter 8.)

_____ 9. Do you know where to look for timely information on projections for future employment? (See Chapter 9.)

_____ 10. Do you understand how to relate your child's interests, aptitudes, and achievements to his/her career planning? (See Chapter 10.)

_____ 11. Do you know the career planning resource persons in your child's school and how best to work with them? (See Chapter 11.)

_____ 12. Do you know ten good resources for further reading about career planning? (See Chapter 12.)

_____ 13. Do you know a fascinating game to sort out your child's career interests? (See Chapter 13.)

_____ 14. Do you know which occupations are expected to have the best employment opportunities over the next ten years? (See Chapter 9.)

_____ 15. Do you know a neat game that can help get across the Data-People-Things concepts to your child? (See Chapter 8.)

_____ Total checks: Score 10 points for each check. (Example: 4 checks = 40 points total.)

TOTAL SCORE

What is your score? The following outline may give you a general idea of where you stand. Top Score is 150. Low score is 0. Now that you have read the book, you should be ready to help your child plan a career.

P.C.Q.	Where You Stand
130-150	You've become an expert.
100-120	You are doing very well.
70-90	You should still be helpful to your child.
40-60	You should re-check the chapters.
0-30	You may want to start over.

Whether your P.C.Q. is that of an "expert" or that of a "parent who may want to start over," you undoubtedly have become aware of many practical ways you can be of help to your child. Your child will be reinforced by your continuing interest and effort. Remember, career planning is not a one time effort; it is not easy, it is a continuing process in which the ultimate goal is realistic career choices with successful placement.

Index

Administrative and Related
  Occupations Outlook 103-104
Air Transportations
  Outlook 110-111
AT&T 83
Apprenticeships 77
Armed Forces Schools 77
Art, Design, and Communication
  Related Occupations Outlook
  123-125
Athletics 76
Banking Occupations
  Outlook 102-103
Bolles, R. 37
Career Awareness 53, 56, 64, 70
Career Exploralism 53, 56, 65, 71
Career Preparation 53, 56, 65, 71
Cleaning and Related
  Occupations Outlook 104
Clergy Outlook 122-123
Clerical Occupations
  Outlook 101
College bound 151
College guides 154
Communications-Related
  Occupations Outlook 125
Community Colleges 78
Computer and Related
  Occupations Outlook 102-103
Construction Occupations
  Outlook 109-110
Correspondence Schools 77
Counselors 136-137
Counseling Occupations Outlook
  Data, People, Things 40-49,
  50-58, 59-67, 81
Decision-Making (SWING) 37-39
Dental Occupations Outlook 118
Department of Labor 85
Design Occupations Outlook 124
Developmental Phases 19-20
D.O.T. (Dictionary of Occupational
  Titles) 41, 159, 161

Driving Occupations Outlook 112
Edison, T. 38
Education and Related
  Occupations Outlook 107
Engineers Occupations
  Outlook 113-114
Environmental Scientists
  Outlook 114
Faith 15
Food Service Occupations
  Outlook 105
Ford, H. 32
Foundry Occupations
  Outlook 98
Franklin, B. 38
Gallup Poll 11, 135
Gelatt, H.B. 36
Gibran, K. 24
Goethe 24
Great Depression 18
Health Occupations
  Outlook 118-121
Hill, G. 127
Home Study 77
Hoppock, R. 11
Hoy, A. 24
Industrial Production and
  Related Occupations
  Outlook 98-101
Insurance Occupations
  Outlook 103
Interviewing 155-157
Junior College 78
Job Search 155-157
Keffering, C. 36
Krista 30
Labor Market 85-97
Leisure Activities 71-75
Liebow 17
Life Sciences Occupations
  Outlook 111-115
Lopez, N. 37

175

Mathematics Occupations
  Outlook 115
Mechanics and Repairers
  Outlook 116-118
Medical Practitioners
  Outlook 119
Medical Technologist, Technician
  and Assistant Occupations
  Outlook 119-120
Minority Youth (Special
  Help) 150
Nash 12
Nursing Occupations Outlook 120
Office Occupations
  Outlook 101-104
O.J.T. (On Job Training) 77
O.O.H (Occupational Outlook
  Handbook) 88, 98-125, 141,
  145, 161
Parsons, F. 15
Peace Corps 25
Performing Artists
  Outlook 123-124
Personal Service Occupations
  Outlook 105-106
Physical Scientists
  Outlook 115-116
Printing Occupations
  Outlook 98-99
Protective and Related
  Service Occupations
  Outlook 106-107
Proverbs 16
Purckey, Wm. 37
Railroad Occupations
  Outlook 111
Repairers Outlook 116-118

Resources, printed 143-148
Resume writing 115-157
Roe, A. 38
Ringer, R. 38
Rose, P. 37
Sales Occupations
  Outlook 107-108
Scientific and Technical
  Occupations Outlook 112-116
Service Occupations
  Outlook 104-107
Social Scientists Outlook
  121-122
Social Service Occupations
  Outlook 122
Success 30-33
Summer School 76
Teachers, 137-138
Teaching Occupations
  Outlook 107
Technical Institutes 77
Technical Occupations
  Outlook 112-116
Telephone Craft
  Occupations Outlook 116
Tests (Ability, Achievement,
  Aptitude, Interest) 129
Therapy and Rehabilitation
  Occupations Outlook 120-121
Time Magazine 17
Transportation Activities
  Occupations Outlook 110-112
Twain, M. 38
Vocational Schools 77, 133
Weiler, N. 138
Women 85, 148-149
Worthiness Qualities 24-28

Career Sort Cards

01 ARCHITECTURE, ENGINEERING, AND SURVEYING

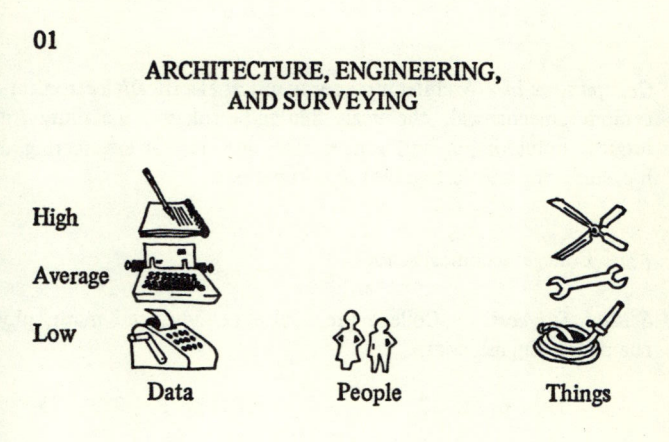

	Data	People	Things
High	■		■
Average			
Low		■	

©Copyright 1979 by Dean Hummel and Carl McDaniels from the book **HOW TO HELP YOUR CHILD PLAN A CAREER** ($6.95 paper, $12.50 cloth, Acropolis Books Ltd., Washington, D.C. 20009)

02 MATHEMATICS AND PHYSICAL SCIENCES

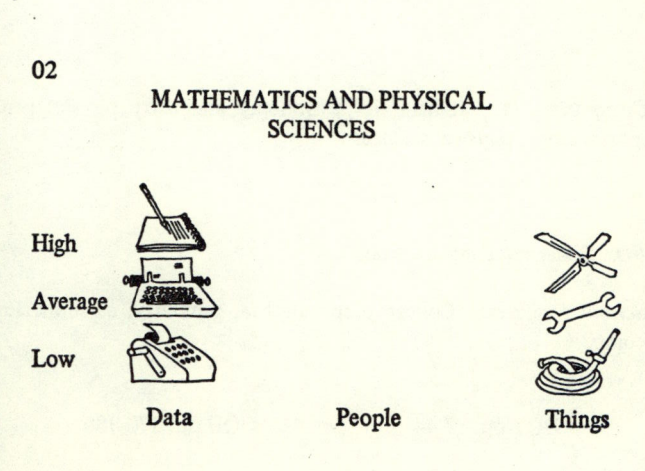

	Data	People	Things
High	■		
Average			■
Low		■	

©Copyright 1979 by Dean Hummel and Carl McDaniels from the book **HOW TO HELP YOUR CHILD PLAN A CAREER** ($6.95 paper, $12.50 cloth, Acropolis Books Ltd., Washington, D.C. 20009)

04 LIFE SCIENCES

	Data	People	Things
High	■		
Average			■
Low		■	

©Copyright 1979 by Dean Hummel and Carl McDaniels from the book **HOW TO HELP YOUR CHILD PLAN A CAREER** ($6.95 paper, $12.50 cloth, Acropolis Books Ltd., Washington, D.C. 20009)

05 SOCIAL SCIENCES

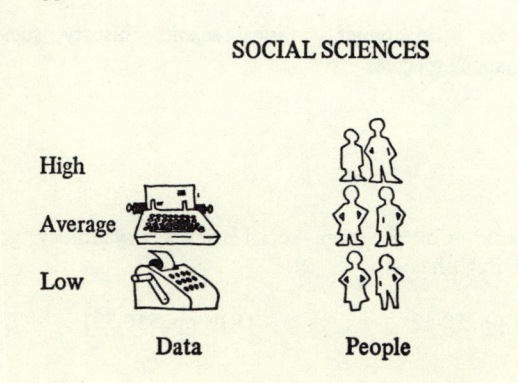

	Data	People	Things
High		■	
Average	■		
Low			■

©Copyright 1979 by Dean Hummel and Carl McDaniels from the book **HOW TO HELP YOUR CHILD PLAN A CAREER** (6.95 paper, $12.50 cloth, Acropolis Books Ltd., Washington, D.C. 20009)

01

Occupations in: Architecture; aeronautics; electrical/electronics; civil, ceramic, mechanical, chemical, mining/petroleum, metallurgy/metallurgical, industrial, agricultural, marine, and nuclear engineering, drafting, surveying and cartographical occupations

ED: College; technical school

School Subjects: College prep.—algebra, advanced math, physics, chemistry, English comp.

DOT pp. 15-37   OOH pp. 331-393, 575

02

Occupations in: Mathematics, astronomy, chemistry, physics, geology, meteorology, physical sciences

ED: College; technical school

School Subjects: College prep.—algebra, geometry, calculus, English comp.

DOT pp. 37-44   OOH pp. 370-380

04

Occupations in: Agricultural, biological sciences; psychology, life sciences

ED: College; technical school

School Subjects: College prep.—algebra, biological sciences, advanced math, earth science, English comp.

DOT pp. 44-50   OOH pp. 355-368

05

Occupations in: Economics, political science, history, sociology, anthropology, social sciences

ED: College

School Subjects: College, prep.—social science, psychology, government, history, English comp.

DOT pp. 50-52   OOH pp. 516-531

07 MEDICINE AND HEALTH

High		
Average		
Low		
Data	People	Things

©Copyright 1979 by Dean Hummel and Carl McDaniels from the book **HOW TO HELP YOUR CHILD PLAN A CAREER** ($6.95 paper, $12.50 cloth, Acropolis Books Ltd., Washington, D.C. 20009)

09 EDUCATION

High		
Average		
Low		
Data	People	Things

©Copyright 1979 by Dean Hummel and Carl McDaniels from the book **HOW TO HELP YOUR CHILD PLAN A CAREER** ($6.95 paper, $12.50 cloth, Acropolis Books Ltd., Washington, D.C. 20009)

10 MUSEUM, LIBRARY, AND ARCHIVAL SCIENCES

High		
Average		
Low		
Data	People	Things

©Copyright 1979 by Dean Hummel and Carl McDaniels from the book **HOW TO HELP YOUR CHILD PLAN A CAREER** ($6.95 paper, $12.50 cloth, Acropolis Books Ltd., Washington, D.C. 20009)

11 LAW AND JURISPRUDENCE

High		
Average		
Low		
Data	People	Things

©Copyright 1979 by Dean Hummel and Carl McDaniels from the book **HOW TO HELP YOUR CHILD PLAN A CAREER** (6.95 paper, $12.50 cloth, Acropolis Books Ltd., Washington, D.C. 20009)

07

Occupations: Physicians and surgeons, osteopaths, dentists, veterinarians, pharmacists, registered nurses, therapists, dietitians, medical and dental technicians

ED: College; technical school

School Subjects: College prep.— algebra, advanced math, physics, chemistry, English comp.

DOT pp. 15-37   OOH pp. 417-512

09

Occupations in: College and university education, secondary school education, preschool, primary school, and kindergarten education, education of the handicapped, home economics, form advising, vocational education

ED: College

School Subjects: College prep.—English comp., subjects in area of teaching interest

DOT pp. 65-72   OOH pp. 210-223

10

Occupations: Librarians, archivists, museum curators and related occupations

ED: College

School Subjects: College prep.—English comp., art, bookkeeping, history, sciences

DOT pp. 72-75   OOH pp. 220-223

11

Occupations: Lawyers, judges; occupations in law and jurisprudence

ED: College (graduate school)

School Subjects: College prep.—history, government, English comp., public speaking

DOT pp. 75-76   OOH pp. 145-148

12 RELIGION AND THEOLOGY

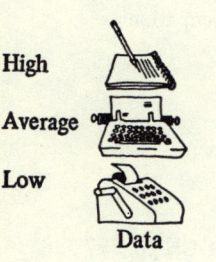

High
Average
Low

Data   People   Things

©Copyright 1979 by Dean Hummel and Carl McDaniels from the book HOW TO HELP YOUR CHILD PLAN A CAREER ($6.95 paper, $12.50 cloth, Acropolis Books Ltd., Washington, D.C. 20009)

13 WRITING

High
Average
Low

Data   People   Things

©Copyright 1979 by Dean Hummel and Carl McDaniels from the book HOW TO HELP YOUR CHILD PLAN A CAREER ($6.95 paper, $12.50 cloth, Acropolis Books Ltd., Washington, D.C. 20009)

14 ART

High
Average
Low

Data   People   Things

©Copyright 1979 by Dean Hummel and Carl McDaniels from the book HOW TO HELP YOUR CHILD PLAN A CAREER ($6.95 paper, $12.50 cloth, Acropolis Books Ltd., Washington, D.C. 20009)

15 ENTERTAINMENT AND RECREATION

High
Average
Low

Data   People   Things

©Copyright 1979 by Dean Hummel and Carl McDaniels from the book HOW TO HELP YOUR CHILD PLAN A CAREER ($6.95 paper, $12.50 cloth, Acropolis Books Ltd., Washington, D.C. 20009)

Occupations in: Clergy, religion and theology

ED: College

School Subjects: College prep.—history, English, English comp., dramatics

DOT pp. 76-77   OOH pp. 544-547

Occupations: Writers, editors (publication, broadcast, and script), interpreters and translators

ED: College

School Subjects: College prep.—English lit., English comp., foreign languages

DOT pp. 77-80   OOH pp. 591-597

Occupations: Commercial art designers and illustrators; graphic artists; environmental, product, and related designers; photographers; fine artists; painters; sculptors; and related occupations

ED: College; special schools

School Subjects: College prep.—art

DOT pp. 80-85   OOH pp. 577-588

Occupations in: Dramatics, dancing, music, athletics and sports, entertainment and recreation

ED: Special schools

School Subjects: College prep. or special school—dramatics, speech, music

DOT pp. 85-91   OOH pp. 566-573

16
ADMINISTRATIVE SPECIALIZATIONS

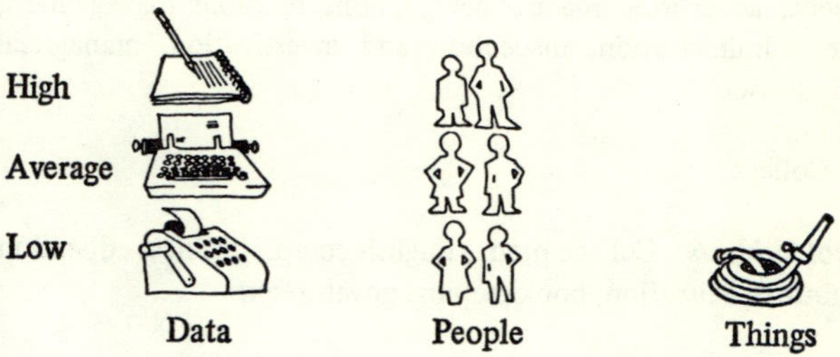

	Data	People	Things
High			
Average	■	♦♦♦	
Low			●

©Copyright 1979 by Dean Hummel and Carl McDaniels from the book **HOW TO HELP YOUR CHILD PLAN A CAREER** ($6.95 paper, $12.50 cloth, Acropolis Books Ltd., Washington, D.C. 20009)

18
MANAGERS AND OFFICIALS

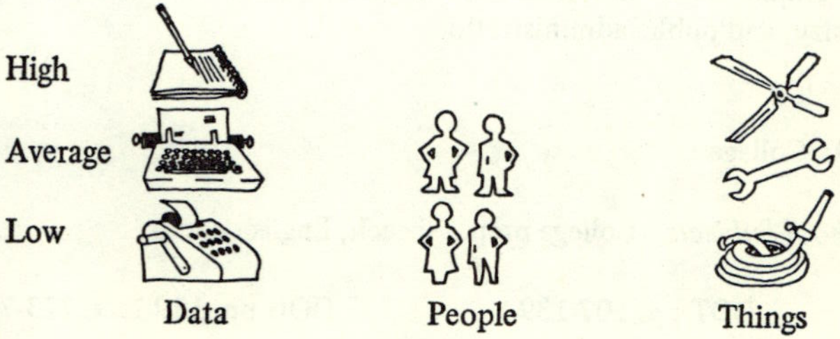

	Data	People	Things
High			
Average	■	♦♦♦	✂ 🔧 ●
Low			

©Copyright 1979 by Dean Hummel and Carl McDaniels from the book **HOW TO HELP YOUR CHILD PLAN A CAREER** ($6.95 paper, $12.50 cloth, Acropolis Books Ltd., Washington, D.C. 20009)

19
MISCELLANEOUS PROFESSIONAL TECHNICIANS AND MANAGERS

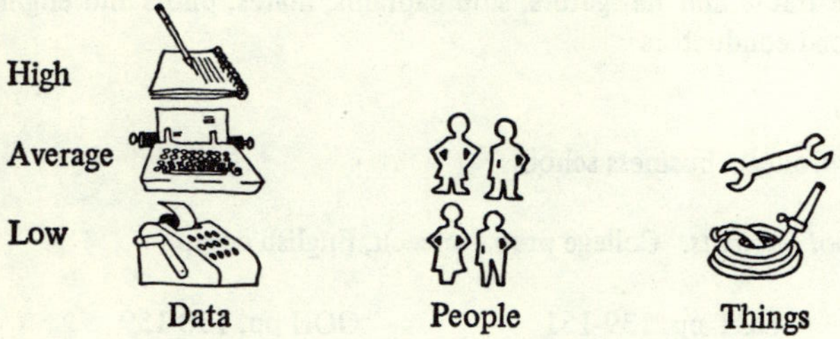

	Data	People	Things
High			
Average	■	♦♦	🔧 ●
Low			

©Copyright 1979 by Dean Hummel and Carl McDaniels from the book **HOW TO HELP YOUR CHILD PLAN A CAREER** (6.95 paper, $12.50 cloth, Acropolis Books Ltd., Washington, D.C. 20009)

20
CLERICAL AND SALES

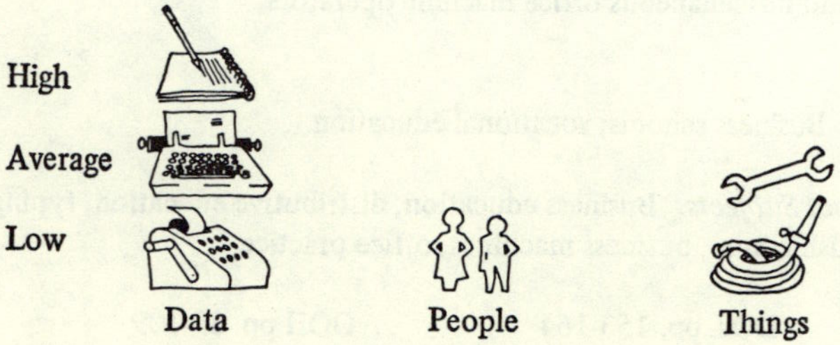

	Data	People	Things
High			
Average	■		🔧 ●
Low		♦	

©Copyright 1979 by Dean Hummel and Carl McDaniels from the book **HOW TO HELP YOUR CHILD PLAN A CAREER** ($6.95 paper, $12.50 cloth, Acropolis Books Ltd., Washington, D.C. 20009)

Occupations in: Accounting and auditing, budget and management systems analysis, purchasing management, sales and distribution management, advertising management, public relations management, personnel administration, inspection and investigation, managerial and public service

ED: College

School Subjects: College prep.—English comp., business education, distributive education, bookkeeping, government

DOT pp. 91-107   OOH pp. 130-145

Occupations: Agents and appraisers; radio operators; sound, film, and videotape recording and reproduction; social and welfare work; airplane pilots and navigators; ship captains, mates, pilots and engineers; railroad conductors

ED: College; business schools

School Subjects: College prep.—speech, English comp.

DOT pp. 139-151   OOH pp. 130-159

Occupations: Managers and officials in agriculture, forestry, fishing industry, mining industry, manufacturing industry, transportation, communication, and utilities, wholesale and retail trade, service industry, and public administration

ED: College

School Subjects: College prep.—speech, English comp.

DOT pp. 107-139   OOH pp. 139-159; 773-784

Occupations: Stenographers, typists, file clerks; secretaries, typewriting operators, interviewing clerks, duplicating machine operators, mailing and miscellaneous office machine operators

ED: Business schools; vocational education

School Subjects: Business education, distributive education, typing, English comp., business machines, office practice

DOT pp. 153-164   OOH pp. 89-109

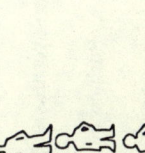

21 COMPUTING AND ACCOUNT RECORDING

High
Average — Data
Low

Average — People

Low — Things

©Copyright 1979 by Dean Hummel and Carl McDaniels from the book **HOW TO HELP YOUR CHILD PLAN A CAREER** ($6.95 paper, $12.50 cloth, Acropolis Books Ltd., Washington, D.C. 20009)

---

22 PRODUCTION AND STOCK CLERKS

High
Average — Data
Low

Low — People

High — Things

©Copyright 1979 by Dean Hummel and Carl McDaniels from the book **HOW TO HELP YOUR CHILD PLAN A CAREER** ($6.95 paper, $12.50 cloth, Acropolis Books Ltd., Washington, D.C. 20009)

---

23 INFORMATION AND MESSAGE DISTRIBUTION

High
Average — Data
Low

Average — People

Low — Things

©Copyright 1979 by Dean Hummel and Carl McDaniels from the book **HOW TO HELP YOUR CHILD PLAN A CAREER** ($6.95 paper, $12.50 cloth, Acropolis Books Ltd., Washington, D.C. 20009)

---

24 MISCELLANEOUS CLERICAL

High
Average — Data
Low

High — People

Low — Things

©Copyright 1979 by Dean Hummel and Carl McDaniels from the book **HOW TO HELP YOUR CHILD PLAN A CAREER** (6.95 paper, $12.50 cloth, Acropolis Books Ltd., Washington, D.C. 20009)

Occupations: Bookkeepers and bookkeeping machine operators; cashiers and tellers; electronic and electromechanical data processors; billing and rate clerks; payroll, timekeeping, and duty-roster clerks; account-recording machine operators; computing and account recording

ED: College; technical school

School Subjects: Bookkeeping, business, math

DOT pp. 164-179   OOH pp. 111-130

Occupations: Production clerks; shipping, receiving, and stock clerks

ED: Vocational education; technical school

School Subjects: Math, speech, distributive education

DOT pp. 179-190   OOH pp. 104-108

Occupations: Hand delivery persons and distributors, telephone operators, telegraph operators, information and reception clerks, accommodation clerks, gate and ticket agents, information and message distributors

ED: High school; vocational education

School Subjects: Speech, distributive education, business education

DOT pp. 190-197   OOH pp. 206-209

Occupations: Investigators, adjusters, government service clerks, medical service clerks, advertising service clerks, transportation service clerks, miscellaneous clerical positions

ED: High school; vocational education

School Subjects: Business education, typing, English comp.

DOT pp. 197-204   OOH pp. 95-109

25 SALES, SERVICES

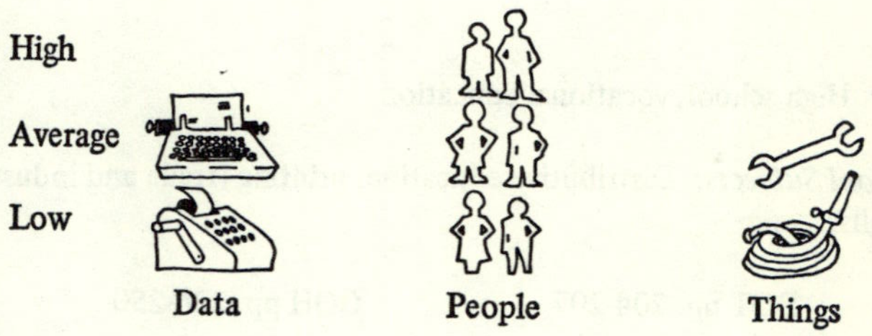

High
Average
Low

Data — People — Things

©Copyright 1979 by Dean Hummel and Carl McDaniels from the book **HOW TO HELP YOUR CHILD PLAN A CAREER** ($6.95 paper, $12.50 cloth, Acropolis Books Ltd., Washington, D.C. 20009)

---

26 SALES, CONSUMABLE COMMODITIES

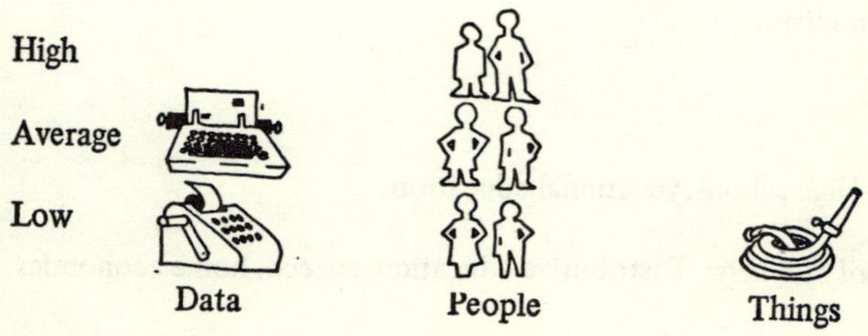

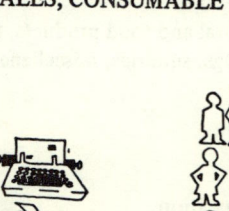

High
Average
Low

Data — People — Things

©Copyright 1979 by Dean Hummel and Carl McDaniels from the book **HOW TO HELP YOUR CHILD PLAN A CAREER** ($6.95 paper, $12.50 cloth, Acropolis Books Ltd., Washington, D.C. 20009)

---

27 SALES, COMMODITIES

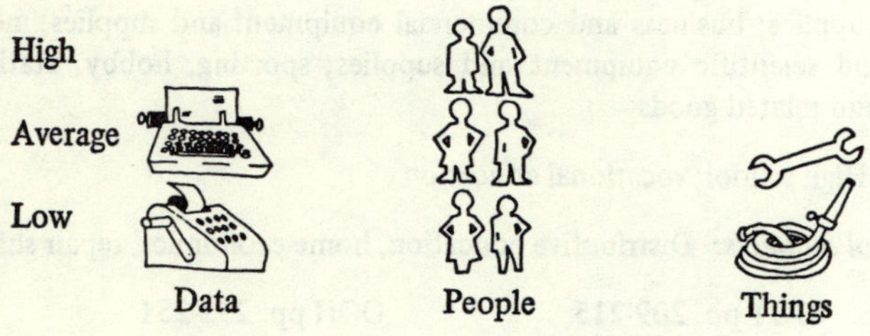

High
Average
Low

Data — People — Things

©Copyright 1979 by Dean Hummel and Carl McDaniels from the book **HOW TO HELP YOUR CHILD PLAN A CAREER** (6.95 paper, $12.50 cloth, Acropolis Books Ltd., Washington, D.C. 20009)

---

29 MISCELLANEOUS SALES

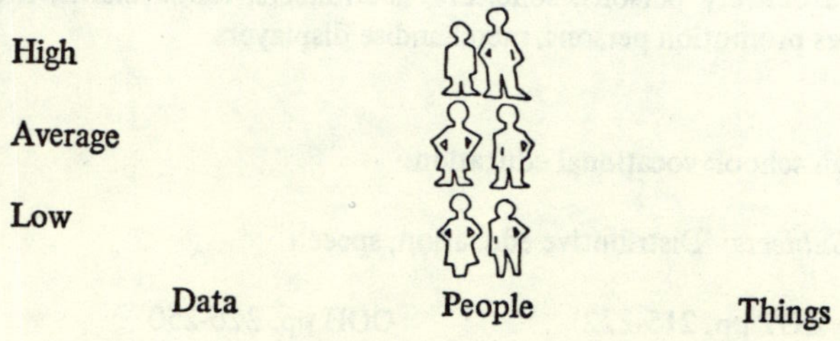

High
Average
Low

Data — People — Things

©Copyright 1979 by Dean Hummel and Carl McDaniels from the book **HOW TO HELP YOUR CHILD PLAN A CAREER** ($6.95 paper, $12.50 cloth, Acropolis Books Ltd., Washington, D.C. 20009)

Sales Occupations in: Real estate, insurance, business, financial services, transportation services, utilities, printing, and advertising

ED: High school; vocational education

School Subjects: Distributive education, printing (trade and industrial), English comp

DOT pp. 204-207   OOH pp. 226-250

Sales Occupations in: Agricultural and food products, textile products, apparel, notions, chemicals, drugs, sundries, miscellaneous consumable commodities

ED: High school; vocational education

School Subjects: Distributive education, speech, home economics

DOT pp. 207-209   OOH pp. 240-250

Sales occupations in: Home furniture; furnishings; appliances; electrical goods; farm and gardening equipment and supplies; transportation equipment, parts, and supplies; industrial and related equipment and supplies; business and commercial equipment and supplies; medical and scientific equipment and supplies; sporting, hobby, stationery, and related goods

ED: High school; vocational education

School Subjects: Distributive education, home economics, repair ship

DOT pp. 209-215   OOH pp. 232-251

Occupations: Sales clerks, vending and door-to-door salespersons, route sales and delivery persons, solicitors, auctioneers, rental clerks, shoppers, sales promotion persons, merchandise displayers

ED: High school; vocational education

School Subjects: Distributive education, speech

DOT pp. 215-222   OOH pp. 226-250

30 DOMESTIC SERVICE

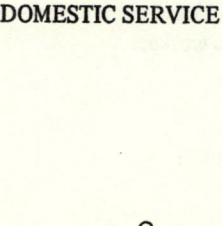

	Data	People	Things
High			
Average			
Low		👤	✂🔧🪢

31 FOOD AND BEVERAGE PREPARATION AND SERVICE

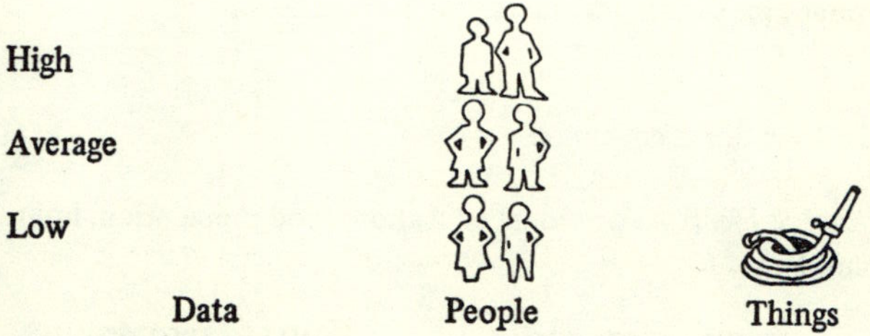

	Data	People	Things
High			
Average		👥👥👥	
Low			🪢

32 LODGING AND RELATED SERVICES

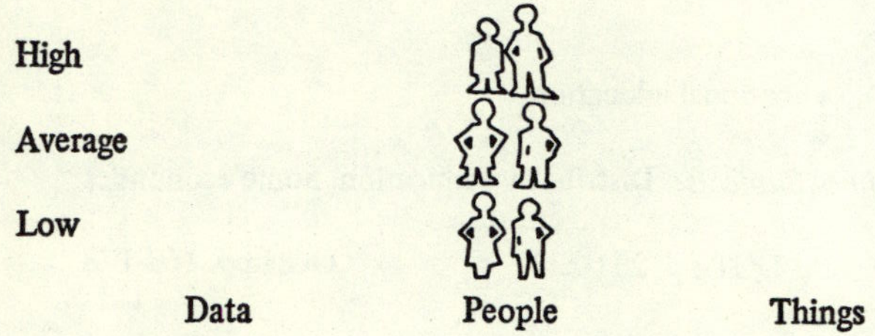

	Data	People	Things
High			
Average		👥👥👥	
Low			

33 BARBERING, COSMETOLOGY, AND RELATED SERVICES

	Data	People	Things
High			
Average		👥👥👥	
Low			🔧🪢

©Copyright 1979 by Dean Hummel and Carl McDaniels from the book HOW TO HELP YOUR CHILD PLAN A CAREER ($6.95 paper, $12.50 cloth, Acropolis Books Ltd., Washington, D.C. 20009)

Occupations: Household and related workers, launderers, private family cooks, domestic workers

School Subjects: Home economics

ED: Vocational education

DOT pp. 223-224　　　　OOH pp. 160-163; 183

Occupations: Hosts, hostesses, stewards/stewardesses, food and beverage servers (except ship stewards/stewardesses), waiters, waitresses, bartenders, chefs and cooks in hotels and restaurants, meat cutters (except in slaughtering and packing houses), miscellaneous food and beverage preparation workers, kitchen workers

ED: Vocational education

School Subjects: Vocational education, food preparation, home economics

DOT pp. 231-233　　　　OOH pp. 163; 178

Occupations: Boarding-house and lodging-house keepers, housekeepers (hotels and institutions), housecleaners (hotels, restaurants, and related establishments), bellhops

School Subjects: Distributive education, home economics

ED: Vocational education

DOT pp. 231-233　　　　OOH pp. 163-178

Occupations: Barbers, manicurists, hairdressers and cosmetologists, make-up artists, masseurs, bath attendants, embalmers

School Subjects: Cosmetology (trade and industrial education)

ED: Vocational-technical school

DOT pp. 233-235　　　　OOH pp. 167; 179; 181

34 AMUSEMENT AND RECREATION SERVICES

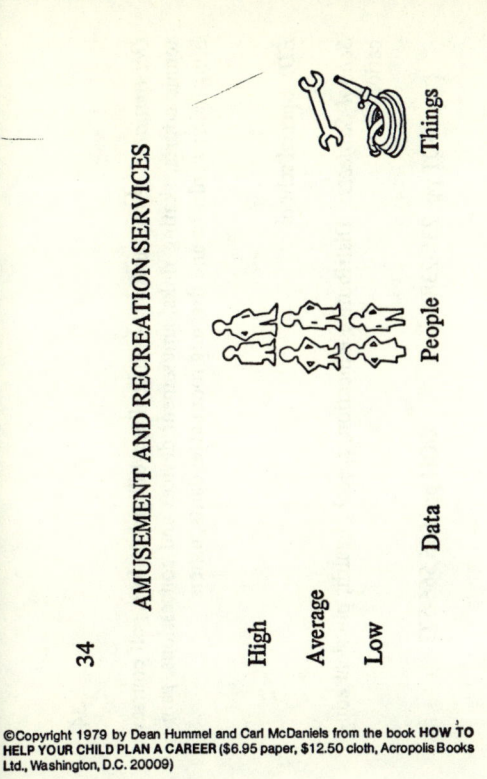

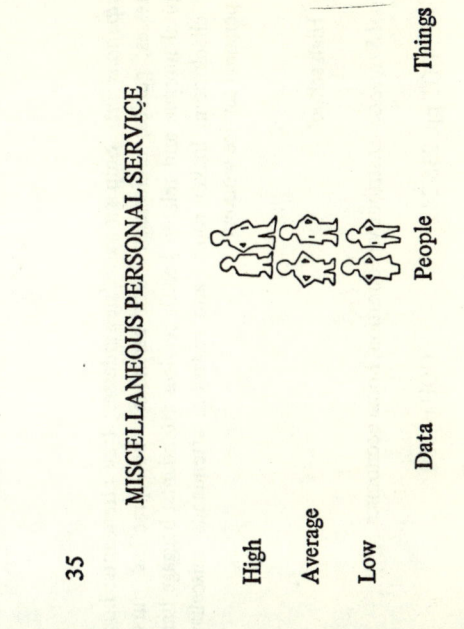

High
Average
Low

Data | People | Things

©Copyright 1979 by Dean Hummel and Carl McDaniels from the book **HOW TO HELP YOUR CHILD PLAN A CAREER** ($6.95 paper, $12.50 cloth, Acropolis Books Ltd., Washington, D.C. 20009)

35 MISCELLANEOUS PERSONAL SERVICE

High
Average
Low

Data | People | Things

©Copyright 1979 by Dean Hummel and Carl McDaniels from the book **HOW TO HELP YOUR CHILD PLAN A CAREER** (6.95 paper, $12.50 cloth, Acropolis Books Ltd., Washington, D.C. 20009)

36 APPAREL AND FURNISHINGS SERVICES

High
Average
Low

Data | People | Things

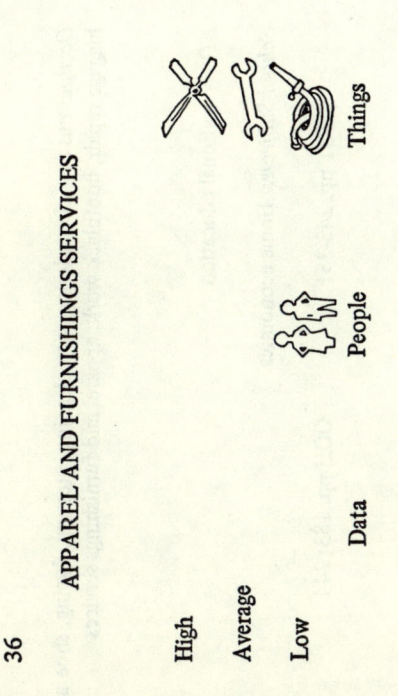

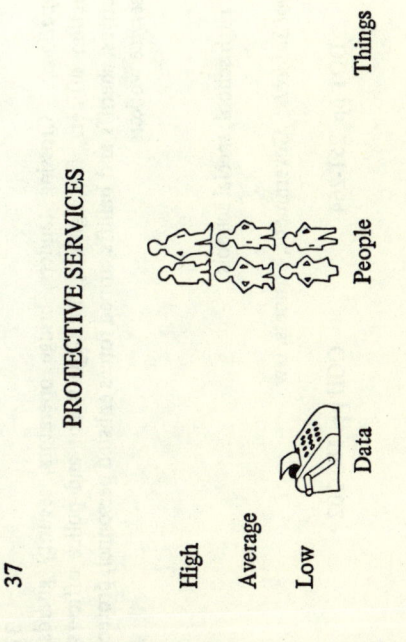

©Copyright 1979 by Dean Hummel and Carl McDaniels from the book **HOW TO HELP YOUR CHILD PLAN A CAREER** ($6.95 paper, $12.50 cloth, Acropolis Books Ltd., Washington, D.C. 20009)

37 PROTECTIVE SERVICES

High
Average
Low

Data | People | Things

©Copyright 1979 by Dean Hummel and Carl McDaniels from the book **HOW TO HELP YOUR CHILD PLAN A CAREER** ($6.95 paper, $12.50 cloth, Acropolis Books Ltd., Washington, D.C. 20009)

Occupations: Attendants at bowling alleys, billiard parlors, golf courses, tennis courts, skating rinks, amusement devices and concessions, gambling halls; wardrobe and dressing room attendants, ushers

ED: Special school

School Subjects: Distributive education, speech, health, physical education

DOT pp. 235-238   OOH pp. 556,566-573

Occupations in: Ship stewards/stewardesses; tray attendants; hosts/hostesses; guides; unlicensed birth attendants and practical nurses; hospital morgue and related health services attendants; baggage handlers; checkroom, locker room, and restroom attendants, miscellaneous personal service workers

ED: High school

School Subjects: Distributive education, home economics

DOT pp. 238-243   OOH p. 550

Occupations in: Laundering, dry cleaning, pressing, dyeing, shoe and luggage repair, bootblack work, apparel and furnishings services

ED: Vocational education

School Subjects: Home economics

DOT pp. 243-251   OOH pp. 183; 244

Occupations: Crossing tenders, bridge operators, security guards, correction officers, fire fighters, fire department and police officers, detectives, sheriffs and bailiffs, armed forces enlisted personnel, protective service workers

ED: High school; special schools

School Subjects: Government, business, law

DOT pp. 251-264   OOH pp. 186-202

BUILDING AND RELATED SERVICES

38

High
Average
Low

Data People Things

©Copyright 1979 by Dean Hummel and Carl McDaniels from the book **HOW TO HELP YOUR CHILD PLAN A CAREER** ($6.95 paper, $12.50 cloth, Acropolis Books Ltd., Washington, D.C. 20009)

PLANT FARMING

40

High
Average
Low

Data People Things

©Copyright 1979 by Dean Hummel and Carl McDaniels from the book **HOW TO HELP YOUR CHILD PLAN A CAREER** ($6.95 paper, $12.50 cloth, Acropolis Books Ltd., Washington, D.C. 20009)

ANIMAL FARMING

41

High
Average
Low

Data People Things

©Copyright 1979 by Dean Hummel and Carl McDaniels from the book **HOW TO HELP YOUR CHILD PLAN A CAREER** ($6.95 paper, $12.50 cloth, Acropolis Books Ltd., Washington, D.C. 20009)

MISCELLANEOUS AGRICULTURE

42

High
Average
Low

Data People Things

©Copyright 1979 by Dean Hummel and Carl McDaniels from the book **HOW TO HELP YOUR CHILD PLAN A CAREER** ($6.95 paper, $12.50 cloth, Acropolis Books Ltd., Washington, D.C. 20009)

Occupations: Porters and cleaners, janitors, building pest control workers, elevator operators, building and related service workers

ED: Vocational and trade schools

School Subjects: Speech, distributive education

    DOT pp. 264-266   OOH pp. 252-286

40

Occupations in: Grain farming, vegetable farming, fruit and nut farming, field crop farming, horticulture, gardening and groundskeeping, diversified crop farming, plant life and related services, plant farming and related services

ED: High school; vocational education

School Subjects: Vocational agriculture, earth sciences, chemistry, horticulture

    DOT pp. 267-275   OOH pp. 603-611

41

Occupations in: Domestic animal farming, domestic fowl farming, game farming, lower animal farming, animal services, animal farming

ED: High school; vocational education

School Subjects: Vocational agriculture, biology

    DOT pp. 275-280   OOH pp. 603-611

42

Occupations in: General farming, miscellaneous agriculture services

ED: Vocational education

School Subjects: Vocational agriculture

    DOT p. 280   OOH pp. 603-611; 368

44 FISHERY AND RELATED OCCUPATIONS

High
Average
Low

Data — People — Things

©Copyright 1979 by Dean Hummel and Carl McDaniels from the book **HOW TO HELP YOUR CHILD PLAN A CAREER** ($6.95 paper, $12.50 cloth, Acropolis Books Ltd., Washington, D.C. 20009)

45 FORESTRY

High
Average
Low

Data — People — Things

©Copyright 1979 by Dean Hummel and Carl McDaniels from the book **HOW TO HELP YOUR CHILD PLAN A CAREER** ($6.95 paper, $12.50 cloth, Acropolis Books Ltd., Washington, D.C. 20009)

46 HUNTING, TRAPPING, AND RELATED OCCUPATIONS

High
Average
Low

Data — People — Things

©Copyright 1979 by Dean Hummel and Carl McDaniels from the book **HOW TO HELP YOUR CHILD PLAN A CAREER** ($6.95 paper, $12.50 cloth, Acropolis Books Ltd., Washington, D.C. 20009)

50 METAL PROCESSING

High
Average
Low

Data — People — Things

©Copyright 1979 by Dean Hummel and Carl McDaniels from the book **HOW TO HELP YOUR CHILD PLAN A CAREER** ($6.95 paper, $12.50 cloth, Acropolis Books Ltd., Washington, D.C. 20009)

Occupations: Net, seine, and trap fishers; line fishers; aquatic life cultivators; sponge and seaweed gatherers

ED: College; vocational education

School Subjects: Biology, chemistry, math

DOT p. 283 OOH p. 361

Occupations in: Tree farming, forest conservation, harvesting forest products, logging, log grading, scaling, sorting, rafting

ED: High school or college

School Subjects: Vocational agriculture, horticulture

DOT pp. 283-286 OOH pp. 334-336

Occupations in: Hunting and trapping

ED: High school

School Subjects: Biology, math

DOT p. 286 OOH p. 355

Occupations in: Electroplating; dip plating; melting, pouring, casting; pickling, cleaning, degreasing; heat-treating; metal spraying, coating; metal processing

ED: Vocational education

School Subjects: Metalworking (trade and industrial), vocational education

DOT pp. 287-298 OOH pp. 33-36; 57-58

51 ORE REFINING AND FOUNDRY

High
Average
Low

Data People Things

©Copyright 1979 by Dean Hummel and Carl McDaniels from the book **HOW TO HELP YOUR CHILD PLAN A CAREER** ($6.95 paper, $12.50 cloth, Acropolis Books Ltd., Washington, D.C. 20009)

52 FOOD, TOBACCO, AND RELATED PRODUCTS PROCESSING

High
Average
Low

Data People Things

©Copyright 1979 by Dean Hummel and Carl McDaniels from the book **HOW TO HELP YOUR CHILD PLAN A CAREER** ($6.95 paper, $12.50 cloth, Acropolis Books Ltd., Washington, D.C. 20009)

53 PAPER AND RELATED MATERIALS PROCESSING

High
Average
Low

Data People Things

©Copyright 1979 by Dean Hummel and Carl McDaniels from the book **HOW TO HELP YOUR CHILD PLAN A CAREER** ($6.95 paper, $12.50 cloth, Acropolis Books Ltd., Washington, D.C. 20009)

54 PETROLEUM, COAL, NATURAL AND MANUFACTURED GAS, AND RELATED PRODUCTS

High
Average
Low

Data People Things

©Copyright 1979 by Dean Hummel and Carl McDaniels from the book **HOW TO HELP YOUR CHILD PLAN A CAREER** ($6.95 paper, $12.50 cloth, Acropolis Books Ltd., Washington, D.C. 20009)

51

Occupations in: Mixing, separating, filtering, melting, roasting, pouring and casting, crushing and grinding, molding, coremaking, ore refining, and foundry work

School Subjects: Vocational education, trade and industrial education, math

ED: Vocational education

DOT pp. 298-314   OOH pp. 31-36; 617-619

52

Occupations in: Mixing, compounding, blending, kneading, shaping, separating, crushing, milling, chopping, grinding; culturing, melting, fermenting, distilling, saturating, pickling, aging; heating, rendering, melting, drying, cooling, freezing; coating, icing, decorating; slaughtering, breaking, curing; cooking and baking; processing food, tobacco, and related products

School Subjects: Biology, math, vocational education, trade and industrial education, home economics

ED: Vocational education; college

DOT pp. 314-368   OOH pp. 167; 379

53

Occupations in: Grinding, heating, and mixing; cooking and drying; cooling, bleaching, screening, washing; calendering, sizing, coating; forming

School Subjects: Vocational education

ED: Vocational education

DOT pp. 368-376   OOH p. 696

54

Occupations in: Mixing and blending; filtering, straining, and separating; distilling, subliming, and carbonizing; drying, heating, and melting; grinding and crushing; reacting

School Subjects: Biology, chemistry, vocational education

ED: Vocational education

DOT pp. 376-384   OOH pp. 617-618

55
CHEMICALS, PLASTICS, SYNTHETICS, RUBBER, PAINT, AND RELATED PRODUCTS

High
Average
Low

Data | People | Things

©Copyright 1979 by Dean Hummel and Carl McDaniels from the book **HOW TO HELP YOUR CHILD PLAN A CAREER** ($6.95 paper, $12.50 cloth, Acropolis Books Ltd., Washington, D.C. 20009)

56
WOOD AND WOOD PRODUCTS

High
Average
Low

Data | People | Things

©Copyright 1979 by Dean Hummel and Carl McDaniels from the book **HOW TO HELP YOUR CHILD PLAN A CAREER** ($6.95 paper, $12.50 cloth, Acropolis Books Ltd., Washington, D.C. 20009)

57
STONE, CLAY, GLASS, AND RELATED PRODUCTS

High
Average
Low

Data | People | Things

©Copyright 1979 by Dean Hummel and Carl McDaniels from the book **HOW TO HELP YOUR CHILD PLAN A CAREER** ($6.95 paper, $12.50 cloth, Acropolis Books Ltd., Washington, D.C. 20009)

58
LEATHER, TEXTILES, AND RELATED PRODUCTS

High
Average
Low

Data | People | Things

©Copyright 1979 by Dean Hummel and Carl McDaniels from the book **HOW TO HELP YOUR CHILD PLAN A CAREER** (6.95 paper, $12.50 cloth, Acropolis Books Ltd., Washington, D.C. 20009)

Occupations in:: Mixing and blending; filtering, straining, and separating; distilling; heating, baking, drying, seasoning, melting, and heat treating; coating, calendering, laminating, and finishing; grinding and molding; extruding; and reacting

School Subjects: Biology, math, chemistry, vocational shop

ED: Vocational education

DOT pp. 384-442   OOH pp. 66, 256-286

Occupations in: Mixing, wood preserving, saturating, coating, drying, seasoning, grinding, and chopping

ED: Vocational education

School Subjects: Industrial arts

DOT 432-438   OOH pp. 73, 257, 674

Occupations In: Crushing, grinding, and mixing; separating; melting; baking, drying, and heat-treating; impregnating, coating, and glazing; and forming occupations

School Subjects: Vocational education

ED: Vocational education

DOT 438-455   OOH pp. 255-260; 269

Occupations in: Shaping, blocking, stretching, and tentering; separating, filtering, and drying; washing, steaming, and saturating; ironing, pressing, glazing, staking, calendering, and embossing; mercerizing, coating, and laminating; singeing, cutting, shearing, shaving, and napping; felting and fulling; brushing and shrinking

School Subjects: Industrial arts, home economics

ED: Vocational education

DOT pp. 455-478   OOH pp. 57; 637

59
PROCESSING OCCUPATIONS

High
Average
Low

Data People Things

60
METAL MACHINING OCCUPATIONS

High
Average
Low

Data People Things

61
METALWORKING OCCUPATIONS

High
Average
Low

Data People Things

62
MECHANICS AND MACHINERY REPAIRERS

High
Average
Low

Data People Things

©Copyright 1979 by Dean Hummel and Carl McDaniels from the book HOW TO HELP YOUR CHILD PLAN A CAREER ($6.95 paper, $12.50 cloth, Acropolis Books Ltd., Washington, D.C. 20009)

Occupations in: Processing products from assorted materials; miscellaneous processing occupations

ED: Vocational education

School Subjects: Home economics

DOT pp. 478-485   OOH pp. 57-81

Occupations in: Toolmaking; gear machining; abrading; turning; milling; shaping, and planing; boring; sawing

ED: Vocational-technical school

School Subjects: Vocational metal shop, trade and industrial, industrial arts

DOT pp. 487-512   OOH pp. 38-45

Occupations in: Forging, hammer forging; press forging; sheet and bar rolling; extruding and drawing; punching and shearing; fabricating machine occupations; forming occupations; miscellaneous metalworking occupations

ED: Vocational-technical school

School Subjects: Vocational metal shop, trade and industrial

DOT pp. 513-536   OOH pp. 38-45

Occupations: Motorized vehicle and engineering equipment mechanics and repairers; aircraft mechanics and repairers; rail equipment mechanics and repairers; farm mechanics and repairers; engine, power transmission, and related mechanics; metalworking machinery mechanics; printing and publishing mechanics and repairers; textile machinery and equipment mechanics and repairers; and special industry machinery mechanics

ED: Vocational-technical school

School Subjects: Auto and machine repair, vocational education

DOT pp. 536-549   OOH pp. 393-445

MECHANICS AND MACHINERY REPAIRERS

63

High
Average
Low

Data | People | Things

©Copyright 1979 by Dean Hummel and Carl McDaniels from the book **HOW TO HELP YOUR CHILD PLAN A CAREER** ($6.95 paper, $12.50 cloth, Acropolis Books Ltd., Washington, D.C. 20009)

PAPERWORKING OCCUPATIONS

64

High
Average
Low

Data | People | Things

©Copyright 1979 by Dean Hummel and Carl McDaniels from the book **HOW TO HELP YOUR CHILD PLAN A CAREER** ($6.95 paper, $12.50 cloth, Acropolis Books Ltd., Washington, D.C. 20009)

PRINTING OCCUPATIONS

65

High
Average
Low

Data | People | Things

©Copyright 1979 by Dean Hummel and Carl McDaniels from the book **HOW TO HELP YOUR CHILD PLAN A CAREER** (6.95 paper, $12.50 cloth, Acropolis Books Ltd., Washington, D.C. 20009)

WOOD MACHINING OCCUPATIONS

66

High
Average
Low

Data | People | Things

©Copyright 1979 by Dean Hummel and Carl McDaniels from the book **HOW TO HELP YOUR CHILD PLAN A CAREER** ($6.95 paper, $12.50 cloth, Acropolis Books Ltd., Washington, D.C. 20009)

Occupations: Special industry machinery mechanics; general industry mechanics and repairers; powerplant mechanics and repairers; ordnance mechanics and repairers; business and repairers; business and commercial machine repairers; utilities service mechanics and repairers; miscellaneous occupations in machine installation and repair

ED: Vocational-technical school

School Subjects: Mechanical repair, trade and industrial

DOT pp. 549-557   OOH pp. 393; 403-424

Occupations in: Paper cutting, winding, and related occupations; folding, creasing, scoring, and gluing

ED: Vocational education

School Subjects: Industrial arts, shop

DOT pp. 557-566   OOH pp. 57; 696-698

Occupations in: Typesetting and composing; printing press occupations; printing machine occupations; bookbinding-machine operation; typecasting

ED: Vocational education; technical school

School Subjects: Art, vocational printing, English Comp.

DOT pp. 566-578   OOH pp. 47-55

Occupations in: Cabinetmaking; patternmaking; sanding, shearing, and shaving; turning, milling, and planing; boring, sawing

ED: Vocational education

School Subjects: Industrial arts, vocational shop

DOT pp. 578-592   OOH p. 73

67
MACHINING STONE, CLAY, GLASS, AND RELATED MATERIALS

High
Average
Low

Data   People   Things

©Copyright 1979 by Dean Hummel and Carl McDaniels from the book HOW TO HELP YOUR CHILD PLAN A CAREER ($6.95 paper, $12.50 cloth, Acropolis Books Ltd., Washington, D.C. 20009)

68
TEXTILE OCCUPATIONS

High
Average
Low

Data   People   Things

©Copyright 1979 by Dean Hummel and Carl McDaniels from the book HOW TO HELP YOUR CHILD PLAN A CAREER ($6.95 paper, $12.50 cloth, Acropolis Books Ltd., Washington, D.C. 20009)

69
MACHINE TRADES OCCUPATIONS

High
Average
Low

Data   People   Things

©Copyright 1979 by Dean Hummel and Carl McDaniels from the book HOW TO HELP YOUR CHILD PLAN A CAREER (6.95 paper, $12.50 cloth, Acropolis Books Ltd., Washington, D.C. 20009)

70
FABRICATION, ASSEMBLY, AND REPAIR OF METAL PRODUCTS

High
Average
Low

Data   People   Things

©Copyright 1979 by Dean Hummel and Carl McDaniels from the book HOW TO HELP YOUR CHILD PLAN A CAREER ($6.95 paper, $12.50 cloth, Acropolis Books Ltd., Washington, D.C. 20009)

67

Occupations in: Stonecutting, abrading, turning, planing and shaping; boring and punching, chipping, cutting, sawing

ED: Vocational education

School Subjects: Industrial arts, vocational shop

DOT pp. 592-600   OOH p. 255

68

Occupations in: Carding, combing, drawing, twisting, beaming, warping; spinning; weaving; hosiery and other knitting occupations; punching, cutting, forming; tufting

ED: Vocational education

School Subjects: Home economics, industrial arts

DOT pp. 600-623   OOH pp. 709-710

69

Occupations in: Plastics, synthetics, rubber, and leather working; fabrication of insulated wire and cable; fabrication of products from assorted materials; modelmaking; patternmaking; fabrication of ordnance, ammunition, and related products

ED: Vocational education; technical school

School Subjects: Industrial arts, drafting, vocational machine shop, trade and industrial

DOT pp. 623-649   OOH pp. 38-45

70

Occupations in: Fabrication, assembly, and repair of jewelry, silverware; fabrication, assembly, and repair of tools; assembly and repair of sheetmetal products; engraving, etching; filing, grinding, buffing, cleaning, and polishing; metal unit assembly and adjustment

ED: Vocational education; technical school

School Subjects: Industrial arts, vocational machine shop

DOT pp. 651-668   OOH pp. 57-60

71
FABRICATION AND REPAIR OF SCIENTIFIC, MEDICAL, PHOTOGRAPHIC, OPTICAL, TIME-KEEPING, AND RELATED PRODUCTS

	Data	People	Things
High			
Average			
Low			

©Copyright 1979 by Dean Hummel and Carl McDaniels from the book **HOW TO HELP YOUR CHILD PLAN A CAREER** ($6.95 paper, $12.50 cloth, Acropolis Books Ltd., Washington, D.C. 20009)

72
ASSEMBLY AND REPAIR OF ELECTRICAL EQUIPMENT

	Data	People	Things
High			
Average			
Low			

©Copyright 1979 by Dean Hummel and Carl McDaniels from the book **HOW TO HELP YOUR CHILD PLAN A CAREER** (6.95 paper, $12.50 cloth, Acropolis Books Ltd., Washington, D.C. 20009)

73
FABRICATION AND REPAIR OF PRODUCTS MADE FROM ASSORTED MATERIALS

	Data	People	Things
High			
Average			
Low			

©Copyright 1979 by Dean Hummel and Carl McDaniels from the book **HOW TO HELP YOUR CHILD PLAN A CAREER** ($6.95 paper, $12.50 cloth, Acropolis Books Ltd., Washington, D.C. 20009)

74
PAINTING, DECORATING, AND RELATED OCCUPATIONS

	Data	People	Things
High			
Average			
Low			

©Copyright 1979 by Dean Hummel and Carl McDaniels from the book **HOW TO HELP YOUR CHILD PLAN A CAREER** ($6.95 paper, $12.50 cloth, Acropolis Books Ltd., Washington, D.C. 20009)

Occupations in: Fabrication and repair of instruments for measuring, controlling, and indicating physical characteristics; optical instruments; surgical, medical, and dental instruments and supplies; ophthalmic goods; photographic equipment and supplies; watches, clocks, and parts; engineering and scientific instruments and equipment

ED: Vocational education, special schools

School Subjects: Industrial arts, shop

DOT pp. 668-691   OOH pp. 414-428

Occupations in: Assembly and repair of radio and television receiving sets and phonographs; motors, generators, and related products; communications equipment; electrical appliances and fixtures; winding and assembling coils, magnets, armatures; assembly of light bulbs and electronic tubes; assembly and repair of electronic components and accessories; assembly of storage batteries; fabrication of electrical wire and cable

ED: Vocational education; technical schools

School Subjects: Industrial arts, vocational electrical repair, physics

DOT pp. 691-709   OOH pp. 403, 405, 420

Occupations in: Fabrication and repair of musical instruments and parts; games and toys; sporting goods; pens, pencils, and office and artists' materials; notions; jewelry; and ordnance and accessories; fabrication of ammunition, fireworks, explosives, and related products

ED: Vocational education; technical school

School Subjects: Industrial arts

DOT pp. 709-739   OOH p. 403

Occupations in: Painting (brush or spray), staining, waxing, decorating, and related occupations

ED: Vocational education; technical school

School Subjects: Home economics, art

DOT pp. 738-741   OOH pp. 278-280

75 FABRICATION AND REPAIR OF PLASTICS, SYNTHETICS, RUBBER, AND RELATED PRODUCTS

High
Average
Low

Data   People   Things

©Copyright 1979 by Dean Hummel and Carl McDaniels from the book **HOW TO HELP YOUR CHILD PLAN A CAREER** ($6.95 paper, $12.50 cloth, Acropolis Books Ltd., Washington, D.C. 20009)

---

76 FABRICATION AND REPAIR OF WOOD PRODUCTS

High
Average
Low

Data   People   Things

©Copyright 1979 by Dean Hummel and Carl McDaniels from the book **HOW TO HELP YOUR CHILD PLAN A CAREER** ($6.95 paper, $12.50 cloth, Acropolis Books Ltd., Washington, D.C. 20009)

---

77 FABRICATION AND REPAIR OF SAND, STONE, CLAY, AND GLASS PRODUCTS

High
Average
Low

Data   People   Things

©Copyright 1979 by Dean Hummel and Carl McDaniels from the book **HOW TO HELP YOUR CHILD PLAN A CAREER** (6.95 paper, $12.50 cloth, Acropolis Books Ltd., Washington, D.C. 20009)

---

78 FABRICATION AND REPAIR OF TEXTILE, LEATHER, AND RELATED PRODUCTS

High
Average
Low

Data   People   Things

©Copyright 1979 by Dean Hummel and Carl McDaniels from the book **HOW TO HELP YOUR CHILD PLAN A CAREER** ($6.95 paper, $12.50 cloth, Acropolis Books Ltd., Washington, D.C. 20009)

75

Occupations in: Fabrication and repair of tires, tubes, tire treads, and related products; laying out and cutting; fitting, shaping, cementing, finishing, and related occupations; fabrication and repair of rubber and plastic footware; fabrication and repair of miscellaneous plastics products

ED: Vocational education; technical school

School Subjects: Industrial arts, vocational shop

DOT pp. 741-749   OOH p. 403

76

Occupations in: Bench carpentry; laying out, cutting, carving, shaping, and sanding wood products; assembling wood products; fabrication and repair of furniture; cooperage occupations

ED: Vocational education; technical school

School Subjects: Industrial arts

DOT pp. 749-759   OOH pp. 70; 257

77

Occupations in: Fabrication and repair of jewelry, ornaments, and related products; stone cutting and carving; glass blowing, pressing, shaping; coloring and decorating brick, tile; fabrication and repair of pottery and porcelain; grinding, filing, polishing, frosting, etching, cleaning; fabrication and repair of asbestos and polishing products, abrasives, and related materials; modelmaking, patternmaking, moldmaking, and related occupations

ED: Vocational education

School Subjects: Industrial arts, chemistry, drafting

DOT pp. 759-770   OOH pp. 271-274

78

Occupations in: Upholstering; fabrication and repair of stuffed furniture, mattresses; laying out, marking, cutting, and punching; hand sewing, mending, embroidering, knitting; fur and leather working; fabrication and repair of hats, caps, gloves; tailoring and dressmaking; garment and nongarment sewing machine operation; fabrication and repair of footwear

ED: Vocational education

School Subjects: Home economics, art

DOT 770-801   OOH pp. 403-437

BENCH WORK OCCUPATIONS

High
Average
Low

Data People Things

79

©Copyright 1979 by Dean Hummel and Carl McDaniels from the book **HOW TO HELP YOUR CHILD PLAN A CAREER** ($6.95 paper, $12.50 cloth, Acropolis Books Ltd., Washington, D.C. 20009)

METAL FABRICATING

High
Average
Low

Data People Things

80

©Copyright 1979 by Dean Hummel and Carl McDaniels from the book **HOW TO HELP YOUR CHILD PLAN A CAREER** ($6.95 paper, $12.50 cloth, Acropolis Books Ltd., Washington, D.C. 20009)

WELDERS, CUTTERS, AND RELATED OCCUPATIONS

High
Average
Low

Data People Things

81

©Copyright 1979 by Dean Hummel and Carl McDaniels from the book **HOW TO HELP YOUR CHILD PLAN A CAREER** (6.95 paper, $12.50 cloth, Acropolis Books Ltd., Washington, D.C. 20009)

ELECTRICAL ASSEMBLING, INSTALLING, AND REPAIRING OCCUPATIONS

High
Average
Low

Data People Things

82

©Copyright 1979 by Dean Hummel and Carl McDaniels from the book **HOW TO HELP YOUR CHILD PLAN A CAREER** ($6.95 paper, $12.50 cloth, Acropolis Books Ltd., Washington, D.C. 20009)

Occupations in: Preparation of food, tobacco, and related products; fabrication of paper products; gluing occupations

ED: Vocational education

School Subjects: Industrial arts, home economics

    DOT pp. 801-804   OOH p. 57

Occupations in: Riveting; fitting, bolting, screwing; tinsmithing, coppersmithing, and sheet metal work; boilermaking; transportation equipment assembly and body work; miscellaneous occupations in metal fabricating

ED: Vocational education; technical school

School Subjects: Industrial arts, vocational machine shop

    DOT pp. 805-824   OOH pp. 57-73

Occupations: Arc welders and cutters; gas welders; resistance welders; brazers, braze-welders, and solderers; solid state welders; electron-beam, electroslag, thermit, induction, and laser-beam welders; thermal cutters and arc cutters

ED: Vocational education; technical school

School Subjects: Industrial arts, vocational machine shop, math

    DOT pp. 824-830   OOH pp. 85; 628-634

Occupations in: Assembly, installation and repair of generators, motors accessories, and related powerplant equipment; transmission and distribution lines and circuits; wire communication, detection, and signaling equipment; lighting equipment and building wiring; transportation and equipment; industrial apparatus; large household appliances and similar commercial and industrial equipment; fabrication, installation, and repair of electrical and electronics products

ED: Vocational education; technical school

School Subjects: Industrial arts, physics, vocational electrical shop, electronics

    DOT pp. 830-846   OOH pp. 264; 393

84
PAINTING, PLASTERING, WATERPROOFING, CEMENTING, AND RELATED OCCUPATIONS

	Data	People	Things
High			
Average			
Low			

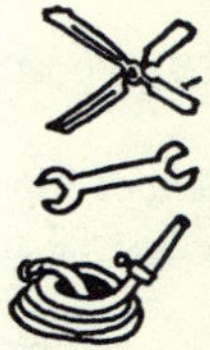

©Copyright 1979 by Dean Hummel and Carl McDaniels from the book **HOW TO HELP YOUR CHILD PLAN A CAREER** ($6.95 paper, $12.50 cloth, Acropolis Books Ltd., Washington, D.C. 20009)

85
EXCAVATING, GRADING, PAVING AND RELATED OCCUPATIONS

	Data	People	Things
High			
Average			
Low			

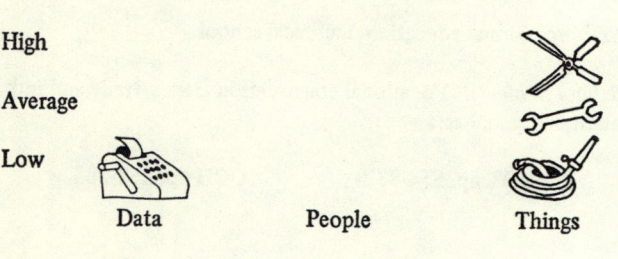

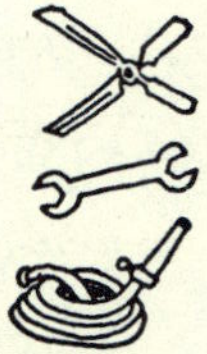

©Copyright 1979 by Dean Hummel and Carl McDaniels from the book **HOW TO HELP YOUR CHILD PLAN A CAREER** ($6.95 paper, $12.50 cloth, Acropolis Books Ltd., Washington, D.C. 20009)

86
CONSTRUCTION OCCUPATIONS

	Data	People	Things
High			
Average			
Low			

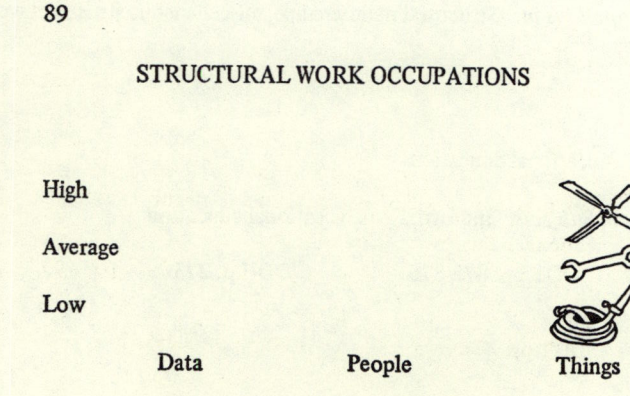

©Copyright 1979 by Dean Hummel and Carl McDaniels from the book **HOW TO HELP YOUR CHILD PLAN A CAREER** (6.95 paper, $12.50 cloth, Acropolis Books Ltd., Washington, D.C. 20009)

89
STRUCTURAL WORK OCCUPATIONS

	Data	People	Things
High			
Average			
Low			

©Copyright 1979 by Dean Hummel and Carl McDaniels from the book **HOW TO HELP YOUR CHILD PLAN A CAREER** ($6.95 paper, $12.50 cloth, Acropolis Books Ltd., Washington, D.C. 20009)

Occupations in: Construction and maintenance painting; paperhanging; plastering; waterproofing; cement and concrete finishing; transportation equipment painting

ED: Vocational education; technical school

School Subjects: Vocational construction trades, trade and industrial, industrial arts, math

DOT pp. 846-850   OOH pp. 259; 278-286

Occupations in: Excavating, grading; drainage; paving occupations (asphalt and concrete)

ED: Vocational education

School Subjects: Industrial arts

DOT pp. 850-854   OOH pp. 261; 276

Occupations: Carpenters; brick and stone masons and tile setters; plumbers, gas fitters, steam fitters; asbestos and insulation workers; floor laying and finishing workers; glaziers; roofers

ED: Vocational education; technical school

School Subjects: Vocational construction trades, trade and industrial, math, industrial arts

DOT pp. 854-872   OOH pp. 252-288

Occupations in: Structural maintenance; miscellaneous structural work occupations

ED: Vocational education

School Subjects: Industrial arts, vocational education

DOT pp. 872-876   OOH p. 273

90 MOTOR FREIGHT OCCUPATIONS

	Data	People	Things
High			
Average	●		
Low		●	●

©Copyright 1979 by Dean Hummel and Carl McDaniels from the book **HOW TO HELP YOUR CHILD PLAN A CAREER** ($6.95 paper, $12.50 cloth, Acropolis Books Ltd., Washington, D.C. 20009)

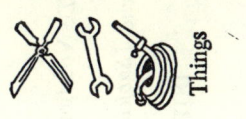

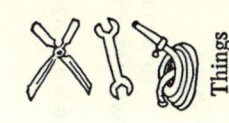

91 TRANSPORTATION OCCUPATIONS

	Data	People	Things
High			
Average	●		
Low		●	●

©Copyright 1979 by Dean Hummel and Carl McDaniels from the book **HOW TO HELP YOUR CHILD PLAN A CAREER** ($6.95 paper, $12.50 cloth, Acropolis Books Ltd., Washington, D.C. 20009)

---

92 PACKAGING AND MATERIALS HANDLING OCCUPATIONS

	Data	People	Things
High			
Average			
Low			●

©Copyright 1979 by Dean Hummel and Carl McDaniels from the book **HOW TO HELP YOUR CHILD PLAN A CAREER** ($6.95 paper, $12.50 cloth, Acropolis Books Ltd., Washington, D.C. 20009)

---

93 EXTRACTION OF MINERALS

	Data	People	Things
High			
Average			
Low	●		●

©Copyright 1979 by Dean Hummel and Carl McDaniels from the book **HOW TO HELP YOUR CHILD PLAN A CAREER** (6.95 paper, $12.50 cloth, Acropolis Books Ltd., Washington, D.C. 20009)

Occupations: Drivers of concrete-mixing trucks, dump-trucks, inflammables trucks, trailer-trucks, heavy trucks, light trucks

ED: Vocational education

School Subjects: Driver's education, business education

DOT pp. 877-879   OOH pp. 219-227; 289

Occupations in: Railroad, water, air, and passenger transportation; pumping and pipeline transportation; parking lots and automotive service facilities (attendants and servicers)

ED: Vocational education

School Subjects: Distributive education, business education, trade and industrial

DOT pp. 879-891   OOH pp. 289-329

Occupations in: Packaging; hoisting and conveying; moving and storing materials and products

ED: Vocational education

School Subjects: Vocational education

DOT pp. 891-910   OOH p. 698

Occupations in: Earth boring, drilling, cutting; blasting; loading and conveying operations; crushing; screening and related occupations

ED: Vocational education

School Subjects: Industrial arts, vocational education

DOT pp. 910-919   OOH pp. 612-618

95 PRODUCTION AND DISTRIBUTION OF UTILITIES

	Data	People	Things
High			
Average			
Low			

©Copyright 1979 by Dean Hummel and Carl McDaniels from the book **HOW TO HELP YOUR CHILD PLAN A CAREER** (6.95 paper, $12.50 cloth, Acropolis Books Ltd., Washington, D.C. 20009)

96 AMUSEMENT, RECREATION, MOTION PICTURE, RADIO AND TELEVISION OCCUPATIONS

	Data	People	Things
High			
Average			
Low			

©Copyright 1979 by Dean Hummel and Carl McDaniels from the book **HOW TO HELP YOUR CHILD PLAN A CAREER** ($6.95 paper, $12.50 cloth, Acropolis Books Ltd., Washington, D.C. 20009)

97 GRAPHIC ART WORK

	Data	People	Things
High			
Average			
Low			

©Copyright 1979 by Dean Hummel and Carl McDaniels from the book **HOW TO HELP YOUR CHILD PLAN A CAREER** ($6.95 paper, $12.50 cloth, Acropolis Books Ltd., Washington, D.C. 20009)

Occupations in: Stationary engineering; firing; generation, transmission, and distribution of electric light and power; production and distribution of gas; filtration, purification, and distribution of water; disposal of refuse and sewage; distribution of steam

ED: Vocational education

School Subjects: Industrial arts, distributive education

DOT pp. 919-928　　　OOH p. 82

Occupations: Motion picture projectionists; models, stand-ins, and extras; motion picture, television, and theatrical production workers

ED: Special schools

School Subjects: Industrial arts, art, dramatic arts, speech

DOT pp. 928-932　　　OOH pp. 566-574

Occupations: Art workers (brush, spray, or pen); photoengravers; lithographers; hand compositors, typesetters, electrotypers, stereotypers; darkroom workers; bookbinders

ED: Vocational education; special schools

School Subjects: Industrial arts, drafting, art, vocational printing, trade and industrial

DOT pp. 932-946　　　OOH pp. 577-588